Ghostwriting Legislation

State legislators introduce more than 100,000 bills per year and the resulting statutes that become law govern every aspect of life and business in those states. But who exactly writes these laws? In *Ghostwriting Legislation*, Mary Kroeger delves into the central and often-overlooked role that interest groups, think tanks, companies, and bureaucrats play in writing state law. While legislators are not expected to draft and pass legislation without the input of outside actors, Kroeger argues that a democratic defect may arise if elected officials must rely substantially on non-legislators to craft high-quality bills. *Ghostwriting Legislation* explores the disconnect between legislative power and legislative capacity, providing key data and insights for those who care about democracy and the separation-of-power dynamics in state legislatures.

Mary Kroeger is Assistant Professor of Political Science at the University of North Carolina at Chapel Hill. Her research focuses on US state politics, American political institutions, bureaucratic–legislative interactions, and policy diffusion. She has been published in leading journals including the *American Journal of Political Science* and *The Journal of Politics*.

Cambridge Studies in American Legislatures

Cambridge Studies in American Legislatures publishes research that confronts major questions affecting the study of legislative politics and political representation in the United States. The series advances problem-driven work that significantly advances theoretical understanding of legislative processes at the national, state, and local levels as well as scholarship that compares the U.S. to deliberative institutions around the world. It is comprised of studies that employ a diverse set of methodological tools that help researchers develop original insights into legislatures' role in American democracy.

Other Books in the Series

Michael P. Olson, *Stolen Representation: Black Disfranchisement and State Legislative Politics in the American South*
Jennifer R. Garcia, Christopher T. Stout, and Katherine Tate, *Black Voices in the Halls of Power: Race and Rhetorical Representation in Congress*

Ghostwriting Legislation

How the Unelected Write State Policy

MARY KROEGER
University of North Carolina at Chapel Hill

CAMBRIDGE
UNIVERSITY PRESS

Shaftesbury Road, Cambridge CB2 8EA, United Kingdom

One Liberty Plaza, 20th Floor, New York, NY 10006, USA

477 Williamstown Road, Port Melbourne, VIC 3207, Australia

314–321, 3rd Floor, Plot 3, Splendor Forum, Jasola District Centre,
New Delhi – 110025, India

Cambridge University Press is part of Cambridge University Press & Assessment,
a department of the University of Cambridge.

We share the University's mission to contribute to society through the pursuit of
education, learning and research at the highest international levels of excellence.

www.cambridge.org
Information on this title: www.cambridge.org/9781009710107
DOI: 10.1017/9781009710145

When citing this work, please include a reference to the
DOI 10.1017/9781009710145

First published 2026

A catalogue record for this publication is available from the British Library

Library of Congress Cataloging-in-Publication Data
NAMES: Kroeger, Mary (Author of Ghostwriting legislation) author
TITLE: Ghostwriting legislation : how the unelected write state policy /
Mary Kroeger, University of North Carolina, Chapel Hill.
DESCRIPTION: Cambridge, United Kingdom ; New York, NY : Cambridge
University Press, 2026. | Series: Cambridge studies in american
legislatures | Includes bibliographical references and index.
IDENTIFIERS: LCCN 2025053453 (print) | LCCN 2025053454 (ebook) |
ISBN 9781009710138 hardback | ISBN 9781009710107 paperback |
ISBN 9781009710145 ebook Subjects: LCSH: Legislative power – United States – States |
Legislation – United States – States | Separation of powers – United States – States
CLASSIFICATION: LCC KF4933 .K76 2026 (print) | LCC KF4933 (ebook)
LC record available at https://lccn.loc.gov/2025053453
LC ebook record available at https://lccn.loc.gov/2025053454

ISBN 978-1-009-71013-8 Hardback
ISBN 978-1-009-71010-7 Paperback

To Tyler, Henry, and Theo.

Contents

Figures

Tables

Acknowledgments

This book has taken me a long time to write and has stopped and started. Because of that, I'm very grateful to see it through and also think about the incredible help that I've received through every step. So many people have helped me with specific parts of this book or general encouragement.

This project started as my dissertation at Princeton. It was heavily shaped and improved by my dissertation committee: Nolan McCarty, Brandice Canes-Wrone, Chuck Cameron, and Dara Strolovitch. Each of my committee members expertly served a different role and took their job as guide and mentor very seriously. During graduate school, Marty Gilens, Georg Vanberg, Omar Wasow, LaFleur Stephens-Dougan, Tali Mendelberg, Paul Frymer, and Chris Achen were shining examples of how to be kind and generous with their time and care to a graduate student who was not their own. Throughout graduate school and beyond, my friends provided academic support: Tyler Pratt, Kelsey Pratt, Saurabh Pant, Daniela Barba Sanchez, Dayna Judge, Song Ha Joo, John P. DiIulio, and Adam Thal. Michele Epstein looked out for me and is such a force of nature.

Next, the project moved with me to the University of Rochester where I started as an assistant professor from 2017 to 2020. I am forever grateful to my time at Rochester for giving me a start in the profession. Larry Rothenberg, Jack Paine, Gretchen Helmke, Lynda Powell, and Gerald Gamm provided helpful feedback.

Moving to be an assistant professor at the University of North Carolina (UNC) – my undergraduate institution and close to my family – was a dream come true. My interest in state politics started at UNC with Justin Kirkland and Virginia Gray, who have been excellent mentors. As an assistant professor, the department has provided the space, time, and encouragement for me to finish up this project. The department sponsored a formative and friendly book conference where Chuck Shipan, Rachel Potter, and Shanna Pearson-Merkowitz gave me incredible feedback. My UNC colleagues – Marc Heterington, Alexander Sahn, and Tim Ryan – made the experience fun and productive. Jason Roberts and Chris Clark deserve special mention for reading and heavily editing large portions of this manuscript. They truly went above and beyond. Allen Wilson provided expert research assistance on the survey chapter.

Given the length of time I've spent working on this book, I've presented parts in a number of speaker series and conferences: University of Chicago, Harris Political Economy Seminar, Duke University Political Science speaker series, Vanderbilt Center for the Study of Democratic Institutions, Yale American Politics and Policy Workshop, Columbia University, Texas A&M Conference on the Political Economic Implications of Legislative Institutions, Conference on Institutions and Lawmaking at Emory University, Harvard University, Notre Dame Rooney Center, University of Southern California, State Politics and Policy Conference, and the Midwest Political Science Association Conference. I am grateful for the feedback that I've received over the years in these venues.

For the use of the ASAP survey data in Chapter 3, I gratefully acknowledge the contributions of Professor Deil Wright, the Earhart Foundation of Ann Arbor, Michigan, and the University of North Carolina-Chapel Hill; Professor Cynthia Bowling, Professor Theodore Arapis, and Auburn University; Professor Susan Webb Yackee and the University of Wisconsin–Madison; and the dozens of students and colleagues who drafted questions and collected data across the years.

Dan Alexander and Trish Kirkland need special mention for being the best academic sounding boards and texting friends. Life in this profession and working on this book would be very lonely without them. Hye Young You made sure I had office space when I was going wild working on this book in our NYC studio apartment and gave me encouragement that meant a lot. Molly Ritchie, Hye Young You, Lucy Martin, Frank Baumgartner, Jennifer Selin, George Krause, Sarah Treul Roberts, Kenneth Lowande, David Fortunato, Maria Silfa, Ashley Anderson, Sharece Thrower, Alex Bolton, Adam Thal, Andy Karch, and Dan Carpenter gave me very helpful comments on various sections of this book. Laurel Harbridge-Yong has been an excellent series editor. I received two incredibly helpful reviews of the book, and I'm grateful to Rachel Blaifeder for making the process so smooth.

This book happened because of the people supporting me and my family. The wonderful caregivers for my children enabled me to focus on the task: Linda Hughes, Jess Batson, Jomaya Reynolds, and Lea Finestone. My in-laws – Jay and Lori Cook – are lovely and supportive. My Aunt Audrey sends me support from afar and I always know she's got me in her thoughts. Most importantly, my Mom has unwavering belief in me and makes the best meals and care for Henry and Theo; she's simply the best in small and big ways. My Dad helped me in ways that I can't describe here and is a rock. My sister Nicole is the best human and sister you could ever dream of, providing cheer, advice, listening, or nephew love depending on what I needed.

Last, but definitely not least, my three favorite people are the most important for life and everything I do is for them. The book is dedicated to them. Tyler Cook, my partner since meeting our first year at UNC as undergraduates, has had unfailing confidence and optimism about this project even when I wavered. My sons, Henry and Theo, have not contributed sleep or time to this book, but much more importantly have brought me indescribable joy and make everything way more fun.

1

Introduction

Marion Hammer is not a legislator and has never been elected to public office, yet she often speaks about "her" bills and amendments in the Florida state legislature. She talks confidently about doing the job most think is reserved for those elected to do it: legislating. This book establishes that legislators are not the only ones legislating. Hammer is a National Rifle Association (NRA) lobbyist and a politically powerful operative in the state's legislature. In the wake of the tragic Marjory Stoneman Douglas High School shooting in 2018, her interaction with the lawmaking body and its staffers garnered increased scrutiny.

Email exchanges – made public through the state's Sunshine Law – revealed that legislative staff viewed Hammer as an essential partner in shaping laws. A news article exposing the email trove states:

> When government policy analysts suggested even minor adjustments to the bill's language, they made sure to receive Hammer's approval. In an e-mail to Hammer about three draft amendments, an analyst wrote, "Marion, I've spoken with you about the first one," and went on to note that a different staffer "said she'd spoken with you about the others." The e-mail concluded, "Let me know what you think."[1]

The article concludes that "Hammer is not an elected official, but she can create policy, see it through to passage, and use government resources to achieve her aims."[2] When questioned about how her bills are doing, Hammer confidently replied:

[1] https://tinyurl.com/24anh64x
[2] https://tinyurl.com/24anh64x

All of my bills are doing very well. We never file legislation or ask to have legislation filed that isn't needed, and when we file it, we plan to pass it. If people were not taking actions averse to the rights to keep and bear arms and to the rights of our members, we would never have to file legislation. But the reality is that there is somebody out there always trying to impose their will on you in violation of your rights. That's what it's all about, and we're working hard trying to pass all three of them.[3]

This exchange provides smoking gun evidence that this is a mutual relationship between legislators who agree with the organization's intent and groups that wish to make legislative changes. It reveals that Hammer considers herself a quasi-legislator: she discusses "her" bills and the choice to "file legislation." Introducing bills and offering amendments are actions reserved for legislators; Hammer does not appear to struggle to find legislators willing to introduce her bills. Non-legislative actors want to make sure their interests are represented at the initial stage of the legislative process and ensure their demands are included in statutory law. This book examines the role of outside actors like Marion Hammer in crafting the legislative agenda. It explores whether such actors are more successful at shaping the legislative agenda and outcomes under certain partisan and capacity conditions.

Clair Burgener, who served in the California State Assembly from 1963 to 1967 and the State Senate from 1967 to 1973, estimates that "Most bills, 99 percent, come from other than your own mind." She credits a range of sources:

They come from the schools or a business or a labor union or a constituent or somewhere. You don't sit there thinking up bills; you wouldn't have time. Mine came from the [California Association for] Retarded Children, many of them, or social welfare, [the] business community, schools. But once you introduce this bill, it's got your name on it. Occasionally, somebody else will have an identical measure, but that's quite rare. Lobbyists give you bills, too, on behalf of their industry or labor union or whatever.[4]

This revelation that legislators "don't sit there thinking up bills" may not surprise legislative scholars or close observers, but speaks to a broader question: If legislators are not dreaming up these bills and ideal policies, who is? This book answers that question.

I argue that legislative and legislator capacity and constraints are central to the partnerships that form at the system level of the legislature.

[3] https://tinyurl.com/bdbjmc5m

[4] https://archives.cdn.sos.ca.gov/oral-history/pdf/burgener.pdf

Partisan alignment also shapes lawmakers' interactions with certain types of outsiders. I look at two levels of actors: individual legislators and state legislatures. Legislators and outsiders form more complex partnerships than system-level patterns. When bills or outside information are bespoke or designed with the state's needs in mind, more experienced or powerful legislators may be more likely to partner with outsiders. Widely disseminated "model" bills that are not tailored to the specific state's needs are more popular among less experienced legislators. This book illuminates the scope of how various types of outsiders contribute to the legislative agenda and the body of law across states.

1.1 REPRESENTATION CONSIDERATIONS: NORMATIVE CONCERNS ABOUT OUTSIDERS WRITING LEGISLATION

As the opening example illustrates, a gun lobbyist seems to be calling the shots on gun legislation in Florida. Yet *legislators* are the ones elected to legislate. A central component of the job of representing their constituents is to come up with laws to address the state's problems. They have paid staff and legislative research bureaus to help translate legislators' desires into legislation. I establish in this book that various outside interests write the bulk of state legislation. What does this mean for representation? Mansbridge (1992) describes the dynamic that may arise if interest groups are left unchecked as "a *laissez-faire* market in interest representation gives different interests very unequal power in the negotiations that take place both in and out of the formal governmental arena." The conduit from groups to prepackaged legislation, described in the following chapters, may amplify these unequal voices. Legislators may abdicate their representational duties in the realm of legislating if they put forward outsiders' legislation without fully considering the consequences for the district or state.

This book uses three data sources to answer an age-old question – Who holds power in political institutions? – in the context of state legislatures. Various actors' relative success in transforming their petitions into statutory law is essential to understanding whose voices are heard in this important branch of state power. Pluralists would argue that the fact that many groups are engaged in this process demonstrates that legislators listen to a large range of groups. However, the volume of the input may demonstrate that the legislators are not appropriately checking power. The variation in the utilization of outsider input illustrates that elected legislatures and legislators require more or less of certain types of information depending on their internal resources. We therefore do not know the extent to which non-legislators help create statutory law. This book identifies which institutions and types of legislators protect against the use of unchecked outside input.

This input may be good, bad, or ugly, depending on one's political views or concerns about outsider influence. At the least problematic end of the spectrum, the group that offers legislation may be comprised of constituents in the legislator's district, and the bill may solve a constituent problem with public service provision in the area. Or the state's Department of Agriculture may offer its expertise in bill form on a matter that costs taxpayers money and does not contribute to the state's overall social welfare. In a more questionable example, the legislation could come from a group that does not represent the majority of the district ideologically; it could provide an easy pathway for a legislator to introduce legislation that does not perfectly represent constituents. At the most problematic end of the spectrum, a company could propose a bill that writes a rent-seeking provision into state law, and a legislature may fail to fully vet the bill and accept the text wholesale. The implications for representation hinge on both (1) the types of bills and groups offering the legislative text and (2) the vetting of the bills by the legislators and legislature.

Beyond describing the extent to which legislators rely on outsiders and variation in this use, I explore the normative consequences of the process behind the consideration of outsiders' bills and public opinion. These investigations focus on the extent to which the legislature vets outsiders' bills. I demonstrate that bureaucrat-sponsored bills are more complex and less subject to change compared to those not offered by bureaucrats. Not only are these executive branch actors requesting bills of the legislature, they mostly get what they want after the bill traverses through the legislative process. Moreover, the bills that subject matter experts – bureaucrats – write may be too complicated for generalist legislators to understand and fully foresee the consequences.

I also examine the democratic angle using a survey experiment that informs respondents of outsider involvement in drafting legislation via a news article that mirrors real news coverage to reflect how the most interested public learns about politics. This awareness of outside involvement may have downstream effects on politicians, as well as the trust constituents will have in the processes of the most basic function of legislators: to legislate. Support for the legislation is not meaningfully affected by adding an outside sponsor in the vignette, but mentioning an interest group sponsor significantly reduces perceptions of the process's legitimacy and of the legislator acting in the public's best interest. Providing an "expertise" cue – stating that these outsiders supply valuable information – has no measurable effect on support, legitimacy, or perceptions of the legislator's motives. Legislators may see outside groups as useful partners who can provide specialized knowledge, but the public appears unconvinced of these benefits. Even if public opinion is unlikely to alter legislative behavior in low-information statehouse contexts, these results suggest that when citizens are informed, they view interest-group involvement as a threat to the integrity of the legislative process. This pattern reveals a legitimacy gap: Lawmakers' reliance on interest groups for expertise risks eroding public views on the legislative process. Over time, these perceptions can fuel cynicism toward representative institutions.

1.2 EXAMPLES OF OUTSIDERS' INVOLVEMENT

When Jenna Adams and Andrew Kalloch met working in the New York City Comptroller's Office in 2014, she was the Director of State Legislative Affairs and he was the Deputy Policy Director. They bonded over their shared dedication to public service and love letters.[5] When they were married, their *New York Times* wedding announcement noted that they were both bill drafters. Neither was employed by the state legislature at the time they were drafting legislation. The announcement reports that the groom is "responsible for trying to get short-term-rental legislation favored by Airbnb passed in New York City" and that the bride works for the New York City Department of Transportation, where she is "responsible for drafting legislation and advocating its passage in the City Council and the State legislature."[6] Identifying which bills they advocated for (or against) on behalf of this company and the city department is opaque and not recorded in the state's government records, which is why I triangulate data sources in the chapters that follow. This couple's announcement hints at the prevalence of non-legislators drafting bills, the range of government levels that groups draft for, and the variety of groups that draft legislation: a company and a city department. The subsequent chapters dive into state-level legislation that comes from bureaucrats and interest groups and shapes the nature of state lawmaking.

5 https://oregonbusiness.com/17656-power-couple/
6 https://tinyurl.com/msypycpm

The League of American Bicyclists has a Legal Affairs Committee comprised of "bicycle lawyers from across the country," which drafts model legislation on recommended practices from states and legal innovations. These laws include the Vulnerable Road User Model Law, the Where to Ride Model Law, and the Safe Passing Model Law. The league's advocacy work has received less attention than the NRA's lobbying and drafting efforts, but both organizations use similar strategies to promote their aims. While the NRA provides detailed and tailored legislative aid to Florida state legislators, the League of American Bicyclists makes information publicly available to state legislators who are searching for an easy solution to a specific issue or a bill to introduce. This strategy and its varying success are the focus of my book.

In California, each piece of state legislation has an accompanying "bill analysis" that lists the source of the bill. This is a unique and relatively transparent reporting institution: Non-legislative sources of legislation may be listed as the bill's "sponsor" or "source" on the bill analysis. The bill analysis for S. B. 860 from the state's 2007–2008 session lists Taser International as the "source" of the legislation. Conveniently, the specifications for permissible stun guns detailed in the bill perfectly align with Taser International's product. In the same bill analysis, Taser International's main competitor, Stinger Systems, strongly objects to these parameters. Stinger Systems, a direct competitor to Taser International, forcefully states that it "sells products that directly compete against Taser. Stinger's products sell for much less than Taser's and I can only speculate that Taser is concerned about competition and is trying to have the California Senate create a monopoly for them."[7] While this bill did not make it out of the committee stage, it took up agenda space and time for legislators to introduce and consider. Taser International's repeated attempts to secure the bill demonstrate that this type of interest group activity is sometimes used for blatant attempts at rent seeking. More surprising than the company's maneuvers to secure a legislative advantage for their product is state legislators' willingness to partner with it and introduce its preferred bill that would reduce competition within the state in obvious ways.

This example also illustrates the importance of studying how groups get their legislation into *specific* state legislatures. While model bills are designed to appeal across states, some groups operate some or all of the time within single or small groups of states. Focusing on

[7] https://tinyurl.com/yznmwucr

national strategies by national-level groups will generate a warped picture of which groups (and potentially which legislators) are promulgating interest group legislation.

Interest groups and companies are not the only actors that seek to get specific language passed into law. State-level bureaucrats also often request legislation. The written testimony for the Connecticut state legislature's S. B. 868, concerning the regulation of a jet pack, includes a striking picture of the device. This 2015 bill "introduces operational safety rules for an attractive, but potentially dangerous emerging type of vessel, which we call a Jetted Articulated Vessel."[8] To legally regulate these devices, the state's Department of Energy and Environmental Protection needed to expand the definition of a vessel. The legislature's Environment Committee raised this bill at the department's request: The department had noticed a gap in statutory law combined with a potentially dangerous device, and worked with the legislature to ensure it would have the statutory authority to issue regulations on the topic. While this example of bureaucratic involvement in the legislative process is more entertaining than most, it represents a larger trend: using bureaucratic input in the legislative agenda-setting process. This interaction may be surprising given the typical understanding of the separation of powers and statutory control of the bureaucracy.

These instances of outsiders' involvement in the legislative process exhibit the range of outsiders and the varying reliance of different types of insiders on the information provided. Capacity and expertise differ dramatically across legislators and legislatures in ways that may alter the information needs of (and thus shape the relationship between) legislators, constituents, and outside groups when it comes to introducing legislation. Systematically mapping these relationships is the main task of the book.

1.3 SCOPE OF OUTSIDERS

I consider a broad range of outsiders that propose bills to state legislators, including interest groups, companies, state-level agencies, national-level groups that produce model legislation, and state agencies. To limit the scope of the book, I exclude other well-known sources of input such as other states and direct democracy initiatives. The main distinction I draw is between *groups* and *bureaucrats*. Within and across these categories,

[8] https://tinyurl.com/4khatn9f

outsiders and legislators have different motivations to work with each other, which I discuss in Chapter 2. The various actors are unified by two main characteristics. The first is the (purported) expertise and time they offer legislators in an attempt to include legislation on the agenda. Second, both types of outsiders have a vested interest in the state legislation or at least a perspective on how they would like it to look. Businesses may seek to benefit from the bill, while a department may be charged with implementing it.

1.3.1 Groups

Since a multitude of interests wish to see their preferred legislation have its day in the legislature, I consider a broad array of entities to be *groups*; I also refer to them as "interest groups." A group is typically defined as "an organized body of individuals who share some goals and who try to influence public policy" (Berry 1989, p. 4). I include organizations that fall under this umbrella, as well as groups of firms and corporations. In examining the interests that propose legislation, I make a similar conclusion to Schlozman (2010): "the majority of organizations in the pressure system are not associations of individuals."

Groups can consist of national-level organizations that do not target individual states (as in the model bills case) or seek to influence policy within a single state or smaller set of states. In some cases, I consider cities and substate actors to be a group because they represent constituents and behave strategically. In later chapters, I classify groups into subtypes. Examining the entities across and within states reveals that an eclectic set of groups is vying for legislative agenda space.

1.3.2 Bureaucrats

Throughout the book I interchangeably refer to state-level governmental actors: *bureaucrats*, *bureaucracies*, *agencies*, and *departments* (and their bills). These bureaucratic entities do not overlap with the groups above, but their tactics and expertise unite both types of actors in the theoretical discussion. I include bureaucrats who are operating in their official capacity as employees of the department when they propose bills and speak for the agency.

The range of agencies varies by state. For example, Hawaii has a Department of Hawaiian Home Lands, but North Carolina has no parallel department. I classify agencies by functional category following long-standing practices in the American State Administrators Project (Yackee and Yackee 2020). While state agencies might have different names and slightly varied mandates, this grouping highlights similarities and differences across states in which agencies are successful in their legislative pursuits.

1.4 WHY STUDY OUTSIDERS IN THE STATES?

This book focuses on the use of group and bureaucratic legislation at the US state level. Decisions made by state legislators and the resulting set of statutory law that governs state citizens are clearly important in and of themselves. Since the US Supreme Court's *Dobbs* decision in 2022 overturned *Roe v. Wade*, state legislators have made frequent and consequential decisions about reproductive rights, bolstering James Madison's point in *Federalist No. 45* that "The powers reserved to the several States will extend to all the objects which, in the ordinary course of affairs, concern the lives, liberties, and properties of the people, and the internal order, improvement, and prosperity of the State." The resulting state laws constrain the actions of state bureaucrats and cities, spread across the states, alter businesses' incentive structures, and shape the carceral and educational outcomes of millions of citizens. According to a report by the Brennan Center for Justice, "[s]tate legislatures increasingly hold the keys to the civil rights of American's citizens. Voting, reproductive freedoms, economic rights, the right to carry firearms, and other individual rights – with the exception of free speech – have more and more been the subject of federal court deference to the states" (Gaskins 2012). Powers are increasingly flowing toward the states, either because of court cases or federal gridlock; about 95 percent of cases are filed in state courts.[9] Evaluating how states make these policies is essential for understanding politics in the United States. Little and Ogle (2006) write that the:

> vast majority of laws that affect the daily lives of Americans are passed not in Washington, DC, but in places such as Bismarck, North Dakota; Springfield, Illinois; Columbus, Ohio; Sacramento, California; and Montgomery, Alabama. States are responsible for governing how people drive, what students learn in school, the quality of the air they breathe, the quality of the food they eat, the safety of the buildings in which they work.[10]

[9] www.courtstatistics.org/FlashMicrosites/CSP/images/CSP2009.pdf
[10] Madison 1788*a*.

The law created in state legislatures shapes the daily functioning of American society. Though many of the laws they pass are mundane, their composition uniquely alters citizens' experience with government. Understanding the set of actors who play a role in the creation of the law, and the parameters under which they can shape the law, is key to understanding state legislatures. Individual state legislatures also oversee massive amounts of money: If California were a country, it would have the eighth largest gross domestic product in the world (Masunaga 2015).

The decisions made in one state, using input from groups or bureaucrats, can shape what other states or levels of government do. This diffusion dynamic creates a multiplier effect for non-governmental actors seeking to put their bills on the agenda. Unlike groups that are successful at the federal level, where the Supremacy Clause means that the law takes precedence over state laws, groups that operate in the states have a potentially lower hurdle to action, but the law only applies to that state. Many groups only want to get their bill passed or considered in one state; this can reduce the cost of action in other states. By securing a policy win in one state, the policy can see momentum take over and speed the spread of the group's preferred policy (Grumbach 2022).

Since attention to and scrutiny of state politics is lacking, we may expect the role that groups or bureaucrats play in the legislative process to be even more important and less examined. Steve Rogers' work illustrates the striking lack of attention to the actions of state politicians, and the normatively troubling implications of this lack of responsiveness for statehouse democracy (Rogers 2017, 2023). State legislators' tendency to turn to outside groups for help legislating or coming up with ideas may be related to this lack of attention to their actions. Other work by Jeffrey Lax and Justin Phillips shows that, in the states, "policy is congruent with the majority will only half the time" (Lax and Phillips 2012, p. 148). Most research on the congruence between constituents and politicians analyzes votes and public opinion. However, the legislation and agendas that state politicians set with the help of outsiders are central to citizens' well-being and lives. This book examines the *origins* of the policies on states' agendas.

Examining state legislatures can provide important insights into the study of Congress. Many members of Congress previously served as state legislators. In the 113th Congress (2013–2015), forty-three senators and 219 of the representatives previously served in state legislatures.[11] Berkman (1993) shows that state legislators who progress to the US

[11] www.ncsl.org/Portals/1/Documents/statefed/fsl113.pdf

House of Representatives have "mastery over both institutional politics and particular areas of public policy," but that this information is conditioned by the state legislature's professionalism, the positions of power they held, and the amount of lawmaking they did at the state level. These former state legislators' propensity to work with groups may shape their ability to get things done in Washington and can determine the amount of campaign contributions they can secure to run for Congress in the first place. State legislatures are common breeding grounds for national representatives (Treul and Porter 2025). Learning about state legislators and their connections to interest groups may provide insights into the network of information providers they will turn to in Congress. Interest groups and corporations spend billions of dollars lobbying federal legislators: OpenSecrets reports that federal lobbying expenditures totaled $4.09 billion in 2022.[12] Yet we generally do not know which bills these entities seek to shape.[13] State legislatures are fertile grounds for interest groups to test out strategies and attempt to get their preferred policies implemented in an environment subject to less scrutiny. According to the director of the US Conference of State Legislatures, "gridlock in Washington" increases the burden at the state level "to do something."[14]

Beyond the inherent importance of state politics, states provide fascinating cases for studying *why* legislators seek group input. Variation across states in levels of legislative staff and resources, institutions, and partisan configurations provides ideal grounds on which to test theories about the relationship between resources, institutions, and reliance on group products. For instance, in 2015 the New York state legislature had 2,865 legislative staffers while Delaware's had 158.[15] These staffers provide research, framing, and bill drafting services for legislators. If legislators do not have staffers, they are likely to turn elsewhere for these resources. For example, some states have adopted term limits. I leverage differences in these shared features to investigate the relationship between institutions and outcomes.

1.5 WHERE DOES THIS BOOK FIT?

This book contributes to a long line of scholarly research on interest groups and the interaction between branches of government. I combine

[12] https://tinyurl.com/mv9h328c
[13] Hye Young You's work on the Foreign Lobbyists database is an exception (You 2023).
[14] www.nytimes.com/2007/01/12/us/12calif.html
[15] https://tinyurl.com/ms4sbkek

the rather disparate lines of study to highlight the need for information in legislatures and the dynamics of partnerships across a broad range of actors. The executive–legislative relationship and lobbyist–legislative interactions are unified by legislatures' limited capacity and desire for information.

According to Schattschneider's (1960) canonical work, interest groups have developed more rapidly than parties due to the need for information. His study assesses how lobbyists specified the text of the 1947 Taft-Hartley Act. Other scholars leverage institutional variation and map the interest group environment at the state level (Gray and Lowery 1996). A branch of this research examines the relationship between group preferences and policy change (e.g., Baumgartner and Leech 1998; Baumgartner et al. 2009). I build on this work and consider interest groups and bureaucrats as essential to understanding policymaking in state legislatures. In line with the subsidy-based theory (Hall and Deardorff 2006; Hirsch and Shotts 2018) of lobbying (over a quid pro quo line of influence), I theorize that legislatures with less capacity will rely more heavily on bill text provided by outsiders.

Much prior work and popular opinion on the role of groups in politics focuses on how money influences the political process. Critics decry the increasing amount of money that floods the policymaking process, while scholars are less certain of its impact. Quantitative research finds it has little influence on roll-call votes (e.g., Wawro 2001*b*). However, a recent randomized study establishes that members of Congress are more likely to meet with an individual if they contributed to their campaign (Kalla and Broockman 2016); this focus is curious given that interest groups spend much more money on lobbying than campaign contributions (de Figueiredo and Richter 2014). This book investigates how information from non-legislators shapes the legislative process. Of course, money helps produce information: Well-resourced groups can hire skilled attorneys to write high-quality legislation, target their appeals to legislators, provide contributions (and information), and hire lobbyists. Previous studies on campaign contributions have not identified the specific role that money plays in mediating the relationship between what the lobbyist wants and what the politician does. Theoretical research has analyzed the nuanced relationship between interest group information provision and legislative action (Schnakenberg 2017). My book merges theory and data to examine exactly how interest groups shape state legislative production.

Recent research has examined how national-level groups influence state politics. Some recent work evaluates how the American Legislative Exchange Council (ALEC) and other conservative groups produce and disseminate model legislation. The most comprehensive is Hertel-Fernandez's (2014) fascinating and weighty study of ALEC's role in furthering conservative goals at the state level. He uses textual analysis to study state utilization of ALEC model legislation and demonstrates the importance of this approach in the study of group involvement in state legislatures. Grumbach's (2022) *Laboratories against Democracy: How National Parties Transformed State Politics* highlights the role of national-level groups in the polarized cross-state spread of policies.

My book instead focuses on the overall level of group involvement and patterns of use in the states. It is the first to identify widespread model bill use across state legislatures. While I find that ALEC is by far the most prolific and successful model bill producer, I also employ data from other groups that produce legislation. Exploring this range of actors helps understand the reliance on outsiders more broadly.

Accounts of federalism are incomplete if they fail to consider the role of outsiders in the state legislative process. This book therefore captures the extent to which state law is derived from national-level groups or other types of outsiders. Jake Grumbach and Alex Hertel-Fernandez make a forceful argument and provide compelling evidence of the importance of national-level groups in state political spheres. The amount of state legislation that comes from outsiders is an important source of variation across states; while less directly related to outcomes such as Medicaid (Michener 2018), this outcome is closely tied to well-being and who gets what (and when) in the states. As Tyler and Gerken (2022, p. 2221) argue, "The laboratories account views state policies as the output of officials working within state governments to promote local interests and working independently from officials in the federal government and in other states. In reality, ideas for many of the most significant state policy experiments come from outside of state governments, serve interests that are national in scope, and are advanced by coordinated political networks." While these groups are important and provide bills that generate considerable attention to state politics, the task of everyday lawmaking is performed by groups and bureaucrats confined to single states. National-level groups are not the only outsiders involved in state-level lawmaking: I show that only considering these groups excludes essential players in the state policymaking sphere. I argue that state-specific groups and bureaucrats are exceedingly involved in the legislative process and generate much of the legislative text. This book therefore offers a more holistic view of state policymaking.

While some groups that propose model legislation may not officially have lobbyists in the state, since they are just posting the legislation, the number of lobbyists who are registered in just one state indicates the state-specific nature of group influence in state legislatures. According to the local news station in Raleigh, North Carolina, "About 10 percent of those registered to lobby in Raleigh list work addresses in other states, including Virginia, Georgia, California, and Washington, D.C."[16] Many lobbying groups, and all state bureaucratic agencies, only attempt to influence a single state's legislation. While this makes cross-state analysis more difficult, it highlights the importance of focusing on *all* law sources within particular states to determine the extent of outsider involvement in lawmaking.

Related to my theory of capacity and separation-of-powers dynamics, I advance previous work on models of delegation from the legislature to the bureaucracy, which do not account for the set of choices available to legislators or the cost of developing these choices. This book demonstrates that policies are not frictionless and costless to draft. For example, Huber et al. (2001, p. 332) write: "lack of confidence in the agency may give the legislature the incentive to write detailed legislation ... However, the extent to which it will be able to write detailed legislation is also dependent on ... capacity, or ability, to write such laws. That is, it must have the necessary skill and knowledge to know what to write." I show that the bureaucracy also plays a substantial role in helping the legislature draft statutory law, some of which constrains or expands the bureaucracy's statutory authority. The information provided by outsiders boosts the capacity of the legislature. I argue that understanding state-level policymaking requires examining the actors involved in drafting legislation. The relationship between the executive and legislative branches of government animates much of the scholarly separation-of-powers literature. I add to our appreciation of this interaction by emphasizing the reversed agenda-setting stage of the legislative process.

1.6 THE FUNDAMENTAL COUNTERFACTUAL

Some may argue that legislators would have come up with bills proposed by outsiders without their involvement. By offering prepackaged

[16] https://tinyurl.com/4nyuzktx

legislation or lobbying in support of a bill, the outside group provides the legislative sponsor with a subsidy of information and frees up the lawmaker's time to work on other bills, provide constituency service, or run for re-election. I am certainly not arguing that groups or bureaucrats that provide legislation *force* the legislators to introduce the bill. Instead, I view this relationship as a collaborative endeavor between legislators and non-legislators.

It is difficult to argue that legislators would have generated the exact wording found in model bills without outside input. For example, while a legislator may have wished to introduce legislation on charter schools, the specific wording of the model bill may alter the contours of the legislation. According to California state legislator Anthony Beilenson,

> even if you can agree in general about the main outlines of your proposal ahead of time. . .when you get down to actually writing legislation it becomes unbelievably complicated and difficult, because the specific way you write means that this is going to happen or this is going to happen. You can describe it in general terms, but it's not adequate to the purposes when you get down to actually writing legislation.[17]

Since a single word may significantly shape the interpretation and effects of statutory law, providing the exact text may have a considerable impact on the state's legal context, especially since legislators are unlikely to read every word of the proposed text.

Other legislators credit bureaucrats, interest groups, or specific lobbyists for bringing them ideas that they would not have considered or fought so strongly for otherwise. Former California Assembly member Eugene Chappie discusses his decision to introduce several bills that sought to remove architectural barriers and increase mobility for persons with disabilities.[18] A lobbyist for the Easterseals – a nonprofit that promotes services for those with disabilities – accused Chappie of "doing nothing for Easter Seals."[19] When a representative of the network visited Chappie in Sacramento, a child who used a wheelchair and the Easterseals lobbyist "related the problem he had getting the youngster in the capitol." Chappie recounts learning about these barriers as problems he could help ameliorate via legislation. He subsequently introduced five

[17] https://archives.cdn.sos.ca.gov/oral-history/pdf/oh-beilenson-anthony-v1.pdf, pp. 244–245.

[18] https://archives.cdn.sos.ca.gov/oral-history/pdf/chappie.pdf), p. 94.

[19] ibid.

bills to improve accessibility in the 1967–1968, 1969–1970, and 1971–1972 sessions.[20] Three of these bills were passed into law despite intense pushback from the building community; he remembers that they came out "guns ablazing" (p. 95). He considers these bills "common sense" and credits "the Easter Seal girl" with drawing his attention to the issue (p. 99). This vignette illustrates an interest group motivating a legislator to become active in a new policy area. The provision of information and specific language made this legislator a committed advocate for the group's bills. These examples do not prove that all outsiders' legislation comes from their own volition, without the first suggestion coming from the legislator, or that the legislator would have failed to craft a similar law if the outsider had not handed them the bill. However, it does show that legislators do often credit outsiders with the idea. We should take these labels seriously when we consider the origins of state-level legislation.

1.7 OUTLINE OF THE BOOK

Chapter 2 introduces a capacity theory on the interaction between groups, legislators, and legislatures in offering bills to introduce. This theory hinges on the tradeoff that legislators face between (1) sponsoring legislation close to their ideological position that does something useful electorally or for their district and (2) capitalizing on groups' policy and political expertise. I generate several hypotheses based on this theory. The main hypotheses hinge on the capacity or constraints imposed on the legislature, partisan alignment between branches, and individual legislators' positions of power or experience. The expectations differ depending on the type of outsider and the kind of information provided.

Chapter 3 applies this theory to examine a separation-of-powers question about bureaucrats' role in creating laws. It analyzes state-specific indicators in eleven representative states for whether a bill was introduced at the request of a department and a long-running survey of state-level administrators that queries the amount of legislation that comes from their agency. I find that bureaucratic actors are cited as the source for a large percentage of the laws passed in the sample of states. This unexpected finding may alter our understanding of the interaction between the legislative and executive branches.

Chapter 4 examines the case of California. This important state legislature shows the extent of group involvement in the legislative process

[20] ibid.

and allows me to look at the individual legislator level more closely. The second dataset used in this book leverages a unique informal reporting institution in the California state legislature: The group that drafts and advocates for the bill is listed as the "sponsor," and the legislator who introduces the bill is the "author." Group involvement is central to the state's legislative outputs: Almost 60 percent of the bills passed have an extra-legislative group sponsor. This project quantifies the extent to which legislation comes from outside sources. Legislators use fewer group bills and craft more of their own legislation as they gain experience, supporting the proposition that the principal–agent relationship between group and legislator varies with the cost to legislators of generating independent legislation.

While groups' relative influence over policy outcomes is of normative importance, previous scholarship has struggled to connect group activities to policy outcomes. To address this gap, Chapter 5 examines model bills (prepackaged legislation disseminated to state legislators by national-level groups) and how legislatures and legislators use them in all fifty states. State legislators' utilization of model legislation reflects an important degree of interest group influence in the early stages of policymaking. I evaluate model bills drafted by fifty-nine national-level organizations. Using an original dataset containing the text of all versions of bills considered in state legislatures from 2009 to 2020, I detect the use of these groups' model bills within all fifty state legislatures. State-level variation in institutions such as term limits and resources allows me to examine which institutional structures are associated with greater uptake of model bills. I establish that model legislation uptake decreases as legislative capacity increases.

Each of the studies addresses weaknesses in the other. While the model bill study allows me to assess the varying use of group input across states, it does not permit me to make claims about the extent to which the body of law draws on group input. Studying model bills also generates an incomplete picture of which groups are successful at getting their preferred laws enacted at the state level. If a group decides not to use model legislation, or targets a specific state, a study of model legislation will not tell us about their involvement in state politics. Nor can I calculate the percentage of state law that relies on group input from this study of model bills since state-level interest groups do not produce national model legislation and I do not have the full universe of model legislation. The California case study of group input allows me to examine a more complete set of bills that draw on group input, but I cannot determine state-level variation across institutions. Together, these two chapters indicate that interest groups heavily contribute to the body of introduced bills in state legislatures, and that the use of this input varies systematically by capacity at the legislature and legislator levels.

Throughout each of these chapters, I find that groups and bureaucrats are deeply involved in drafting statutory law in the states. This involvement varies along important partisan configurations and resource constraints. The core of this book assesses how interest groups, bureaucrats, and legislators interact, and how resources and partisanship shape these relationships.

Chapters 6 and 7 explore the implications of what this extensive involvement means for democracy from several dimensions. Chapter 6 examines the text of the bills that outsiders propose to determine whether they systematically write more complex bills and if those bills are heavily scrutinized during the legislative process. These metrics can capture outsiders' intent to overcomplicate legislation and if differential democratic procedures are used on legislation proposed by outsiders.

Using a series of textual analyses, I establish that bills written by outsiders are more complex and more likely to be preserved throughout the legislative process than those that are not. These measures and tests of the obfuscation in bills written by bureaucrats and outsiders in California suggest that outsiders strategically write different bills than legislators. Departmental bills in low-professionalism states (those with less experienced legislators) are written in simpler language than those in high-professionalism states. This finding indicates that departments in states with lower professionalism might tailor their bills to the legislative context (or deal with less complex material). Normative concerns about outsider involvement may be amplified regarding businesses or business groups that write bills. I find that bills with business sponsors are significantly less "readable" than those with no sponsor. Looking at the scrutiny that outsiders' bills receive suggests legislators are less able or willing to modify these bills throughout the legislative process. This finding speaks to the normative considerations across groups: It could indicate the expertise that groups bring to the table, or that groups retain special provisions in their preferred legislation.

To bring in the role of voters, Chapter 7 presents the results of a survey and embedded survey experiment to assess how learning about the role of interest groups and bureaucrats affects constituent assessments of legislators and the legislative process. A combination of legislators' reliance on interest groups and constituents' distrust of lobbyists leads me to probe the implications for democratic accountability. Since policymaking does not occur within a vacuum, it is difficult to separate the causal effects of interest group input, partisanship, and expertise on public opinion. In an experimental setting, I assess how voters judge legislators and policies when outsiders provide draft legislation. Process concerns about the role that groups play in legislating may trouble some voters or potential voters. In turn, public opinion about process may indirectly influence legislative action.

I conclude the book by discussing the implications of this action. Based on my interviews with organizations and archival evidence, producing these model bills and the associated lobbying is costly. To pursue this tactic and contribute to the body of state law, groups must have (and spend) a significant amount of money. Groups' relative ability to produce and promote model legislation may mean that their success in enacting their preferred legislative wording follows the "upper-class accent" found throughout the literature on interest groups. Groups that have the resources to produce model bills are those that see more success. Moreover, I empirically show that unelected officials play an important but conditional role in setting the state legislative agenda.

1.8 SUMMARY

The following chapters triangulate where state legislators get a significant portion of their laws. I first determine which bills originate from non-legislators and then study the predictors of reliance on groups and bureaucrats. To explore the democratic implications of this involvement for trust in state politicians, policy, and government, the final empirical chapter uses a survey experiment.

I close the book in Chapter 8 by questioning the distress surrounding the group provision of laws in states. Certainly, this practice could violate democratic norms of accountability and fairness if an unrepresentative group has outsized influence over the legislative process. However, banning outside involvement in development legislative text would not necessarily produce legislation that is better for the public interest.

I find that legislators who are under greater time pressures than their counterparts rely more heavily on model legislation or group legislation in California given the accessibility and ease of introducing a prepackaged bill. These findings imply that institutions that lead to decreasing levels of legislator expertise may encourage more input from outside groups. If group bills represent constituents' interests, then this may not jeopardize representative democracy. Indeed, the groups are often experts in the areas in which they write bills and consult many players in their development of bills, so this method of writing legislation may produce laws that better achieve the desired purpose and benefit citizens. However, previous research on groups' priorities suggests that their composition and concerns do not necessarily match with those of the average constituent (e.g., Schattschneider 1960; Verba et al. 1995; Strolovitch 2008; Schlozman et al. 2012; Gilens and Page 2005). When then, will legislators and legislatures turn to outsiders? Chapter 2 establishes the expectations about party alignment and capacity and uptake of these bills.

2

A Theory of the Interaction between Legislator, Legislature, and Groups

State legislatures hold enormous power in the United States. They decide how much the state will invest in public goods such as universities, public schools, highways, state parks, and public safety. They also set policies on how elections are conducted; how businesses are regulated; charter, create, destroy, fund, or take over local governments; and how alcohol is distributed and sold within their borders, among other things. In addition, legislatures authorize and fund the bureaucracy to enforce these provisions, and decide how much to tax the state's citizens and businesses to pay for these decisions. These decisions affect anyone who lives, visits, or does business in a state. A myriad of actors ranging from individuals to interest groups to state bureaucrats therefore compete to try to influence legislators' decisions on which policies to consider and how they should be crafted. This creates a complex information environment for state legislators, who are expected to be responsive to the concerns and desires of those who interact with the government. Yet adjudicating between competing claims and distinguishing authentic concerns from rent seeking can be difficult. Unfortunately, as I detail below, most legislatures do not provide their members with the necessary resources to effectively govern their states. This disconnect between *legislative power* and *legislative capacity* creates an opening for outside actors to partner with legislators in an effort to secure their desired policy outcomes.

Many legislators have tried to remedy this disconnect. Former Washington state Representative Tom Copeland once stated, "if the legislative branch of government was to remain in its present position, we were heading into calamity. You either had to change the ability of the legislative branch of government or you had to give up and say, 'Okay, here bureaucrat, you take and run the damn thing.' "[1] Representative Copeland later played a key role in modernizing the state's legislature so it could keep up with the various outsiders and stand a shot at running "the damn thing" more independently.

Such efforts may have helped enhance legislative capacity in Washington state, but state legislatures' resources still vary greatly. Chapters 3–5 empirically demonstrate that external actors set a large portion of the agenda in state legislatures. I analyze some of the most important documents in politics – bills – to establish that a substantial portion of what becomes law originates outside of legislatures. The main thrust of the book is that several types of outsiders have substantial positive agenda-setting power across state legislatures. This chapter first describes the motivations and goals of legislators, bureaucrats, and interest groups. It then uses these to develop a theoretical framework to predict the conditions under which interest groups and bureaucrats will be most successful at influencing legislative outcomes.

2.1 INTRODUCTION TO THE PROCESS

Outsiders have been bringing legislation to legislators and working to pass it for more than a century. In the early 1900s, Reinsch (1907) noted the prevalence of outside interests crafting legislative products: "[t]he legislature itself originates comparatively few laws. Most of them are suggested by outside influences, and are taken over and made their own by legislators. Legislatures indeed rather shun originality … really new departures in legislative experiments, original solutions of legislative problems, are mostly suggested by active men or organizations outside the legislative bodies" (Reinsch 1907, p. 275). Alan Rosenthal made similar observations decades later. After a lengthy immersion in Florida's legislature, Rosenthal (1986) observed that "[n]early a third of all bills introduced focus on special interests. Such bills are advanced by a group wanting to use governmental authority to promote its professional, occupational, or economic interests. Another third are 'agency bills,' containing the legislative programs of executive branch departments and agencies. Most of these concern noncontroversial matters of administration, organization, and implementation." In Congress, Bressman and Gluck (2014) use interviews to put these percentages of first drafts at 25 percent from the White House and government agencies and 34 percent

[1] https://apps.leg.wa.gov/oralhistory/copeland.pdf

from "policy experts and outside groups, like lobbyists" (p. 758). These are strikingly similar observations across time and legislature.

This book systematically studies when, where, and why legislators introduce more (or fewer) outsiders' bills. I scale these observations up to analyze bill origins across several states. Identifying state-level legislation written by interest groups and bureaucrats directly connects outsider information provision to a legislative product or bill, and its subsequent success. The next section introduces the process I employ throughout the book. Various types of groups can write bills with different state legislatures in mind, whereas bureaucrats tend to write legislation for their own state.

2.1.1 Interest Groups Writing Bills

This book investigates two ways in which interest groups write bills. First, specific groups (or lobbyists) in each state draft legislation that they wish to see introduced and eventually passed. While groups can lobby across states, they often target a single state when writing this type of legislation, either because they operate exclusively within that state or because they are interested in shifting policy within the state. In Chapter 4 I focus on the process in California, where legislators can list the outside group that brought them the bill as its "sponsor."

Second, model bills are written without a specific state legislature or sponsor in mind. National-level groups, generally nonprofits, post suggested legislative language on their websites, which any interested state legislators can copy or incorporate into a draft bill. Hall and Deardorff (2006) call model bills "info-drops" from groups to legislators who are searching for bills to introduce. While in some cases the organization that produces model bills may wine and dine the legislators they wish to introduce these bills, this is generally a hands-off endeavor.

2.1.2 Bureaucrats Writing Bills

The bill writing process differs considerably for bureaucratic actors as they often have more procedural hoops to jump through. The process through which bureaucrats submit their preferred bills to the legislature varies from state to state. For example, Idaho clearly maps out the process: "All legislation an agency is involved in must be reviewed and approved by the Governor's Office and the Division of Financial Management ('DFM') to determine consistency with gubernatorial policies and to assess the impact on state agencies and the public."[2] In Virginia, the governor's office has an online system through which the agencies submit their legislative proposals. Departments in Maryland must run their legislation by the Governor's Legislative Office before submitting it to the legislature.[3] All states that publicize this process have a mechanism through which the governor's office signs off on bills from executive branch agencies before they are sent to the legislature.

The draft bills introduced by bureaucrats aim to accomplish several distinct goals for the departments and agencies they work for. They may seek to codify current departmental practices, expand the department's authority, coordinate between departments or specify the authority held by specific departments, or authorize departmental action. For instance, when the Idaho state legislature held a hearing about agency bills in 2017, the director of the state's Department of Transportation, Grant Levi, stated the department's bill requests intend to: "1. Meet federal rules and requirements. 2. provide better service to the public. 3. Enable the department to be more effective and efficient." The legislators and departments view these bills as helpful legislative products because the bureaucrats are the government actors closest to the problems that arise out of statutory law and are the most adept at proposing solutions.

2.2 INTRODUCTION TO THE ACTORS AND THEIR MOTIVATIONS

The following sections explore the motivations of the actors involved in this insider/outsider game of legislative politics to describe the context of my theory of how these groups interact. The groups, departments, and legislators operating in different legislative contexts have various self-interested (sometimes overlapping) motivations.

2.3 INTEREST GROUP PREFERENCES AND MOTIVATION

Interest groups that have developed expertise or have many employees on hand to draft bills are at an advantage because they can craft high-quality bills for reelection-seeking legislators. An article in *Nonprofit Quarterly* describes the modern lobbyist as "more like an adjunct staffer than like a sales rep."[4] It also highlights the merits of pre-drafting

[2] https://tinyurl.com/3pdasm3m, p. 2.

[3] http://mhcc.maryland.gov/mhcc/pages/home/meeting_schedule/documents/minutes/MHCC_min_20140116.pdf

[4] https://nonprofitquarterly.org/nonprofits-can-write-legislation-heres/

legislation for the legislature: It helps legislators and gives outside groups control over exact wording, and allows interest groups to sway the narrative surrounding an issue and mobilize:

> Drafting a legislative solution to a social problem is a great way to take some control over the legislative process. Having a bill in the public arena can frame an issue and rally supporters. The proliferation of for-profit and nonprofit public interest law firms means that even small nonprofits can find legislative drafting expertise. Keep in mind the need to be careful when using tax-exempt dollars to promote legislation, but don't be afraid to act.[5]

Setting the scene by providing legislative text is very appealing to interest groups because it lets them "frame an issue" as the quote above suggests. In the same way that internal legislative actors can change the conversation by innovating and introducing new legislation, outsiders can (and do) use this tactic. Groups have recently proposed and pushed model legislation on anti-transgender topics; in this area, "Many bills contain nearly identical language, suggesting a common template."[6] Model legislation can give national-level groups exactly what they want in terms of policy, or even if a bill fails in a particular session, it can redefine the terms of the debate or what their constituents know to request of their legislators.

Groups find this tactic appealing: Nownes and Freeman (1998) report that 96 percent of state lobbyists and 88 percent of state organizations they surveyed said they had helped draft legislation. The supply side of providing these bills also highlights the importance of studying the tactic.

Various groups may propose legislation to pursue different goals. As described in Chapter 1, Taser International wrote legislation to secure a special advantage for the company. Trade organizations like the California Medical Association (CMA) want to protect their members' interests, but this goal may also indirectly serve the interests of the state. For example, the CMA sponsored a bill in 2025 to "streamline the process for licensing out-of-state physicians looking to practice in California."[7] This bill is intended to help members by making it easier to work in the state, but it may also help the people of the state by speeding up wait times for doctors and providing needed medical care. Non-profit or public interest organizations like the League of American Bicyclists discussed in Chapter 1 also seek to advocate for the general interests of

5 https://nonprofitquarterly.org/nonprofits-can-write-legislation-heres/
6 www.nytimes.com/2023/01/25/us/politics/transgender-laws-republicans.html
7 https://tinyurl.com/2jfub7tm

the organization. While some of these may overlap with the general public interest, that is not a guarantee and may distract the legislature from considering more pressing matters. While the groups are distinct, they all push for their own interests, which unifies the study and highlights the normative concerns associated with unelected individuals engaging in this essential legislative function. While the legislature may check the interests presented before it, that also requires time and attention that may be in short supply.

While groups may be pleased to see their bill introduced and go no further in the legislative process, I assume and argue that the goal is generally to change state law. This begs the question: What types of legislators will groups wish to partner with, all else equal? My hypothesis following from Hall and Deardorff's 2006 (p. 76) theory of interest group subsidization is that "Lobbyists will lobby legislative allies with the most productive enterprises." Similarly, Rosenthal (2009, p. 159) provides insights into which partnerships are attractive to the group:

> If lobbyists are backing a bill, they must decide which legislator to ask to be a sponsor. Normally, they would choose a member of the majority party, and ideally they would recruit a member of the leadership team to take on sponsorship. They could obtain no better sponsor than the chair of the standing committee to which the bill is being referred. Occasionally, a bill can be drafted so that it falls within the jurisdiction of a chosen committee. Lobbyists usually focus their efforts on the chair and members of the committee with jurisdiction over their issues.

Outsiders know that legislators in leadership positions (e.g., committee chairs) exhibit greater capacity in resources and experience and can thus more effectively shape legislative outcomes than their less powerful counterparts, such as first-term legislators. Fouirnaies and Hall (2018) find that committee leaders are targets for campaign donations. Interest groups also give strategically to committee chairs given their ability to accomplish goals more effectively than rank-and-file members. I argue that committee chairs are also attractive partners for outsiders: Bureaucrats will give them bills due to their increased ability to overcome legislative hurdles and guide the bills into law. If an outsider has the choice between a novice and a powerful legislator to introduce their bill, the committee chair will, all else equal, be the chosen target.

2.4 AGENCY PREFERENCES AND MOTIVATION

Bureaucrats have multiple motivations for wanting to contribute to the body of statutory law. My examination of bills proposed by bureaucrats indicates that they offer these bills in an attempt to secure greater control over the policy implementation process, gain more discretion, legalize certain norms and practices (thus elevating the department's standing on particular issues within the court system), and simplify their jobs. Since it is costly to draft a bill and agencies' goals are less public facing than those of many groups, bureaucrats' end goal is to see their measures introduced and eventually passed into law. Many state agencies have legislative liaisons and policy experts dedicated to working with the legislature to pass bills. In the course of carrying out their duties, these actors identify gaps in statutory law and work with relevant stakeholders to rectify these omissions.

North Dakota's Assistant Commissioner of the Department of Financial Institutions conveys the importance of bureaucratic involvement in the legislative process, stating that "[b]ased on our understanding and familiarity of these laws and their applications and their interconnectivity with federal laws, as well as the industries that we charter and license, *we are capable and well-suited to draw up and introduce legislation on their behalf.* ... [We] examine and amend to get a good quality product to introduce" (emphasis added).[8] This testimony strongly resembles Carpenter's (2002) conception of bureaucratic autonomy, which maintains that bureaucrats believe they are uniquely positioned to craft solutions. This North Dakota bureaucrat highlights the complicated nature of crafting laws that deal with the department given the subject matter and interaction with federal laws. This sentiment demonstrates that some bureaucrats believe they have the capacity and expertise to craft *better* legislation than the legislature on particular topics.

A number of goals animate individual bureaucrats, including career advancement (Teodoro 2011), budget maximization (Niskanen 1971), and policy advancement. Involvement in the legislative process may help further each of these goals. By introducing bills to the legislature, individual bureaucrats establish themselves as subject matter experts and potential candidates for legislative or executive branch appointments. Or if they want to work in the private sector in the future, they can point to successful inter-branch relationships and skills gathered while bringing bills to the legislature. By streamlining the tasks required of the agency or removing obsolete provisions of law, the agency may free up room in the budget for its own use. By garnering favor with the legislature by presenting easy to introduce and pass bills, the bureaucracy may also increase legislative support to boost its budget. Moreover, simplifying

[8] www.legis.nd.gov/files/resource/65-2017/library/hb1397.pdf

the statutory law or closing gaps can make the bureaucrat's job easier or more pleasant. Specifying exact legislative language can further each of these goals for the collective bureaucracy and the individual bureaucratic legislative liaison.

However, bureaucrats who directly lobby the legislature must avoid angering actors who may have substantial control over their departmental budgets or day-to-day work (Bradley 2014). Bradley (2014) shows that in the area of state Medicaid policy, bureaucrats work through interest groups to lobby for their preferred policies. This circuitous interaction is related to the direct lobbying process between bureaucrats and legislators that I examine here.[9]

Shobe (2017, p. 501) interviews federal agency actors and concludes that "When an agency is the initial drafter, it has more control of the statutory text." This control reflects state bureaucrats' sentiment that providing legislative language furthers their aims. By writing the statutes, the bureaucracy can avoid legal challenges to their actions, contour the parameters of their discretion, and make their operation easier. Bureaucrats have the best information about how specific statutory wording can affect their day-to-day operations and authority. This information asymmetry between the agency and the legislature, combined with the department's motivations to control the initial version of legislation, makes it a compelling tactic under certain circumstances.

While a partnership between bureaucrats and lawmakers can be mutually beneficial, a more adversarial relationship may form if different parties control the various branches of government. At the federal level, agency staffers "noted that congressional staff from the same party as the president are more likely to accept agency comments to draft legislation and to use agency-originated language as the starting point rather than their own draft" (Shobe 2017). Under a unified government, spending time crafting legislation on state legislators' behalf may be productive for bureaucrats. Moreover, the governor may be more supportive of partnerships with the legislature given that the bureaucracy needs the governor's sign-off on these bills. When government is divided, however, governors often have few incentives to facilitate the legislative agenda of an out-party legislature. They may therefore be reluctant to take steps that would facilitate cooperation between bureaucrats and lawmakers.

[9] As I discuss in Chapter 3, the study of bills introduced at the request of these actors represents the lower bound of outsiders' involvement in the legislative process.

Beyond partisan alignment between branches, state agencies' capacity varies within and across states. Legislatures may strategically reduce the capacity of specific agencies or the executive branch writ large depending on the alignment between branches. This low bureaucratic capacity may reduce the will to follow the legislative directives (Huber and McCarty 2004). This book examines agencies with lower capacity – state agencies, which may have a reduced ability to write legislation even if the legislature would agree to sponsor the bill. The observation that divided government is associated with fewer bureaucratic bills may be compounded by the agencies' lower capacity to produce legislation.

2.5 LEGISLATOR PREFERENCES AND MOTIVATION

A North Carolina legislative aide once quipped during a round-table, "Legislators want to pass laws and spend money." This sentiment echoes Mayhew's 1975 canonical prediction that if members of Congress are single-minded re-election seekers, they will dedicate their time to advertising, credit claiming, and position taking. Introducing and passing legislation can, of course, help achieve all of these goals. Many legislators seek office, at least in part, to shape the policy process. Even where voters have low levels of knowledge about state politicians' activities, elections often motivate legislators to introduce more bills and participate in more votes (Fouirnaies and Hall 2022). State legislators thus connect the act of *legislating*, which includes introducing bills, to their overriding electoral concerns. Members are therefore likely to welcome help in drafting legislation.

Legislators apply their diverse backgrounds and skill sets to the tasks of legislating in a variety of ways. Their ability and capacity to create quality legislation vary in two main ways. The first is differences in legislative acumen based on experience, expertise, or innate talent. The second source is resources or capacity provided by the legislature. Carnes (2013) demonstrates that legislators come to office with a variety of prior work experience. In an oral history interview, Oklahoma state Representative Wanda Jo Peltier (1986–1996) described applying her research experience to the task of legislating: "Along the way, I owned a research and technical writing business for about... I think it was about eleven years, so I knew where to go and how to find things."[10] Her research

[10] https://dc.library.okstate.edu/digital/collection/legislature/id/90

and technical writing skills helped her navigate the complicated legislative legalese and leverage the legislature's resources. Rosa Franklin was a rehabilitation nurse before her illustrative career in the Washington state legislature. She said her work as a nurse came in handy in the legislature given the parallel needs for "people skills to connect across many forms of difference, while maintaining a level of respect for others' humanity."[11]

Legislators also learn on the job. From the mundane logistics of filing a bill, to figuring out how to work with internal staff, to grasping the complicated leadership politics, legislators gain competence from serving. Some skills from their prior experience will translate to the legislative sphere, while others are unique to this setting. In Washington state, Ray Moore was elected to his first term at the age of 66. He recounts lacking institution-specific knowledge despite his long background in political campaigning and organizing in Washington state politics: "Physically, I kind of knew my way around. But, there were parliamentary maneuvers that I didn't understand, didn't know about, because the Senate has its own rules as opposed to Reed's or Roberts'. So, you can know a lot and still not know much."[12] This sentiment applies to many aspects of the legislative setting. The organizational dynamics are complicated, and the minutia of working with limited legislative resources to craft a bill that accomplishes a specific goal is difficult. While other jobs may prepare legislators for the organizational challenges, research tasks, or interpersonal interactions, the combination of tasks and the constant time demands make the job unique. It also has a steep learning curve that ranges from mundane tasks such as finding the mail to the complex twists of navigating a bill to passage.

While some legislators may claim to gain this type of expertise sooner or prioritize other types of learning, many acknowledge the learning curve. For example, while discussing term limits, Moore talks about how long it took him to figure out legislative processes and relationships:

> I had been here about four years before I was able to detect the wheat from the chaff. After six or eight years, I had most of the bureaucrats figured out. I could tell from their answers whether they were lying or not – I don't think a legislator who's limited to eight years in the Senate is going to be able to do a real job.[13]

Former Missouri state legislator Edwin Dirck, Sr. recounts a similar timeline: "the eighth year (somewhere along in there, between the fourth to

[11] https://app.leg.wa.gov/oralhistory/franklin.pdf, p. 64.
[12] https://app.leg.wa.gov/oralhistory/moore.pdf, p. 71.
[13] https://app.leg.wa.gov/oralhistory/moore.pdf, p. 113.

eighth year) is when you really get into the workings of the government. It takes a while."[14]

New members, in particular, are thus often looking for help. In California, for example, "a few new members confessed that in their first year, over 90 percent of their bills were drafted or given to them by lobbyists" (Cain and Kousser 2004). This shockingly high percentage of input from groups illustrates how members rely on outside help to make up for their lack of experience. On-the-job experience teaches legislators how to assess group bills, work with bill drafting services, and otherwise craft high-quality legislation.

Legislators emphasize the difficulty of navigating relationships with internal and external actors. It generally takes time to figure out who to trust and how to work these partnerships. It is possible to track an individual's increasing legislative prowess over the course of their time in office. For example, North Carolina's Phil Berger was ranked the most effective legislator in the state in 2015, but during his first term he was forty-fourth out of fifty.[15] Previous work has established that a legislator's 'years of consecutive service' proxies for experience and is associated with the number of bills they sponsor (Keefe 1968; Squire 2007). i Miquel and Snyder Jr (2006) find that North Carolina state legislators' effectiveness "rises sharply with tenure, at least for the first few terms" (p. 348).

Legislators acknowledge the tradeoffs inherent in their relationships with lobbyists and outside groups. Oral histories and news stories based on interviews with state legislators indicate that many legislators see lobbyists as akin to staffers. In a surprisingly candid interview, Missouri state Senator Ed Emery, a Republican from Lamar, told the *St. Louis Post-Dispatch* that "I look at lobbyists as unpaid staff."[16] Robert Barengo served as a legislator in the Nevada Assembly from 1972 to 1982 and later became a lobbyist. In an oral history commissioned by the state legislature, when asked about the differences between being a legislator and a lobbyist, Barengo responded that as a lobbyist, "[y]ou're more of a staffer, I think is what it is. You're an advocate for a position, and you've got to find a legislator who either agrees with your position or [shows]

[14] Edwin L. Dirck, Sr., Will Sarvis, February 23, 1996, Transcript, and The Oral History Program of the State Historical Society of Missouri, Politics in Missouri Oral History Project, https://digital.shsmo.org/digital/collection/ohc/id/530/.

[15] https://nccppr.org/wp-content/uploads/2017/02/2016legislativerankings_0.pdf

[16] https://tinyurl.com/msfyxpfn

that they might agree with your position."[17] This also speaks to the large informational lobbying literature on who groups lobby. Another Nevada state legislator from 1992–2006, Lynn Hettrick reflects that

> For the most part, I think the interaction is good. You simply cannot be an expert on everything. I really see this body acting as a board of directors. You have a group who comes to you and says they need this or that, and then you have another group who says they don't want any changes, or if you're going to change that, you need to change this, too.[18]

Former California legislator Quentin Kopp praises department liaisons as "the people I depended upon for information and knowledge in committee... Those three agencies would have at least one sometimes two liaison people at every one of my committee meetings and they were just stupendous."[19] This legislator's glowing praise of the aid from the agency shows the mutual dependence of these actors.

However, at least some legislators recognize that collaborating with outside actors can resemble a double-edged sword. Former member of Congress, Tom Davis admits that "lobbyists play an important role" in crafting legislation, but noted that staff with long-term expertise would be better able to "'second guess' the legislative language lobbyists provide."[20] Another state legislator from Washington, Lorraine Wojahn, discusses the dual nature of such interactions: "Anytime anyone asks me about it, I tell them that we could not survive without lobbyists. They offer technical information. The only thing you have to be able to do is to know whom you can trust and who you can't, and that's a matter of being able to judge character. That comes with maturity."[21] Other legislators are less sanguine about the nature of the relationship: "The elimination of experienced policymakers will lead to lobbyists and employees of state agencies becoming 'the custodians of institutional knowledge,' Andrist said."[22]

Legislators also highlight the need for independent capacity to counter or fact-check information from lobbyists. They talk about the sentiment that lobbyists cannot expect to get *everything* they ask for from the legislature. Former Nebraska state legislator and lobbyist Fred Settelmeyer recounts:

[17] www.leg.state.nv.us/Division/Research/LegInfo/OHP/transcripts/Barengo.pdf
[18] www.leg.state.nv.us/Division/Research/LegInfo/OHP/transcripts/Hettrick.pdf
[19] https://ia600104.us.archive.org/33/items/oh2003-03-kopp/oh2003-03-kopp.pdf
[20] https://rollcall.com/2019/05/02/lobbyists-to-congress-pay-staffers-better/
[21] https://apps.leg.wa.gov/oralhistory/wojahn/WojahnOralHistory.pdf
[22] https://tinyurl.com/yh9tddzj

at one time, the railroad employees, they came in with something that was known as the bill, the 'surrey with the fringe on top,' and so forth. It was demanding legislation that the handcars that were used by section workers should have tops on them. I didn't approve of it completely because I felt this should be negotiated in their contract of employment, rather than have to come to the legislature for legislation.[23]

While outsiders can ask for an exact wish list, the legislature sometimes provides a check on the interests.

Legislators' ability to introduce a bill and guide it to passage is widely considered an important aspect of being an effective legislator. Introducing high-quality bills – from a policy or political perspective – can help legislators demonstrate their accomplishments to constituents. Rosenthal (1981) describes an interview with a state legislator describing the dynamic that legislators face: "Constituents have valued the production of bills and we have responded to them by introducing more bills in order to get the limelight… Let's face it, we've got to look for payoffs. We're all politicians and we're all concerned about how we will be perceived by the public and whether we are appreciated" (quoted in Rosenthal 1981, p. 118). Moreover, effective legislators receive an electoral advantage as they are less likely to be challenged in primaries (Treul et al. 2022). Bills authored by groups or bureaucrats can help legislators in this regard.

Craig Volden and Alan Wiseman's widely used measures of legislative effectiveness incorporate the various stages of passage (Volden and Wiseman 2014). The first step in the lawmaking process is, of course, to have bill text to introduce. As I show in Chapter 4, bills sponsored by outsiders have a higher chance of passage than similar bills without an outside sponsor. Sponsored bills can also help legislators accomplish their goals. The *Ohio Capital Journal* describes model legislation as "a kind of skeleton key for state lawmakers. It's relatively easy to convey what you want a law to do. But actually drafting it to do so can be tricky. Groups like [the American Legislative Exchange Council] step in to provide the means to achieve those ends."[24] While a legislator could ask the bill drafting services to come up with statutory text on a particular topic to accomplish a certain goal, the quality will likely be lower than that of a model bill drafted by an interest group. In addition to demonstrating their effectiveness to constituents, legislators wish to signal to interest

[23] https://archive.org/stream/SettelmeyerFred/Settelmeyer%2C%20Fred_djvu.txt

[24] https://bit.ly/45XLf8J

groups that they are taking action in a policy area. What better way to do so than introducing the group's bill?

2.6 LEGISLATIVE CONTEXT

Each legislature's rules of the game and partisan configurations structure, constrain, and empower legislators to craft their own legislation and turn to outsiders for help. The general structure of state legislatures (excluding Nebraska) is the same, with bicameral legislatures and separation-of-powers institutions. Yet, many features such as session length, compensation, and term limits vary widely across states. Some legislatures are highly resourced with numerous staffing agencies, while others are impoverished institutions that rely on legislators performing legislative work for pennies. The context within which legislators operate shapes all aspects of the experience including their motivation to engage with outsiders and the incentives associated with legislating. I detail some of the institutions that vary across the states below with a focus on those related to capacity. I argue that the legislative institution's capacity to develop internal information and analysis can disincentivize reliance on outside sources and allow legislators to effectively evaluate the quality of information they receive from outsiders.

Although New Hampshire is the forty-first state in terms of population, it has by far the largest state legislature: 424 legislators, split unevenly between the lower (with 400) and upper (with twenty-four) chambers (Egbert and Fistek 2009). The legislature takes pride in its citizen legislature status; Squire (2017) rank it the least similar institution to the US Congress. Members must hold outside jobs or be independently wealthy as they are paid only $100 per year (Egbert and Fistek 2009). Members of the upper chamber do not get their own offices, and lower chamber members have no office space (Egbert and Fistek 2009). As of 2021, the entire legislature was allocated only 139 permanent staff and nine session-only staff; fewer than half a staffer per member.[25] Legislators therefore struggle to find high-quality information.

At the opposite extreme, the California state legislature is ranked the most similar to the US Congress in terms of professionalism (Kousser 2005; Squire 2017). California legislators need not hold outside jobs since they are paid $122,694 per year.[26] In 2021, there were 2,764

[25] www.ncsl.org/about-state-legislatures/size-of-state-legislative-staff

[26] https://ballotpedia.org/Comparison_of_state_legislative_salaries

staffers available to the state's 120 legislators.[27] California does have term limits, however, so overall legislative experience has dropped in recent decades.

In addition to variance in capacity, the demand for legislation in state legislatures also differs greatly. Laws that pass in California often spread to other states and countries. As a result, the California legislature is more saturated with interests vying for bills than the New Hampshire legislature. These rules of the game are often endogenous to the very state legislatures, and the institutions are not static within states. This variation generates the empirical analyses in the subsequent chapters of the book. The rest of this section details three types of institutional arrangements that vary across states and shape legislative capacity and partisan interactions: professionalism, term limits, and the presence of divided government.

2.6.1 Professionalism

The examples of New Hampshire and California reveal the importance of considering the development of professionalism in state legislatures. While these bodies are still considered backwaters by some standards, state legislatures have come a long way since the 1960s. For example, powerful former Speaker of the House, Jesse Unruh, is credited with professionalizing California's legislature. A biography of his rival, Phillip Burton, writes this about Unruh's role:

> Unruh believed that information and knowledge equaled power, and he set out to ensure that elected officials were able to get the data and expertise they needed to be effective. Information-starved legislators were at a perpetual disadvantage because they were dependent on lobbyists who always supplied facts and figures that benefited their clients. The governor's office, moreover, had an entire executive branch to compile data he needed to make policy. To correct that imbalance, Unruh very deliberately began to professionalize the assembly, hiring more and better trained staff, permitting members larger budgets to hire their own aides, expanding the number of interns. (Jacobs 1995, p. 93)

The politically savvy Unruh was motivated to increase the legislature's resources due to the branch's lack of power compared to interest groups and the executive branch. Reinsch (1907) similarly observed over 100 years ago that "The members of the legislature, having an unpolluted source of information at their command, gain self-reliance and

[27] www.ncsl.org/about-state-legislatures/size-of-state-legislative-staff

confidence, they are able to meet the pleader for special interests with strong arguments drawn from their independent armory" (p. 297). Their logic underlies the theory I develop in this chapter regarding the role of internal capacity and external relationships. When there is a vacuum of resources within the legislature, legislators will turn elsewhere for information in the form of bills drafted by outsiders from interest groups and the executive branch.

Staff are central to the functioning of legislatures. They help legislators manage their office and agenda, conduct casework, develop legislative ideas, and create political and legislative strategies. According to respected state politics scholar and observer Rosenthal (1986), "More than any other factor, the expansion of professional staffing has contributed to capacity" (p. 402). In California, a committee consultant relayed a story about a new chair who told the staffer: "I am ambitious, but have no agenda, that is what you are for; what will my agenda be?"[28] While the other components of legislative professionalism relate to legislators' motivation and time to do their jobs, internal capacity is most directly driven by the legislative resources available to review external information. The length of the session and legislator salary may not necessarily capture the time legislators spend on the job; they may be more indicative of the nature of the individuals who are able to do this nominally part-time job. In North Carolina, legislators note the full-time nature of the job, without full-time pay.[29] The number of days that these legislators meet does not always reflect the time they spend fulfilling their duties.

Staff do not automatically insulate the legislature from outside influence; they can sometimes be conduits for outside voices. In a fascinating series of interviews with staff, Warden-Washington (2010) reports that a chief consultant for the Assembly Arts, Entertainment, Sports, Tourism and Internet Media Committee in California described lobbyists as "de facto staff for the Legislature, even filling out background sheets for staff."[30] Even when highly qualified staff are available, including the committee consultants in California's legislature, lobbyists still provide valuable information. Staffers, especially those who are new to the job, are also hungry for aid given the complexity of their jobs and the time

[28] https://tinyurl.com/3crndx4n
[29] https://tinyurl.com/38h4hc6j
[30] https://tinyurl.com/3crndx4n

demands. Inexperienced staff "may be more willing than committee staff to accept what an agency drafts without question" (Shobe 2017, p. 475). Shortcuts, such as lobbyist information in clean forms, help staffers; this type of information seems to be most important for legislatures wishing to develop capacity.

2.6.2 Term Limits

Introducing term limits into a state legislature shakes up its composition and function in many ways, some of which may be unanticipated. Most term limits were imposed via ballot initiatives in the 1990s. Proponents claimed they were a panacea for many of the state legislative woes of the time. California's Proposition 140 from 1990 imposed a lifetime term limit on legislators and other offices and cut the legislature's budget. Supporters and critics of the initiative both claimed that term limits would either increase or decrease the influence of special interest groups. The former said term limits would "put an end to the life-time legislators, who have developed cozy relationships with special interests."[31] They were referring to the long-serving Speaker of the Assembly Willie Brown and the Senate Leader, David Roberti, since "[l]obbyists and power brokers pay homage to these legislative dictators, for they control the fate of bills."[32] Critics rebutted that the proposition "upsets our system of constitutional checks and balances, forcing our representatives to become even more dependent on entrenched bureaucrats and shrewd lobbyists."[33] In a similar logic, scholars argue that term limits can change the nature of representation by reducing legislators' internal knowledge and will to work for their constituency.

Studies of term limits have generally found evidence that they are associated with a host of the ills that their opponents predicted. Examining both individual legislators' trajectories and system-wide outcomes, this work concludes that term limits alter the behavior of individual legislators, the composition of the legislature, and aggregate activity in the legislature (Mooney 2009). Other research finds more qualified or limited connections between term limits and the predicted outcomes. For example, Carey et al. (2000) survey legislators across states with and without

[31] https://tinyurl.com/bde5jbkf

[32] ibid.

[33] ibid.

term limits and find that some of the expectations bear out while others do not. Kousser (2005) finds some evidence that the legislature's ability to negotiate with the governor on the budget drops after term limits are imposed. Governors seem more powerful after term limits are passed, which change the inter-branch dynamics (Carey et al. 2000; Carey et al. 2006). System-wide, Olson and Rogowski (2020) demonstrate that parties become more important after term limits. Fouirnaies and Hall (2022) report that a variety of metrics capturing legislative productivity drop in a legislator's final term.

These arguments and a variety of evidence highlight the importance of considering term limits in the interaction between interest groups, the bureaucracy, and the legislature in the analyses that follow. The bottom-line finding from all of this work is that term limits constrain the legislature by reducing institutional knowledge and reducing individual-level motivation for legislators to legislate.

2.6.3 Divided Government

Each state has a separation-of-powers system. No legislature can unilaterally enact its desired policies. The partisan composition of a state's legislature and executive branch shapes the nature of policymaking and cooperation between the branches. The governor and legislature adjust their actions based on the political dynamics at play in the other branches. This mutual reliance means that outside groups – especially bureaucrats aligned with the executive branch – may have different levels of success based on the partisan alignment between branches.

Understanding and capturing the dynamics of divided government is thus essential to analyzing the lawmaking process and actors' motivations. Huber et al. (2001) and Huber and Shipan (2002) also examine state-level legislative text, exploring levels of bureaucratic discretion granted via words added to statutes. This innovative study finds that legislatures increase statutory control when they have a divided government and more legislative resources. A main argument of this book is that bureaucrats get involved in crafting the statutes that govern their behavior. Though the interaction I model and capture is less about control of the bureaucracy and more a partnership between the bureaucracy and legislature, the same dynamics apply. The relative preferences and alignment of each institution's political motivations are essential for understanding these partnerships.

2.7 LOGIC OF THE INTERACTIONS BETWEEN PLAYERS

The above sections explore the motivations and constraints of the various relevant actors and institutions separately. However, when, why, and how these actors come together at the legislative agenda-setting stage is most important for this study. I argue that individual capacity, institutional capacity, and political dynamics interact to create the conditions under which these actors will engage. Demand and supply from legislators and the outsiders providing bills, respectively, drive the flow of outside legislation and the subsequent behavior of individual legislators and legislatures.

The trade-offs that legislators experience when working with outsiders drives my predictions about the conditions under which they should be more likely to accept and introduce group bills. Like college students writing papers, the choice to take shortcuts and use generative AI or plagiarize using online sources often depends on the time crunch. While I am not equating legislators using outsiders' information with student plagiarism, the same trade-offs apply. When legislators are time crunched, or the costs of legislating are higher, they are less able to manage the complicated task of legislating. Institutional capacity can provide a buffer between legislators and outsiders.

When do legislators need help? And what kind of help do they want? As discussed in Section2.5, legislators want to introduce and pass effective bills and claim credit for them without taking too much from time away from other activities. Bills that stray too far from their intended purpose can be embarrassing for legislators and potentially be used as ammunition in an opposition campaign. Authoring a bill, especially one on a complicated topic, that has the intended policy effect is costly. Legislators therefore need strategies to help reduce these costs. This work is even more difficult for legislators with few resources or little experience. In some cases, the legislator may give up some control over the direction or content of a bill in order to end up with one that can survive the legislative process. This trade-off animates the hypotheses surrounding system-level capacity and individual-level experience when bills are provided without tailored help. Sometimes, the goals of the outsider and legislator align when they want the same policy outcomes.

Legislators face different opportunities and limitations, which may create space for outsiders to step in to fill resource vacuums. Curry (2015) describes members of Congress as "legislating in the dark." They maintain that the influx of information flooding members on legislation leads to transfers of power to party leaders, who release summaries and dole out cues on how to act. I argue that at the state level, this lack of internal information leads to a transfer of power to outsiders (rather than party leaders) at the agenda-setting stage. At this stage, the information vacuum creates space for outsiders to write a vortex of bills for legislators to introduce.

My main dependent variables capture the portion of the legislative agenda or statutory session law that comes from outsiders, and the success of these bills. At the individual legislator level, I measure the number or portion of the legislator's agenda that originated from an outside source. These metrics help capture the relationships in the theoretical predictions.

2.7.1 Internal Capacity

Some legislators may be able to craft bills close to their ideal points at low cost. As the above discussion indicates, legislators can gain on-the-job experience in the art of drafting bills and navigating the political dynamics of the legislative process. Individual legislators' tenure seems to be related to their ability to successfully maneuver the complicated legislative process. Inexperienced legislators may jump at the offer of an easy-to-introduce outside bill that may win the approval of an outside group or attention from constituents and future voters. This relationship is conditional upon outsiders providing legislators with bills. As I discuss below, outsiders can find legislators to introduce their bill, but they prefer high-powered legislators to their first-term colleagues. My *Legislator Capacity Hypothesis* predicts that legislators are more likely to rely on group bills when they are in their first term.

I also develop expectations about legislatures' reliance on outside input in the form of prepackaged legislation. At the legislature level, the resources available to legislators within a chamber and the structure of the legislative body shape members' capacity to formulate legislation, and thus alter the attractiveness of model legislation as an alternative to independent drafting. Huber and Shipan (2002) find that professionalism is related to legislatures' ability to address policy issues, and Rogers (2010) concludes that the rate of law adoption is positively related to professionalism. Combined with the assumption that legislators wish to sponsor bills and produce legislation (Rosenthal and Forth 1978; Schiller 1995), members who are more constrained than their counterparts may rely more heavily on outsiders' laws. Legislators' sponsorship of outside legislation allows me to test theories about resources and group influence. All else equal, "information subsidies" from outsiders are more welcome when legislatures have reduced capacity (Hall and Deardorff 2006). Lower-capacity legislatures should also be more likely to introduce outsiders' bills of all types.

As discussed above, various metrics of legislative professionalism and term limits capture a legislature's system-level capacity. These institutional features affect the legislature's ability to operate independently. At the legislature level, this hypothesis applies to bills from the range of sources studied here. Interest groups and bureaucratic actors can fill in the gaps left by a lack of institutional capacity or institutional constraints. These differences across legislatures and incentives for information at the legislature level lead to the *Legislative Capacity* and *Legislative Constraints* hypotheses: I expect that when a legislature has lower capacity or is constrained by term limits, respectively, it will rely more on outsider input.

2.7.2 Divided Government

When different parties control the governor's office and the legislature, the calculations regarding close coordination with executive branch agencies change. When the government is under unified party control, legislators may continue to champion the bills offered by the departments and agencies controlled by the governor. However, a misaligned majority party may block these bills. While group bills come from a range of actors across the ideological spectrum, bureaucrats and the legislature engage in a well-defined and measurable partisan game. The bureaucrats proposing the bills work for agencies led by appointees of the governor. When there is divided government, the legislature exerts more control over the bureaucracy, and at the start of the process there will be less mutually beneficial cooperation.

Legislatures often need the governor's buy-in for legislative support, general goodwill, favors, and public attention, which may give the legislature additional motivation to introduce and adopt bills from bureaucrats. Indeed, powerful legislators may vie to introduce agency bills that have been blessed by the governor. Allied legislatures and executive branches will have mutual goals, and are likely to partner more than when they are divided. According to the *Bureaucrats' Unified Partner* hypothesis, a larger portion of the legislative agenda will be comprised of bureaucrats' bills when the government is unified.

2.7.3 Differences between Types of Outsiders beyond Partisanship

In an open market in which outside bills are available to any legislator, those who need them may use more. As I detail below, some model bills fall into this camp. When the outsiders' bills are in higher demand, more powerful legislators may choose to introduce more of them. Bills from outsiders are sometimes tailored to the political context such as a particular legislator; there are fewer trade-offs involved in these cases. Thus depending on the type of outsider, there are different predictions regarding which legislators will use more outsider bills.

Bureaucrats provide more technocratic and less political expertise than that offered by interest groups and other outside actors. This type of expertise is difficult for legislators to acquire, even more experienced ones (Gailmard and Patty 2013). Since bureaucrats are responsible for executing the laws that legislators pass, they have direct knowledge of what changes would improve a law's implementation. While the legislature can request reports from bureaucrats, directly presenting bureaucrats' bills to the legislature can give legislators an easy win. Abney (1988, p. 914) describes the difference between lobbying for a state agency and being a private sector lobbyist:

> One public lobbyist who had also been a private sector lobbyist described the major difference between the two roles as one of difference in accessibility. This lobbyist noted the difference in terms of the ease with which he now gets information from the state office of planning and budgeting. As a representative of a public agency, he is now considered a member of the team. A greater sense of trust exists. As a lobbyist for a private group he could get information from the budget office, but it did not come nearly as freely. As the lobbyist put it, he had to ask the right questions. Otherwise he would not get what he needed.

In his theory of the "dual dynamics" of information sharing between Congress and the bureaucracy, Workman (2015) argues that the (federal) bureaucracy is viewed as a very different type of information source to Congress compared to interest groups. Workman (2015) compares the tension between the goals of interest groups versus the more aligned goals of bureaucrats and legislators: "The federal bureaucracy holds some distinct advantages in comparison to organized interests in the provision of information to politicians plagued by uncertainty. These advantages are primarily due to the political economy of interest group supply and organization." While I focus on the agenda-setting stage of policymaking by looking at bill introductions, albeit a later agenda-setting stage than in some studies, this type of "information" is unique.

Model bills written by interest groups are simply posted online; any legislator is free to introduce them. Bills written by bureaucrats, however, are doled out by the agency actors. The supply side of bureaucrat-written bills drives predictions about what types of legislators should introduce this type of legislation. Other scholars have found that bureaucrats cozy up to and prioritize relationships with majority-party legislators and committee chairs who have jurisdiction over their policy area (e.g., Lowande 2019). My next hypothesis builds on that research to anticipate which legislators are attractive sponsors for bureaucrats' preferred bills. The *Bureaucratic Power Partner Hypothesis* predicts that legislators will introduce more bureaucratic bills as they gain more power. Unfortunately, I cannot observe which legislators bureaucrats first offer their legislation to. But the observable portion of the equation – which legislators introduce bills written by bureaucrats – tells us a great deal about the legislators bureaucrats chose to partner with. Similar to the logic in Hall and Deardorff (2006), certain legislators will be better able to translate outsiders' efforts into legislative action, so these types of legislators should be especially targeted. This leads to a testable implication: When legislators assume positions of power, which I measure as committee chairs or majority-party membership, they should introduce more bills from bureaucrats.

2.7.3.1 Bill or Group Area

Legislators may want to introduce a bill on a particular topic that is complex, politically important, or potentially subject to legal challenges. Niche groups, such as the National Association of Insurance Commissioners, likely understand insurance law better than legislators or even a state's general bill drafting services. While these state non-partisan offices have professionals who help draft legislation at the request of legislators (Hart 2016) and are essential for the functioning of the states, groups employ or recruit volunteers who are lawyers and experts on the topic. These groups spends a significant amount of time vetting bills offered to legislators with various experts and getting feedback on specific propositions. More ideological groups, like the

American Legislative Exchange Council, may use institutional capacity and memory to translate ideas into legislative language that will lead to their desired outcomes. These groups often examine similar laws in other jurisdictions and implications (e.g., judicial or economic) and tailor the language to achieve the legislator's preferred outcomes. Additionally, state bill drafting services are non-partisan offices. Thus, ideological groups may provide political expertise about the type of reception the bill will receive among the interested public.

Legislators and constituents will view bills provided by some groups or outsiders differently than others. While parts of this book lump together outsiders as varied as General Motors and the Bicyclists' Association, the quality of the bills these groups produce may significantly differ, and affect their uptake.

Given the combination of time demands plus the desire for specialist knowledge, legislators should prioritize groups or bills that provide political or subject-matter expertise. For example, state financial agencies may be much better suited than generalist legislators to draft bills on complicated financial matters. I expect there to be an *Expertise Premium*: Outsiders with expertise in complicated topic areas will be most successful either in getting their bills onto the agenda or passed.

2.8 SUMMARY OF EXPECTATIONS

Table 2.1 summarizes the hypotheses that the remaining chapters will explore. The type of outsider and resources and expertise at the individual legislator and collective legislature levels affect the relationships that will develop as well as the legislative implications.

TABLE 2.1 *Summary of hypotheses*

Hypothesis	Summary of hypothesis
Bureaucrats' unified partner	A larger portion of the legislative agenda will be comprised of bureaucrats' bills when the government is unified.
Bureaucrats' power partner	When legislators obtain positions of power, they will introduce more bills from bureaucrats than before assuming this position and relative to their peers.
Legislative capacity	When the legislature has lower capacity, it will rely more on outsider input.
Legislative constraints	When the legislature is constrained by term limits, it will rely more on outsider input.
Legislator capacity	Less experienced legislators will introduce more group bills.
Expertise premium	Outsiders with expertise in complicated topic areas will be most successful.

2.9 CONCLUSION

The actions taken by legislators, bureaucratic actors, and group representatives help us understand their motivations. Evidence from oral histories, other documents, and scholarly work demonstrates the conditions under which (and why) these outside actors are likely to interact and when we should expect more input from them. Determining where states' bills originate from requires identifying the origins of power in state legislatures – a main contribution of this book. When legislators are deciding where to turn for legislative ideas and bill text, several sources are attractive and likely across legislators, states, and over time.

Does it matter if an outside group came up with the idea or if the legislator initiated it and a group or agency drafted it? It can. I argue that this information provision can distort the overall set of legislation that the legislative body produces. Hall and Deardorff (2006) concludes that information subsidies from outsiders can distort the overall set of policies that a legislature produces. The finding that legislators and legislatures rely more heavily on outsiders' input when they have fewer resources paints a troubling picture about when and why the agenda and resulting laws may be altered.

After establishing the conditional relationships between legislative and legislature capacity and reliance on outsiders, the book examines the processes legislatures use to consider these bills and the public's views on legislatures' reliance on outsiders. My hypotheses that lower-capacity legislatures will rely more heavily on outside bills leads to the troubling normative conclusion that outsiders may seek to target legislatures that cannot adequately vet their draft legislation. Chapter 6 explores this possibility. By measuring the extent to which outsiders' bills are more complicated and more heavily altered than non-outsiders' bills, I assess the extent to which the legislative process serves as a check on these actors. While in some cases the legislature's reliance on information provided by subject matter experts may enhance the quality of the law, there may be process concerns if the legislatures do not check the outsiders' work. In Chapter 7 I examine voters' views to evaluate whether they ultimately care about the process through which these bills come about or just the politics. While public opinion is a downstream consideration, it speaks to the fundamental democratic implications of the legislator's job. What does the public think of legislators relying on outsiders for this input? Does it alter their perceptions of the legislature or their trust in the process? If so, this interaction may be problematic even if the bills that are ultimately passed are of higher quality.

In the following chapters, I employ a wide variety of data sources to evaluate the empirical predictions that flow from these observations. I focus on identifying the bills that originate in agencies, interest groups, and other outsiders to assess the relationship between legislative and legislator capacity in the reliance on this input. First, bureaucrats accomplish several goals by providing legislators with draft text and aiding in the legislative process. Using California as an example, I demonstrate how interest groups can provide legislation to get what they want in many circumstances. Legislators and legislatures will turn to bureaucrats and interest groups under different institutional, individual, and partisan conditions. I examine the sources, dynamics, and implications for representative democracy in the final chapters.

3

Bring in the Bureaucrats

Chapter 2 introduced my theory about the conditions under which outside agencies draft and promote legislation and how likely legislators and legislatures are to consider and pass these bills. Yet even within the same state, agency bills can differ in terms of the scope of actors affected by the legislation. For instance, in 2017 the Idaho Board of Tax Appeals proposed and drafted S. B. 1016, which would have increased board members' "daily compensation."[1] This bill was tailored to the specific interests of the board members, and seems to have been a rent-seeking attempt. S. B. 1005 originated in 2017 in the Idaho Department of Health and Welfare and proposed closing a loophole in the state's Child Protective Act to "increase the state's ability to protect minor[s who are] victims of sex trafficking."[2] This bill proposed altering a technical aspect of the law but had important policy implications. The agency was close to the policy issue and thus the bureaucrats knew the loophole may have had negative legal implications for a vulnerable population. It used its expertise to intervene in the legislative process and correct statutory omissions.

Examining bills requested by state agencies reveals the motivations and extent of the executive branch's involvement in the craft of legislating. These two agency bills in Idaho indicate a larger trend in the state's legislature: many agency bills have been considered and passed.[3] These

[1] https://tinyurl.com/mr4be57a

[2] ibid.

[3] Nearly 20 percent of the 2016 session's bills are estimated to have originated from legislative agencies: https://tinyurl.com/2p9uej9n notices that around 100 of the legislative session's 550 bills originate in legislative agencies.

two agency bills in Idaho's state legislature illustrate the topics covered by these bills and their differing implications and intents.

This chapter first examines the bureaucracy's role in shaping state law to demonstrate how my theory applies in the context of these specialists. While we typically think of groups like the National Rifle Association or the American Legislative Exchange Council as playing active roles in state legislatures, state agencies also have a special interest in being heard in these arenas. Chapters 4 and 5 examine how such lobbying groups influence the legislative process, while this chapter explores the role of the bureaucracy as the first mover. The cross-state and legislator-level nature of my data on bureaucrats' involvement allows me to test my hypotheses about the conditions under which the legislature should interact more or less with outsiders.

Past research on bureaucrats' role in the policymaking process typically concentrates on popular actors' rule-making authority. The typical process is thought to be: (1) the legislature crafts and passes legislation, (2) the governor signs the statute into law, and (3) the bureaucrats draft the necessary rules to implement the legislation. However, the separation of powers principle prohibits each branch of government from performing the functions of the other branches. The Massachusetts Constitution of 1780 mandates that "the legislative department shall never exercise the executive and judicial powers, or either of them: the executive shall never exercise the legislative and judicial powers, or either of them." What is considered a legislative power may be up for interpretation, but writing legislation and advocating on its behalf appears to violate this principle. While the study of variable delegations of political control from the legislature to the bureaucracy is essential for understanding the separation of powers, I argue that it misses the first step of the interaction by failing to consider how bureaucrats help draft bills. This chapter emphasizes the administrative state's role in the democratic process of drafting and advocating for legislation, which adds a wrinkle to a clean separation of powers story.

Using a hand-collected dataset from eleven states that reveals whether an agency proposed the legislation and a decades-long survey of administrators from all fifty states, I establish that bureaucrats play a surprisingly key role at the beginning of the legislative life cycle. The basic description of this process and the findings presented in this chapter complicate a simple separation-of-powers explanation of the lawmaking process and highlight the importance of studying a range of actors' involvement. This chapter describes the origins and process of bureaucrats writing bills for the legislature, introduces the two datasets, and analyzes the bureaucratic intervention and variation across the capacity and partisan factors highlighted in the theory.

3.1 ORIGINS AND PROCESSES

Bureaucrats have been involved in legislating for at least a century. For example, in its biennial report on the period from 1928 to 1930, the North Carolina Department of Agriculture touted its success in the legislature by recounting that "[t]he last Legislature, through the influence and activities of the Commissioner of Agriculture and others, enacted Chapter 325, providing for the production and certification of crop seeds for North Carolina Farmers."[4] Over time, the movement to professionalize state legislatures has altered the inter-branch relationships, but the need for information from the actors carrying out legislative directives remains.

The institutions that have developed around bureaucrats' role in the legislative process provide initial evidence that this bureaucratic function is important to both bureaucrats and the legislature. The interactions between the legislative and executive branches run both ways: the bureaucracy requests bills, and legislators and committees frequently solicit or require information and reports from bureaucrats. While this chapter focuses on bureaucrats' direct involvement in drafting bills, both roles shape the formation of these inter-branch relationships.

At the federal level, agencies "have extensive legislative interests, and have evolved effective machinery, operating within an annual legislative cycle, for converting legislative ideas into legislative language" (Hirsch 1989, p. 1). In the mid-1960s, many federal departments began employing legislative liaisons (Fiorina 1989, p. 63); state agencies also started this practice. North Carolina agencies are now statutorily required to have at least one legislative liaison,[5] and "the Office of the Attorney General has the statutory duty to draft bills at the request of the state's many departments and agencies (called 'agency bills')."[6] The agencies do not keep these interactions secret; they feature their legislative programs online. The institutions and official roles that agencies have established to facilitate their interaction with the legislature demonstrate

[4] https://tinyurl.com/3h4c5wu8
[5] www.ethicscommission.nc.gov/governmental.aspx
[6] http://nchouse117.com/how-the-general-assembly-works/

that these ties are institutionalized and that the bureaucracy privileges such interactions.

3.2 DATA

This chapter employs two unique datasets to develop my theory about the conditions under which legislatures and legislators use the input of state-level bureaucrats. I created the first dataset by collecting information from state legislatures' websites. Several states clearly list which bills are introduced at the request of a state department or agency (i.e., they originate outside of the legislature), which allows me to connect the bills to specific legislators who choose to introduce bills from bureaucrats. This dataset expands our knowledge of bureaucratic involvement at the state and individual legislator level.

The second dataset, released by Jason and Susan Webb Yackee, draws on a long-running and comprehensive survey of state administrators. It covers administrators from all fifty states and queries their involvement in the legislative process at multiple points in time. This information fills a gap in my dataset, which only includes states that disclose information about bill origins. The following sections describe these datasets in detail. Together, they establish that the bureaucracy has a heavy but conditional hand in state lawmaking.

3.2.1 Bureaucratic Bills: Bill-Level Data from the Legislatures

Eleven state legislature websites clearly specify which bills are introduced at the request of a state department or agency (what I call agency bills); they do so in a variety of ways (see Appendix A.2). These states are California, Maryland, Montana, North Carolina, North Dakota, Nevada, New York, Idaho, Oregon, South Dakota, and Washington. Some states list agency bill requests alongside the bill's legislative sponsor. Others do not coherently identify which bills are agency bills. For example, several state agencies in Virginia post a list of the bills they proposed to the legislature, but this information is not available on the legislature's website[7] and is not consistently listed for all state departments. Some agency bill markers in these eleven included states are not obvious and were determined via personal correspondence with various

7 This was determined via email correspondence with the Virginia Legislative Information System.

state legislators or employees. I also collect information on a number of other variables about the bills from the state legislatures' websites, including whether the bill passed into law (*passage*), the number of words in the bill (*length*), and the bill's sponsor (where available). These variables help determine why legislatures and legislators involve bureaucrats and what factors predict their participation.

Ideally, I would have panel data on all fifty states and be able to establish the extent to which each state legislature uses agency bills. However, this analysis is limited to the eleven states that indicate which bills agencies offer. While it is possible that these states may have different patterns of interaction between agencies and legislatures if they openly provide this information, these states reflect the overall population of states in terms of legislative institutions and resources. In the next section, I confirm that the same patterns hold across all states by examining a survey of bureaucrats in all fifty states that asks about their interactions with legislatures.

The eleven states included in the dataset are representative of all states on a number of important dimensions. Nearly a third (30 percent) of the states in the sample have term limits (California, South Dakota, and Montana), just as 30 percent of all states have term limits. The states in the sample are also almost evenly split across the National Conference of State Legislature's classification of full- and part-time legislatures.[8] Furthermore, the states adhere to national trends on deferring to state agencies. Before the US Supreme Court overturned it in 2024, there was a long-standing federal precedent of *Chevron deference* – the notion that agencies' interpretations of legislation should prevail if laws are ambiguous. Hudson (2009) classifies state courts as either (1) recognizing a "strong, Chevron-like deference to state agencies' interpretive efforts," (2) being split on their deference, or (3) not deferring to state agencies. This standard of interpreting the authority of agency actions in each state is important for understanding the motivations and abilities of state-level agencies. In my sample of states that post detailed bill information, one might expect states with court systems that do *not* defer to state agency interpretations to be overrepresented, since these states may give greater preference to agencies on a number of dimensions. However, this is not the case.

[8] https://tinyurl.com/errf45j2

3.2.1.1 Bureaucratic Bills: Volume and Rates

Agency bills comprise a large, but varying, portion of the legislative agenda. Table 3.1 presents the information available for each state and the years for which it is available.[9] Across all eleven states in the same, 35,195 of the 390,906 bills introduced were offered by bureaucrats (9.0 percent of the introduced bills). Bureaucrats' bills pass at a remarkably high rate: 59.4 percent (compared to 22.6 percent of non-bureaucratic bills). Additionally, departmental bills comprise a high portion of the bills that pass into law (20.6 percent). In Oregon and South Dakota, about 35 percent of the passed bills were from departments. Departments shape the legislative agenda, and also propose a sizable portion of the statutory law in some states. Departmental bills pass at a high rate in all states in the sample – over 40 percent in all but Washington. As I discuss in Chapter 4, this high passage rate mirrors the finding about bills sponsored by outsiders in California. Bureaucratic bills' high chance of passage and relative success hints at their appeal to legislators hoping for a legislative victory.

3.2.2 State-Level Predictors of Agency Bill Utilization

In this section, I explore the state- and session-level predictors of agency bill utilization. To assess the theoretical expectation that legislatures with fewer resources will rely more heavily on the bureaucracy for expertise, I estimate models for states' use of bureaucrats' bills as a function of partisan and resource configurations. The unit of analysis is at the state, s, session level, t. The main dependent variables are (1) the proportion of introduced bills that are departmental and (2) the proportion of departmental bills that pass in that state and session. The *Proportion of introduced bills that are departmental* variable indicates the number of bills that are departmental divided by the number of bills introduced in that session of the state's legislature. The *Proportion of departmental bills that pass* is the number of departmental bills that are introduced in that state during that session divided by the total number of departmental bills that pass into law during that session. Finally, *Proportion of passed bills that are departmental* denotes the number of departmental bills that pass into law in that state during that session divided by the total number

[9] Appendix A.3 walks through each state and the percentage of introduced and passed bills that are departmental.

TABLE 3.1 *Data available per state*

State	Years	No. all Bills	No. Departmental bills	% Introduced departmental	No. Bills passed	No. Departmental bills passed	% Passed departmental	% Departmental bills passed
CA	1993–2014	60,989	3,939	6.46	23,840	2,874	12.06	72.96
ID	1999–2010	8,693	1,242	14.29	5,368	951	17.72	76.57
MD	1997–2012	39,862	1,833	4.6	10,873	1,194	10.98	65.14
MT	1991–2018	18,037	2,875	15.94	8,886	2,229	25.08	77.53
NC	2001–2016	26,446	397	1.5	5,641	171	3.03	43.07
ND	1997–2018	11,000	1,824	16.58	6,808	1,553	22.81	85.14
NV	1997–2018	12,283	2,286	18.61	6,246	1,601	25.63	70.04
NY	2005–2016	115,951	2,288	1.97	14,504	942	6.49	41.17
OR	1997–2018	33,843	5,504	16.26	9,828	3,477	35.38	63.17
SD	1997–2016	11,815	2,247	19.02	5,417	1,948	35.96	86.69
WA	1991–2016	51,987	6,060	11.66	3,942	1,056	26.79	17.43
Totals	—	390,906	30,495	—	101,353	17,996	—	—

The table presents the years for which each state has information on departmental bills available. The columns present the number of bills introduced in that state, the number of departmental bills, the number of introduced bills that are departmental, the number of bills that pass through the state legislature, the number of departmental bills that pass, and the percentage of passed bills that are departmental.

of bills that pass into law during that session. These dependent variables account for the total number of bills introduced or passed in a session.

The main independent variables capture the legislature's partisan and resource environment. *Unified government* is an indicator variable assigned a value of 1 if the lower chamber, upper chamber, and governor all belong to the same party, and 0 otherwise. When the same party controls both chambers of the legislature and the governor's office, it may be easier to agree on which policies are acceptable than if the other party controls any of these institutions. I account for the need for partisan agreement to achieve consensus in the legislative setting by looking at the unity of government institutions. Giving another branch a win in the form of getting its preferred legislation introduced and passed is expected to be more difficult when different parties control the branches.

The state legislature's ability to independently generate information and policy also affects the extent to which it relies on the executive branch to prompt legislative ideas. To capture legislative capacity, I use three variables commonly associated with legislative professionalism (Squire 1992, 2007, 2017; Bowen and Greene 2014). The Squire score is a widely used index in state politics research; it uses "the relevant attributes of Congress as a baseline against which to compare those same attributes of other legislative bodies" (Squire 2007, p. 212). Squire uses salary, average number of days in a session, and average staff per member to compare state legislatures to Congress. On his index, a score of 1 indicates that the legislature perfectly resembles Congress and 0 means no resemblance. In later refinements of this score, Bowen and Greene (2014) argue that legislative professionalism should be measured as an index with the components of *session length*, *salary*, and *legislative expenditures*. Rogers (2023) shows that the metrics are related in different ways to state legislators' accountability. Since each of these variables may be distinctly related to legislative interactions with outsiders, I include each component.

As discussed in Chapter 2, I pay particular attention to legislative *Expenditures* to measure the resources available to state legislators across states. This component of state legislative resources is the most closely tied to the drafting of legislation. While the other two additions to the Squire index, salary and session length, may be tied to the legislators' motivation and ability to focus on lawmaking, they are also linked to the types of individuals who will seek election and the value of the seat. The amount of resources flowing in the legislature to the information environment is the measurement most closely related to the theoretical expectation that low-capacity legislatures turn to outsiders due to a lack of internal capacity. This measure captures the resources and demands on the legislative institution to craft legislation.

The presence of term limits varies across states and alters the relationship between state legislatures and outside forces by limiting their individual and collective experience. I therefore include an indicator variable for *Term limits* that denotes whether they were imposed on legislators in that session. While term limits vary in stringency, I include a simple indicator variable for ease of interpretation; previous research indicates that the presence or absence of term limits (rather than their type) is the relevant metric for state legislative motivations (e.g., Carey et al. 2006).

Since this chapter focuses on the interactions between the executive and legislative branches in the crafting of legislation, I need to assess their relative capacity. *Executive and legislative salary difference* from Boushey and McGrath (2016) captures the salary difference between executive branch officials (excluding the governor) and the legislative branch. Larger values indicate greater salary differentials between the two branches. I use this variable to proxy for the difference in capacity between the branches (Boushey and McGrath 2016; Berkowitz and Krause 2018). While I would ideally be able to compare each branch's staffing or employ other metrics similar to the legislative professionalism score, this is the best available measure of the difference in priority between the state legislature and executives.

3.2.3 State-Level Results

In this section, I apply all the considerations about relative partisan alignment and various metrics of legislative capacity institutions to the data I collected on the extent of reliance on bureaucratic bills at various stages of the legislative process. The dependent variables are all proportions to capture the extent of the legislative agenda, success of the bureaucrats' bills, and the formation of successful legislation that is passed by the legislature.

The results highlight interesting state-level patterns about the use and success of bureaucrats' bills across varying state conditions. The first set of models includes a more limited set of variables and the second set contains the more limited availability of the *Executive and legislative salary difference*. Table 3.2 reports the results from beta regressions of the proportion of introduced bills that are departmental and the proportion of

TABLE 3.2 *Beta regression models*

	(1) Prop. depart.	(2) Prop. depart.	(3) Prop. depart. pass	(4) Prop. depart. pass
Unified gov.	−0.17	−0.25	0.29**	0.06
	(0.15)	(0.19)	(0.10)	(0.09)
Term limits	0.36	0.31	1.19*	0.93*
	(0.26)	(0.16)	(0.49)	(0.47)
Log sess. length	−1.25**	−1.06**	0.28	0.13
	(0.45)	(0.36)	(0.66)	(0.51)
Log salary	0.07	—	0.04	—
	(0.21)		(0.25)	
Log expenditures	0.02	−0.01	−0.51*	−0.62*
	(0.07)	(0.10)	(0.22)	(0.29)
Exec. and legi. salary diff.	—	0.00	—	−0.02*
		(0.01)		(0.01)
Constant	3.54*	3.20*	1.68	4.32**
	(1.41)	(1.61)	(1.94)	(1.55)
Phi	3.69***	3.55***	2.13***	2.31***
	(0.33)	(0.35)	(0.30)	(0.28)
Session fixed effects	Yes	Yes	Yes	Yes
Observations	107	80	107	80
Log lik.	181.07	128.22	56.81	48.61

The first two columns model the proportion of introduced bills that are departmental, and columns 3 and 4 model the proportion of departmental bills introduced that pass into law. Robust standard errors are clustered at the state level and all models include session fixed effects.

Standard errors in parentheses.

$^{*}p < 0.05$, $^{**}p < 0.01$, $^{***}p < 0.001$.

departmental bills that pass. I use beta regressions because the dependent variables are proportions and do not assume values of 0 or 1 (Ferrari and Cribari-Neto 2004). I also model the results using ordinary least squares and a generalized linear model with a logit link; the binomial family and results are substantively similar.

Unified government exhibits a strong and positive relationship with the portion of departmental bills that pass in that session and state. However, this variable is not significantly related to the proportion of introduced bills that are departmental. This finding may be explained by legislators introducing departmental bills that have no chance of passing to demonstrate to constituents that they are attempting to work on a topic.

However, *Unified government* is positive and significantly related to a higher proportion of departmental bills passing. This indicates that the partisan structure of the branches relates to the success of bureaucrats' bills, even though other considerations are at play in the formation of such bills as a proportion of the overall legislative agenda.

In all regressions, some metric of legislative professionalism is negatively related to the proportion of introduced bills that are departmental and the proportion of departmental bills that pass. Term-limited legislatures are associated with a higher proportion of departmental bills passing and forming the legislative agenda. When legislatures are constrained by limited expenditures or time considerations in the form of term limits, a higher portion of the agenda comes from bureaucrats, and bureaucrats are more successful at passing their bills. These variables are especially important for the models of the proportion of department bills that pass (Table 3.2, columns 3 and 4). As my theory emphasizes in the *Legislative capacity* and *Legislative constraints* hypotheses, the measures of expenditures and term limits should especially matter for the legislature's reliance on outsiders.

Next, I compare the executive and legislative branches' resources. In Table 3.2, columns 2 and 4, I remove the log of legislative salary measure since both covariates use legislative salary in their construction. Contrary to my expectations, the *Executive and legislative salary difference* is negatively and statistically significantly related to both the proportion of introduced bills that are departmental and the proportion of departmental bills that pass. In the data, when the executive makes more than the legislative branch, a lower proportion of the introduced bills are departmental. This could be due to altered incentives when the legislature's salary increases. While the measure may indicate that the bureaucracy's capacity is stronger than the legislature's, higher legislative salaries may also "dampen the incentives for legislatures to allocate scarce time and effort to influence public agencies" (Krause and Woods 2014). When legislative salaries are lower than bureaucrats' salaries, the legislative opportunity cost of legislating on bureaucratic topics may be lower. Other measures of relative bureaucratic and legislative capacity should be captured in the future to assess this relationship. For example, vacancies in the state bureaucracy may indicate a lower capacity than a fully staffed state legislature.

Table 3.3 models the proportion of passed bills that are departmental. These models exhibit fewer patterns of relationships between partisan or capacity variables than the models of the success of departmental

TABLE 3.3 *Passage Beta regression models*

	(1) Prop. passed departmental	(2) Prop. passed departmental
Unified government	−0.27	−0.29
	(0.14)	(0.21)
Term limits	0.37	0.18
	(0.35)	(0.24)
Log sess. length	−1.28**	−0.99*
	(0.47)	(0.39)
Log salary	0.25	—
	(0.24)	
Log expenditures	−0.04	0.05
	(0.12)	(0.15)
Exec. and legi. salary diff.	—	0.00
		(0.01)
Constant	4.23**	3.09
	(1.57)	(1.79)
Phi	2.98***	2.87***
	(0.36)	(0.36)
Session fixed effects	Yes	Yes
Observations	107	80
Log lik.	115.70	81.78

The columns model the proportion of passed bills that are departmental. Robust standard errors are clustered on the state and all models include session fixed effects.
Standard errors in parentheses.
$^{*}p < 0.05$, $^{**}p < 0.01$, $^{***}p < 0.001$.

bills. The survey data from all fifty states, which specifies the portion of the passed bills *dealing with the specific agency* that originate in the department, shows the expected relationships, which suggests that in the findings using the sample of eleven states, the denominator is inflated. While all bills that pass are important for state functioning, agencies may not have a chance to influence bills on topics beyond their specialist focus.

Overall, these correlations support the hypotheses that legislatures with fewer resources, or those constrained in gaining experience by term limits, will rely more heavily on bureaucrats for statutory ideas and be more willing to pass bills they propose into law. The partisan configuration of unified government also affects the uptake of these bills. When one party controls all branches of government, the legislature allows more of the bureaucrats' proposals to pass into law. The characteristics of the legislature and partisan alignment with the bureaucracy shape this strategic inter-branch interaction. Differences in the institutional environment, partisan conditions, and legislative resources alter legislators' willingness to partner with bureaucrats in this way.

3.2.4 Bill-Level Description

To determine what types of bills departments and agencies propose, and investigate legislators' motivations for accepting this input, this section addresses two components of classifying bills. These classifications capture the intent of the bills and their partisan nature; they shed light on what motivates legislators to accept help from the executive branch of government. What issues are these outsiders successful at shepherding into law? These descriptions speak to both the assumption that these bills would be attractive to legislators wishing to solve problems and the *Expertise premium* hypothesis. This hypothesis posits that outsiders in areas that are complex will see more success. If bills from state agencies are consensus pieces of legislation, they can supply a useful and high-quality product that gives easy and "cheap" wins to legislators and free up their time for other pursuits.

I manually categorize a sample of the bills (n = 400) based on their intent, which varies from housekeeping and cleaning up statutory law to significantly expanding the authority of the bureaucrats who are drafting and requesting the legislation. I then assess the partisan nature of the bills proposed by bureaucrats to determine whether they are controversial. I gather data on the votes taken on bureaucrats' bills to explore partisan conflict. I find that these bills are *not* dividing the parties; they garner votes from the minority party and do not split the party vote.

3.2.4.1 Categorization

Perhaps the most fundamental question about these bills is what they seek to do. I code a random sample of 400 departmental bills across the eleven states in my sample into nine categories as listed in Table 3.4. The largest category is those that clean statutory law; these bills can help close loopholes or make it easier for individuals and businesses to follow the law. Bills that expand the department's authority are the most important category for the book: studying this connection is important for understanding the statutory discretion granted to the bureaucracy. Nearly one-fifth (19 percent) of the bills *requested by bureaucrats* fall into this

TABLE 3.4 *Categorization of random sample of bureaucrats' bills*

Category	Percentage
Cleans statutory law	25
Expands department's authority	19
Adds requirements for entities	16
Appropriations or paying claims	12
Creates/expands board/program	7
Restricts department's authority	5
Regulates employees	3
Memorial	3
Other	10

category. For example, in Washington state, the Department of Agriculture requested H. B. 1462 in 2017, which seeks to allow the department to "regulate sanitary processing of marijuana-infused edibles."[10] Bureaucrats help shape the nature of their directives, which complicates a simple separation of powers dynamic and brings bureaucrats into the legislative process.

3.2.4.2 *Partisan Breakdowns*

In addition to the category of bills and their cost, the partisan breakdown of the votes taken on bills proposed by bureaucrats may reveal insights into the partisan conflict generated by these requests, and the nature of legislative cooperation on the issues the bureaucracy deems important enough to suggest as legislation. To gauge the partisan composition of the votes on bureaucrats' bills, I match the bill-level dataset with LegiScan data on roll-call votes. Complete LegiScan data is available for only a subset of the years and states in my bill-level dataset. Table 3.5 presents the year and state information for which data is available on both bills and votes. LegiScan scrapes and processes data from state legislative websites. It has several CSV datasets per state and session, which present roll-call votes per legislator, legislator characteristics (e.g., party and district), vote description and final tally, and bill information. First, I merge these LegiScan datasets to produce a tally of the number of yea, nay, and absent votes by Republicans, Democrats, and Independents per vote.

[10] https://app.leg.wa.gov/billsummary?BillNumber=1462&Year=2017

TABLE 3.5 *Years of joint roll-call and bureaucratic bills data availability per state*

State	Years available
California	2009–2014
Idaho	—
Maryland	2010–2012
Montana	2011–2018
North Carolina	2011–2016
North Dakota	2009–2018
Nevada	2011–2018
New York	2011–2016
Oregon	2011–2018
South Dakota	2010–2016
Washington	2009–2016

Next, I merge this information with the bill-level data on bureaucrats' bills to generate a vote-level dataset of bills (Table 3.5).

To assess the level of partisanship of these bills and compare departmental vs. non-departmental bills, I create several variables that indicate the bills' partisan slant. To construct these variables, I follow Curry and Lee (2020), which studies the relationship between regular order legislative lawmaking and partisan conflict. These authors use multiple variables to measure partisan conflict, which is the metric I seek to capture. To assess highly partisan votes, I calculate a dichotomous measure that indicates if at least 90 percent of each party votes in a different way than the other party (Curry and Lee 2020, p. 632). To capture a lower threshold of partisan votes, the next variable is a dichotomous measure which indicates that at least 50 percent of each party votes in a different way than the other party (Curry and Lee 2020, p. 632). The final variable is a continuous measure that indicates the level of bipartisan support for a bill (i.e., the percentage of the minority party in favor of its passage).

To explore the relationship between departmental bills and partisanship, I run a series of sparse linear regression models (see Table 3.6). The indicator of whether a department proposed the bill (*Departmental*) is the sole independent variable. The dependent variables evaluate partisan conflict on the vote: *50% Party vote*, *90% Party vote*, and *% Minority party*. All models include state and year fixed effects, which account for baseline differences in partisan conflict across states and sessions.

TABLE 3.6 *Party votes on state bills by departmental status*

	50% Party vote	90% Party vote	% Minority party
Departmental	−0.09***	−0.04***	0.08***
	(0.005)	(0.003)	(0.004)
Constant	0.33***	0.23***	0.68***
	(0.01)	(0.005)	(0.01)
State fixed effects	Yes	Yes	Yes
Session fixed effects	Yes	Yes	Yes
Observations	56,016	56,024	54,779
R^2	0.07	0.08	0.07
Adjusted R^2	0.07	0.08	0.07

*$p < 0.05$; **$p < 0.01$; ***$p < 0.001$.

The results are logical: departmental bills are less likely to split parties because they are consensus based. This strong, negative correlation holds whether party vote is measured at the 50 percent or 90 percent level. Moreover, there is a positive association between departmental bills and bipartisan support. Departmental bills garner more of the minority party vote than those that are not offered by bureaucrats.

Therefore, when legislators are searching for bills that will accomplish a discrete task and pass, those introduced by bureaucrats are attractive options. These bills pass at high rates with little disagreement in the legislature. When legislators are looking for an easy win that solves a clear problem, bureaucrats' bills may be the ideal solution.

3.2.5 American State Administrators Project Survey

The American State Administrators Project (ASAP) Survey complements my observational data about which bills come from state bureaucrats (Yackee and Yackee 2020). Whereas my bill-level data provides information from legislatures, this survey captures the bureaucrats' views and input. Together, these two datasets identify the conditions under which state legislatures and bureaucrats work together on legislation.

Many of the survey questions touch on important aspects of the claims I make in this chapter and provide initial evidence that the state bureaucracy contributes to the body of state law. Those related to the legislative provision of information have not yet been explored in the scholarly literature. While these surveys have been conducted for years, they have only recently been made available via the efforts of Susan Webb Yackee. Thus, they provide an exciting trove of information about the status of agency–legislature interactions.

My observational data cannot assess the portion of bureaucrats' time spent on policymaking. The number and percentage of bills that originate in the bureaucracy are important outcomes, but are perhaps difficult to compare across states. Some states require bills to focus on a single topic, which *may* make bills from these states simpler and more compact compared to states that do not have (or do not enforce) this requirement. Research by Farhang (2021) on the US Congress suggests that comparing the number of statutes passed may obscure their content over time. My focus on the number of bills proposed by bureaucrats could thus also be difficult to compare across states. The amount of time bureaucrats spend on policymaking may reveal more about the executive branch's involvement in lawmaking than the number of bills they craft. Conveniently, ASAP asks bureaucrats what percentage of their time is spent on policy development, specifying that this work can be in concert with the governor, legislators, and boards. I use these survey items to measure bureaucrats' assessments of their reach into state legislative development.

3.2.6 Administrator Assessments of Their Role in Legislating

How do state bureaucrats conceptualize their role in the legislative process? In the question most closely related to the book's intent to gauge the role of non-legislators in crafting state law and the variable conditions under which this relationship changes, state administrators were asked about the origination of state law. Their responses to the query: "Percentage of [introduced/passed] legislation affecting the agency that originates in the agency" reveal high perceptions of agency aid in crafting legislation. Respondents claimed that high levels of bills (affecting the respective agency) came from the agency itself during the 1974–2008 time period. Most legislation that deals with the agency originates in the agency. The percentage of introduced legislation that administrators said originated from the agency hovers around 50 percent: it peaked at 62 percent in 1974 and dropped to only 41 percent in 2008. The percentage of passed legislation that administrators claimed *originated* from the agency is slightly higher than the percentage of introduced legislation.

The straightforward survey items directly address the question regarding what are considered "departmental bills" and corroborate the findings from my observational data. While my data reveals which bills are labeled as coming at the request of the agency, these indicators may vary across states in their completeness or differ in regard to what "originate" in the bureaucracy means. While there is anecdotal evidence that this indication means the idea for the bill and general language came from the department, the meaning of this designation may vary across states. The survey evidence establishes that a high proportion of state legislation and passed laws dealing with the agency "originates in the agency," which confirms that my observational finding reflects the extent to which bills come from the bureaucracy. Another survey question only contained in the 2008 wave asked respondents "Over the past four years, has the respondent's agency influenced the decision-making of the legislature? If so, to what degree from 1 (low) to 5 (high)?" Nearly half (47 percent) of the respondents claimed that their agency had a high or very high degree of influence over the legislature's decision making. The answers to these questions confirm that agencies play a prominent but conditional role in drafting laws.

3.2.7 Which Agencies?

The agencies that are most active in the lawmaking process provide some leverage on the proposed relationships between legislative reliance on outsiders and issue area complexity. As with the observational bill-level data, the categories indicate the type of policy area that the legislation deals with. Respondents' agencies are categorized into thirteen functions (e.g., education, economic development). Appendix A.5 reports the examples given for each category by the ASAP researchers.

The variation in responses across agency categories reveals insights into how expertise shapes perceptions of influence in the state legislature. Figure 3.1 plots responses to questions about the extent to which legislation affecting the agency originates in that agency across the categories. The figure reveals that the top categories differ for the introduced vs. passed bills. According to administrators in transportation-related departments, the highest percentage of *introduced* bills originate in that agency, whereas income security and social services rank the highest for *passed* bills.

In the observational bill data, fiscal and budgetary-related departments are among the most frequent bill requestors. While the types of categories differ across the datasets, income security appears to be similar in intent. This finding bolsters the (*Expertise premium*) theory underpinning

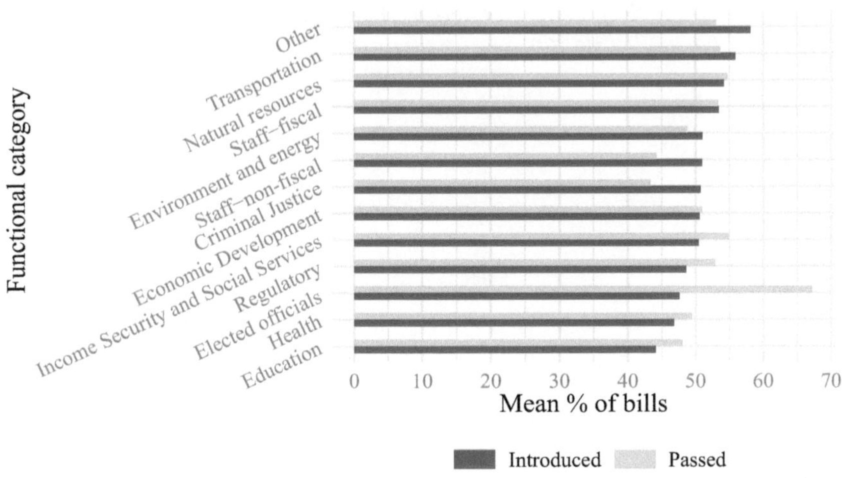

FIGURE 3.1 Mean percentage of introduced and passed bills that affect the originating agency (ASAP respondents).

legislators' use of these bills. When uncertainty over policy area and the need for expertise increase, legislators will become more dependent on outsiders.

Within the bills that affect their agencies, state administrators reported that a mean of at least 40 percent of bills came from their agency, across all functional categories of bureaucracy. This high percentage makes a compelling case for the need to incorporate the bureaucracy into our understanding of state separation of powers. These powers do not seem so separate when we consider the executive branch's role in crafting legislation relevant to their own agency. The survey data thus reinforces the findings from the observational bill data: bureaucrats are very involved in legislating matters that relate to their own agencies.

3.2.8 State-Level Predictors of Administrator Assessments of Bill Sources

Beyond the sheer volume of law coming from bureaucrats, my theory also predicts that there should be partisan and capacity patterns in the relationship between the bureaucracy and state legislature. Under a unified government, more bill writing should be "delegated" to the bureaucracy. However, as the legislature's capacity increases, it should develop more legislation internally. Table 3.7 explores these relationships. The dependent variable in Column 1 is the percentage of introduced bills that affect

TABLE 3.7 *Regression models of the percentage of introduced and passed legislation that originates in the agency from ASAP survey responses*

	% Introduced originates in agency	% Passed originates in agency
Unified government	2.17	5.18*
	(1.16)	(2.26)
Term limits	0.63	2.07
	(2.42)	(2.25)
Log session length	−0.28	1.94
	(2.05)	(2.44)
Log legislative expenditures	−4.81***	−4.06**
	(1.24)	(1.46)
Log legislative salary	−0.69	−0.95
	(1.21)	(1.11)
Constant	87.63***	86.72***
	(9.42)	(13.84)
Functional category fixed effects	Yes	Yes
Appointment category fixed effects	Yes	Yes
Year fixed effects	Yes	Yes
Observations	3,345	1,561
R^2	0.077	0.056
Adjusted R^2	0.070	0.042
Residual std. error	31.353 (df = 3319)	33.358 (df = 1538)

Limited to administrators who are appointed by the governor with legislative consent, appointed by the governor without legislative consent, or appointed by a board or commission with the governor's consent.
$^{*}p < 0.05$; $^{**}p < 0.01$; $^{***}p < 0.001$.

the agency that originate in the agency, and Column 2 lists the dependent variable as the percentage of passed bills that originate in the agency. I run linear regression models since the percentage of bills that administrators identify as originating from the bureaucracy ranges from 0 to 100 percent, including the upper and lower bounds; beta regression analysis is therefore not an option. This analysis only includes administrators who are appointed by the governor with legislative consent, appointed by the governor without legislative consent, or appointed by a board or commission with the governor's consent. The unit of observation is the state administrator per survey. The question about passed legislation was asked in fewer years, so there are fewer observations than for introduced legislation. Year, functional category, and appointment category fixed effects are included, and robust standard errors are clustered at the state level. The variables used in the observational data analyses to capture legislative capacity and divided government are merged with the ASAP dataset to assess the proposed theoretical relationships.

The results reported in Table 3.7 exhibit a similar pattern to that created using the observational bill data: partisan misalignment between branches of government decreases partnerships between the bureaucracy and the legislature. Table 3.2 displays the regression results for the observational data; they reveal a negative relationship between divided government and the passage rate of agency bills. Similarly, Table 3.7 establishes the positive and statistically significant relationship between unified government and the percentage of introduced (and particularly passed) legislation that originates from an agency, according to administrators. When a state has a unified government, the percentage of passed legislation that originates in the agency increases by a statistically significant 5.18 percentage points. When different parties control the executive and legislative branches of government, the partnerships during legislative formation change in substantial and systematic ways.

Some of the variables associated with resources and constraints relate to the legislative agenda and passage as anticipated, but others do not. As expected, there is a negative relationship between legislative expenditures and legislative salary and use of agency bills. When these forms of legislative resources increase, the legislature shifts away from agency-originated legislation as a part of the agenda. I observe a strong finding within the observational data that term limits are associated with significantly greater reliance on agency bills, but I do not find this relationship in the survey data. The analyses using both datasets provide solid evidence that bureaucrats and state legislators work together under specific partisan and resource conditions, in line with my theoretical expectations.

3.2.9 ASPA Data Wrap-Up

This section provides complementary evidence that the fifty states in a different context adhere to the pattern observed using the observational bill-level data from the subset of eleven states. The results are similar in terms of resource and partisan constraints when we explore administrators' perceptions of agency involvement in lawmaking. Combining what state legislatures reveal and what administrators claim provides corroborative evidence that significant portions of laws come from bureaucrats. Both types of data complement each other and indicate that bureaucracies are closely involved in legislative affairs. But this relationship is conditional on partisan alignment between branches and legislative resources.

The survey data is provided by bureaucrats, who may be motivated to overstate how effective they are at getting preferred legislation into the legislature. Their recollections of the percentage of legislation that originates from the agency are likely to be less precise than the observational bill data, and their responses may reflect perceptions of partisanship, resources, or relationships with the legislature. However, the fact that the results between the observational and survey data are similar strengthens my confidence that I am picking up on substantial relationships between partisan alignment between the branches, resources, and reliance on the bureaucracy for legislation.

Next, I explore which individual legislators introduce bureaucrats' bills. Since the survey data does not include information on *which legislators* administrators partner with, we cannot use it to assess which ones are attractive partners for bureaucrats. However, the *types* of legislators bureaucrats successfully partner with tells us about the rationales on both sides of these interactions.

3.2.10 Which Legislators Introduce Bureaucrats' Bills?

While the observational data does not indicate which legislators bureaucrats *approach* to sponsor their bills, it does detail the end result of this matching process. The partnerships that form between individual legislators and bureaucrats highlight individual characteristics that may make legislators appealing partners for bureaucrats. The findings reveal the importance of power for bureaucrats hoping to get their bills passed and the ability of legislators with power to attract offers of help from specialists.

To investigate Abney's 1988 observations revealed in the previous chapter and the theory's prediction that legislators in positions of power will sponsor more bureaucratic bills, I use a difference-in-differences (DID) design to examine the partisan predictors of sponsoring agency bills. This approach allows me to evaluate changes to the conditions that make the legislator a more attractive partner to the bureaucrat and assess whether these changes are associated with greater sponsorship of bureaucrats' bills.

According to the ally principle, we should expect legislators from the governor's party to sponsor more agency bills. From the supply side of which legislators bureaucrats will approach with their legislation, we expect to see majority party legislators sponsor more agency legislation. This analysis is limited to legislators in the California, Montana, and Washington state legislatures. Committees sponsor agency bills in most of the other eleven states in my sample, making this individual-level analysis impossible. The unit of analysis is the legislator-session.

The outcome variable for this analysis is *No. Departmental bills introduced* in a session. The main independent variables are the majority party status of the legislator and an indicator of their shared partisanship with the governor. *In chamber majority* is coded 1 if the legislator is in the majority of their chamber and 0 otherwise. *Gubernatorial copartisans* is coded 1 if the legislator and governor belong to the same party and 0 otherwise. *Tenure* captures how long the legislator has been in office. *Chair* and *Leader* come from Fouirnaies (2018) and Fouirnaies and Hall (2018) and indicate whether a legislator chaired a committee or was a "majority leader, minority leader, minority leader, speaker, president, or president pro tempore" during that session (Fouirnaies 2018, p. 178). I also include a control for the logged number of bills a legislator introduces (*No. Bills introduced*). Together, these variables form a panel dataset of legislator utilization of bureaucratic input.

I follow several recent papers that use this DID design to study legislative behavior or campaign contributions when legislators gain leadership positions (for the latter, see Fouirnaies (2018) and Fouirnaies and Hall (2018)). This design allows me to isolate the effect of becoming a committee chair, or being in the same party as the governor or majority party, on sponsorship of bureaucrats' bills. In other words, what happens when a legislator switches from being a rank-and-file member of the legislature to obtaining a position of power by becoming a committee chair? Does this person become a more attractive partner for bureaucrats and thus receive and introduce more departmental bills? The DID design allows me to answer these questions and empirically examine the theoretical predictions about when legislators should sponsor more bills from the administration.

The DID analysis includes legislator and session fixed effects. The former account for differences in legislators' proclivities to partner with bureaucrats: legislators may have different beliefs about working with bureaucrats or have worked in a bureaucracy before entering elected office. These fixed effects account for legislator-level characteristics that

TABLE 3.8 *Legislator-level bureaucratic bill introductions*

	Number of departmental bills introduced	
Leader	−0.09	−0.03
	(0.25)	(0.24)
Committee chair	0.53**	0.63***
	(0.17)	(0.16)
Chamber majority	0.48*	—
	(0.22)	
Governor copartisan	—	0.56***
		(0.13)
Log introduced	1.59***	1.68***
	(0.15)	(0.15)
Legislator fixed effects	Yes	Yes
Session-state fixed effects	Yes	Yes
Observations	2,980	2,980
Legislators	1,162	1,162

Robust standard errors clustered on the legislator are included. Legislator fixed effects, and session-state level fixed effects are included in the models. The dependent variable is the number of departmental bills that legislator *i* introduced in session *s*.
$^{*}p < 0.05$; $^{**}p < 0.01$; $^{***}p < 0.001$.

do not vary during their time in office. The latter control for shocks within particular legislative sessions that are common to all legislators. *Chamber Majority* is an indicator variable for whether the legislator belongs to the same party as the chamber majority in the session. *Governor Copartisan* indicates whether the legislator belongs to the same party as the governor during that session. From Fouirnaies (2018), *Committee Chair* and *Leader* are variables for whether the legislator served as a committee chair in that chamber and session or a legislative leader, respectively. To control for the size of the legislator's agenda, I include the logged number of bills they introduced in the session, *Log Introduced*. All models include standard errors clustered at the legislator level.[11]

Table 3.8 presents the results of the DID regression analysis. Legislators in positions of power (partisan alignment with the majority/governor or committee chairs) partner with bureaucrats more than those without

[11] Given the session fixed effects, I do not include the tenure variable in these regressions.

such influence. This empirical finding aligns with Abney's 1988 observation that administrative lobbyists prefer to use legislators in positions of power to sponsor their bills and the proposed relationships under the ally principle. Becoming a party leader does not cause legislators to increase their sponsorship of bureaucrats' bills, likely because they are not in primarily policy positions. These results indicate that bureaucrats and legislators who gain positions of policy power work together. Transitioning into the chamber majority party causes an increase of about one more bill coming from the bureaucracy. Becoming a committee chair is associated with about 0.53 more of a bill coming from the bureaucracy in each session.[12] While this is a relatively small effect, it demonstrates that legislators in leadership positions are more attractive partners; it yields roughly the same effect size as switching into the chamber majority or being in the same party as the governor.

When legislators become committee chairs, they are more likely to introduce departmental bills. This relationship between positions of power and the use of bureaucrats' bills provides further evidence that bureaucrats choose to partner with legislators who are more likely to guide the bill into law. This finding constitutes compelling evidence that, from the legislator's perspective (even after they become a committee chair), bureaucrats represent a very appealing source of information and legislation. This chapter establishes that bureaucrats also prefer to work with legislators in leadership positions and that legislators in committee positions are happy to partner with them.

The discovery that powerful or well-resourced legislators partner with bureaucrats may seem inconsistent with the finding at the state level that greater resource constraints increase the use of bureaucratic input. However, at the individual legislator level, bespoke bills from bureaucrats do not present a tradeoff; even powerful legislators are hungry for this type of information and vetted legislation.

Together, these various sources and levels of data analysis suggest that bureaucrats are very involved in legislative affairs. The observational and survey data both demonstrate that legislators rely on state-level departments for a significant proportion of the legislative text they introduce. This finding undermines a strict separation-of-powers view of government in which the legislature legislates, and the executive branch executes

[12] In Appendix A.4, following Fouirnaies (2018), I estimate whether being a committee chair in session *s* is related to sponsoring agency bills in sessions before *s*. I establish that the future role of committee chair is not significantly related to agency sponsorship in previous sessions when the legislator was not a chair.

these laws. This system highlights the importance of partisan dynamics: when the same party controls all three branches of government, motivations align, and bureaucrats' bills succeed at higher rates and create more laws that affect their agencies. In legislatures that have fewer investments in legislative expenditures, a higher portion of their agenda is drawn from the executive branch. Since departments provide targeted information in bill form that is likely to pass and potentially save the state money, powerful legislators are attractive and willing partners with the bureaucracy.

While the results do not uniformly display the patterns due to difficulties associated with refining the observational denominator of which bills deal with the agency, together they demonstrate clear patterns of regular involvement conditional on partisan alignment between branches and legislative resources.

3.3 BEYOND THE DATA: OTHER WAYS BUREAUCRATS GET INVOLVED IN LEGISLATIVE PROCESSES

State-level agencies also lobby for and *against* legislation and work with interest groups to indirectly lobby the legislature. This chapter complicates the traditional separation of powers model in which the legislature is the first mover. Bills that state government departments and agencies bring to the legislature and shepherd to passage are central to lawmaking. These tactics are just one way in which these actors attempt to translate their preferences into law. In this section I note several other entanglements that relate to the introduction of laws, but are beyond the scope of this study.

The budgetary process also involves the input of state-level bureaucrats, which relates to the relationships between legislatures and bureaucrats, and vice versa. Bills that started as "by request" from the agency are sometimes incorporated into the broad budget. For example, the North Carolina State Department of Motor Vehicles (DMV) requested a bill to extend the renewal period for drivers' licenses from eight years to sixteen years. While the proposal was not adopted as a standalone bill, the idea was incorporated into the state's 2023 budget.[13] A legislative oversight hearing was held due to concerns that the proposal might violate federal REAL ID legislation; a blame game ensued. Department of Motor Vehicles Commissioner Wayne Goodwin said the

[13] www.newsobserver.com/news/politics-government/article286051471.html

legislature had come up with the idea, while legislators claimed "We've been thrown under a bus to the media and to the Board of Transportation by someone in your agency, and we were told it was you."[14] This interaction (under divided government) illustrates that discord persists between agencies and legislatures, and partisan and organizational divisions may exacerbate inter-branch conflict over legislative proposals. Including departmental proposals in "must-pass" budget bills is another example of how the strict "by request" definition under counts the full extent of bureaucratic influence on legislation.

The measures of involvement employed in this chapter to evaluate bill origination do not capture general lobbying by state-level departments and agencies. State agencies spend a substantial amount of time and money lobbying state legislatures (and the federal bureaucracy). For example, Rachel Beaulieu, the Legislative Affairs Program Director for the North Carolina Department of Public Instruction and the State Board of Education, spent 100 percent of her time lobbying for these agencies and conducted a wide range of activities; she "develops and writes legislation for introduction and oversees preparation of accompanying descriptive and fiscal impact information; secures sponsors for legislation and sponsors on such proposals and their justification."[15]

A more circuitous pathway between bureaucrats and legislators involves using interest groups as intermediaries. Bradley (2014) and Bradley and Haselswerdt (2016) explore this indirect form of lobbying. Interest groups also bring concerns to the departments, which may lead to a departmental bill. An example of this pathway is S. B. 486 during the 2003 session of the Nevada state legislature; the Department of Agriculture responded to the "concerns of the industry by adding a board member to the State Board of Agriculture to represent the sheep industry."[16] Another example puts this into blunt terms about getting National Association of Insurance Commissioners (NAIC) preferred bills bolstered as agency bills across the states: "when [Commissioners] place NAIC models on their prized list of 'agency bills' every year. Agency bills receive a political 'leg up' in the competition of the legislative process because the proposals are wrapped in the 'disinterested' robes of a public official."[17] Beyond wanting to get a bill introduced into the legislature, securing introduction with the "agency bill" byline can give additional

[14] https://tinyurl.com/yc2ejzsn

[15] https://tinyurl.com/266vx2sv

[16] www.leg.state.nv.us/Session/72nd2003/Minutes/Senate/NR/Final/2578.html

[17] https://roughnotes.com/rnmagazine/2013/july/2013_07p056.htm

credence to the interest group's legislation. The data presented in this chapter is the tip of the iceberg in terms of bureaucrats' role in the legislative process. However, the patterns of partnerships and utilization across varying levels of resources revealed in the chapter shed light on broader questions of bureaucratic input in the legislative marketplace.

3.4 CONCLUSION

State legislatures constitute an ideal setting in which to explore predictions about the relationship between the bureaucracy, the legislature, and policy formation while varying institutions and capacity for two reasons. First, some states provide information about which bills are introduced at the request of bureaucrats. This measure of agency involvement is not readily available at the federal level, complicating efforts to detect which legislative products are shaped by the bureaucracy. Second, the variation in institutions (e.g., term limits and legislative veto of rules) and institutional capacity of legislatures and bureaucracies enable the study since the predictors are not constant. Previous studies have compared state bureaucracies to examine related questions (e.g., Huber and Shipan 2002; Huber et al. 2001; Krause and Woods 2014; Woods 2015). This chapter further demonstrates that states are ripe grounds for examining the collaborative, but contingent, relationship between the bureaucracy and legislative branch.

Questions about bureaucrats' varied responses to statutes that originate in the bureaucracy versus the legislature follow from this initial exploration. Potter (2017) establishes that agencies strategically use timing in the rule-making process to "undermine political oversight by Congress, the president, and the courts." Other scholars find evidence that agencies decide which statues to implement (Acs 2015). At the state level, Boushey and McGrath (2016) find that states with bureaucracies that have better funding than the legislature are more likely to promulgate more rules. This work provides considerable evidence that bureaucrats strategically engage in policymaking via their rule-making decisions. A natural extension of this project would be to determine the bureaucratic response to bills that they draft. Given the substantial groundwork that the agency put into drafting the bill for the legislature, I expect bureaucrats to quickly implement agency bills that pass.

The interdependence between legislators and bureaucrats to create and implement policies, provide information, and carry out constituency service likely has implications for their partnership patterns and communication. Recent work by Ritchie (2018, 2023) finds that legislators request and receive assistance from bureaucrats. Agents then conditionally share this information depending on appointees' politicization (Lowande 2019). Ban et al. (2024) establish that Congress strategically solicits information-packed testimony from the bureaucracy. Fiorina (1989) says that these small favors that legislative liaisons perform for legislators are "a cheap price to pay for [the legislator's] goodwill on a legislative proposal dear to the department's heart" (p. 64). Together, these works spur questions about the link to the bureaucracy's legislative agenda. For instance, do legislators introduce a department's bill after it fulfills a legislator's service request? In hearing testimony, an Illinois state legislator contemplated holding up a department's bill in order to get information on a separate matter. During questioning about H. B. 2720, a bill requested by the Department of Central Management in Illinois's 91st legislative session, Representative Black stated that "sometimes the only way that we can get an agency to respond is to just say we're going to hold your addend Bills [his term for 'departmental bill'] until we get an answer." Representative Black urged the legislature to resist departmental bills and threatened that "we're not going to advance your department agenda until you get some of these question[s] answered, we never can seem to get the questions answered."[18] This exchange demonstrates that bureaucrats' bill requests do not exist in a vacuum; the departments and legislators have repeated interactions. These patterns and relationships can alter the effectiveness of bureaucrats' preferred bills and the attention that legislators can get from bureaucrats. This research on the success of bureaucrats' bills and which legislators sponsor them is a primary link in the systematic study of this chain of interactions in state legislatures.

Some departments even keep scorecards (identical to interest group scorecards) and examine how frequently legislators voted with the department's interests. At the federal level, Parrillo (2013) notes that "the federal government argued for its preferred interpretation of a statute by citing legislative history to show that the agency, in proposing the measure, had put congressmen on notice that it would have that meaning." Examining the relationships between bureaucrats, legislators, and resulting policy would advance this emerging work on these interconnections.

[18] www.ilga.gov/house/transcripts/htrans91/t031099.pdf, p. 149.

While my theory treats the actors as somewhat automated beings with varying characteristics such as professionalism, legislators' experience, and partisan composition, the bureaucrats and legislators are real humans, and we know that identity differences shape interactions within these governmental bodies. Uttermark et al. (2023) examine the "experiences of women of color in leadership roles within state government agencies, their communication with elected superiors, and perceptions of their own policy discretion and communication compared to white men and women, and men of color." The descriptive representation of legislators and resulting partnerships between actors (à *la* Lowande et al. (2019)), especially legislators and bureaucrats who share descriptive characteristics, may reveal interesting patterns in the bill sponsorship data.

The extent of bureaucrats' involvement in the legislative process that I demonstrate using new data on bills introduced at bureaucrats' request contributes to the separation-of-powers literature. Statutory control of the bureaucracy is thought to be a primary form of control of the legislative principal over the bureaucratic agent. However, I establish that bureaucrats secure their preferred legislation. Their role in the legislative process suggests that current metrics of statutory control may imperfectly determine the balance of power between the legislature and agencies since they do not consider the bureaucracy's role in their formation. Bureaucrats are important sources of information for legislators and help set the legislative agenda.

4

Legislating from the Outside in the Golden State

The FBI conducted sting operations in at least eight state legislatures in the 1980s based on allegations that legislators were accepting bribes in exchange for bill introduction or votes.[1] These state legislature scandals suggest a parallel logic of alleged wrongdoing for legislation action in return for money or favors; they prompted retorts that this is how business is done in the states for promoting legislation. Specifically, in California, former state legislator Gwen Moore's legislative aide Tyrone Netters was convicted of "extortion, conspiracy, racketeering, money laundering, and income tax evasion."[2] Netters accepted "$10,500 in illegal campaign contributions" in exchange for introducing A. B. 3773 and A. B. 4203 on behalf of two fake front companies (Gulf Shrimp Fisheries, Inc. and Peach State Capitol, Inc.).[3] These bills passed through both chambers of the state legislature, but did not become law because the FBI alerted Governor Deukmejian who vetoed them[4] due to their rent-seeking nature. The governor cautioned, "I am concerned that this special-interest legislation will benefit one company to the detriment of others that may be similarly situated."[5] The governor's reasoning reflects the general normative concern regarding bills proposed by outsiders. When interested parties write the legislation and the legislature fails

1 These states were California, Illinois, Kentucky, Louisiana, South Carolina, Tennessee, and West Virginia (Rosenson 2005).

2 www.oac.cdlib.org/findaid/ark:/13030/c8ks6trs/entire_text/

3 ibid.

4 There is some speculation that the FBI did not alert the governor, and that he independently chose to veto the bills.

5 www.latimes.com/archives/la-xpm-1988-08-30-mn-1290-story.html

to fully vet it, interests can unilaterally give unfair advantages a legal blessing.

The FBI's fake companies were listed on the bills as their "sponsors" in a stark example of the issue investigated in this chapter: The institutionalization of outsiders in work that seems to be the sole purview of the legislature (see Figure 4.1). This case of group sponsorship is more dramatic than most in the well-resourced legislature but highlights the regularity of the disclosure institution and the range of bills that the California legislature considers to be group sponsored.

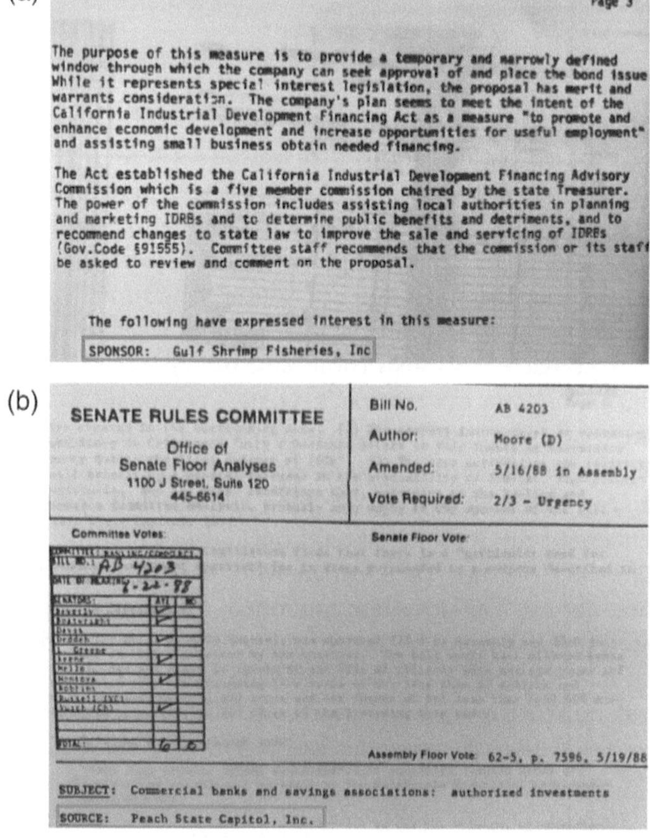
(a)

AB 3773
Page 3

The purpose of this measure is to provide a temporary and narrowly defined window through which the company can seek approval of and place the bond issue While it represents special interest legislation, the proposal has merit and warrants consideration. The company's plan seems to meet the intent of the California Industrial Development Financing Act as a measure "to promote and enhance economic development and increase opportunities for useful employment" and assisting small business obtain needed financing.

The Act established the California Industrial Development Financing Advisory Commission which is a five member commission chaired by the state Treasurer. The power of the commission includes assisting local authorities in planning and marketing IDRBs and to determine public benefits and detriments, and to recommend changes to state law to improve the sale and servicing of IDRBs (Gov.Code §91555). Committee staff recommends that the commission or its staff be asked to review and comment on the proposal.

The following have expressed interest in this measure:

SPONSOR: Gulf Shrimp Fisheries, Inc

(b)

SENATE RULES COMMITTEE

Office of
Senate Floor Analyses
1100 J Street, Suite 120
445-6614

Bill No. AB 4203
Author: Moore (D)
Amended: 5/16/88 in Assembly
Vote Required: 2/3 - Urgency

Committee Votes:

BILL NO.: AB 4203
DATE OF HEARING: 7-22-88
TOTAL: 6 0

Senate Floor Vote:

Assembly Floor Vote: 62-5, p. 7596, 5/19/88

SUBJECT: Commercial banks and savings associations: authorized investments

SOURCE: Peach State Capitol, Inc.

FIGURE 4.1 Excerpts from bill analyses for A. B. 3773 (A) and A. B. 4203 (B). These bills were proposed by the FBI, fronting as Gulf Shrimp Fisheries, Inc. and Peach State Capitol, Inc., in the late 1980s. Despite the illicit activities surrounding the introduction of these bills, the fake entities are clearly listed on the bill analyses.

The FBI's justification for this years-long sting operation highlights the nature of group–legislative relations. The operation culminated in a court case that reveals fascinating background information about the culture of group relations in the state capitol (*U.S. v. Freeman*, 6 F.3d 586 (9th Cir. 1993)):

> In 1986, the FBI initiated an undercover investigation into suspected corruption in the California legislature. The investigation arose as the result of conversations in 1982 between Marvin Levin, who was working as a citizen informant for the FBI, and Freeman, who was then employed as a legislative staff member for the California Assembly. During these conversations, *Freeman made statements indicating that special interest legislation could be purchased in the California legislature and that he expected to be paid for his efforts as a staff member. (emphasis added)*

While the bill analyses were not available online prior to 1993, the prevalence of group bills in the 1990s and 2000s indicates that the phenomenon was widespread at the time of the sting. Figures 4.2 and 4.3 chart the success rates and volume of these sponsored bills in the California state legislature. While this book does not explore the nature of corruption or rent seeking that arose during these FBI stings, the dramatic instance of a group-sponsored bill speaks to the widespread nature of the provision of bills by outsiders in this important state legislature.

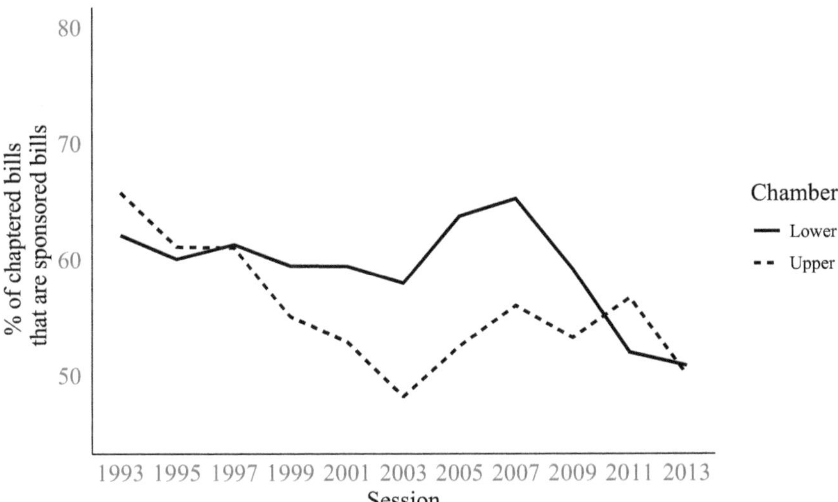

FIGURE 4.2 Percentage of *chaptered* bills that are sponsored bills, per session and chamber, 1993–2014.

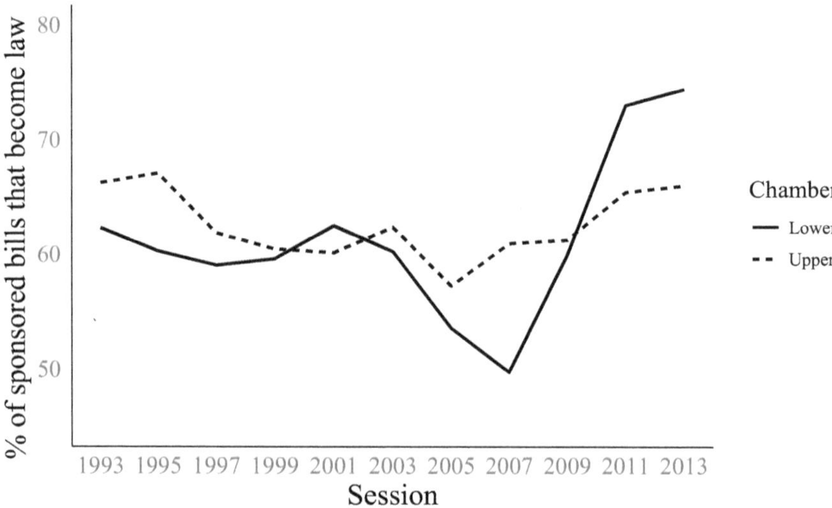

FIGURE 4.3 Percentage of *sponsored* bills that are chaptered, per session and chamber, 1993–2014.

Moreover, the reason the legislative aide gave for transmitting the bill to Representative Moore was: "because [the bill] supported a small business and had the potential for generating jobs for minorities and women."[6] While perhaps motivated reasoning, this rationale speaks to the desire to use these outsiders' bills for the good of the representative's constituents and legislative goals. While Representative Moore had been in office for several years before the sting, the data indicates that legislators tend to introduce more group bills in their first term than in later terms; this allows inexperienced legislators to show voters and groups that they are actively representing their interests.

The range of groups and types of actors present in the dataset demonstrates that simply studying the involvement of national-level groups in state politics overlooks an important aspect of the state policymaking story. In this chapter, I explore the types of groups that sponsor bills in the California state legislature. While I do not classify them as "national" or not, state agencies and municipal entities are well represented as sponsors. By definition, these types of groups are not national and contribute many bills to the California legislature.

[6] https://law.justia.com/cases/federal/appellate-courts/F3/6/586/577009/

In a typical example of a legislator partnering with a group to sponsor a bill, in 2013 California State Senator Kevin de León proudly touted his introduction of S. B. 402, a bill about breastfeeding protocols in hospitals, in a press release on his personal website. Reporters were directed to the bill's sponsor, the California Women, Infants, and Children Association, for further information about the bill (Rosenhall 2013).

Sometimes legislators introduce bills on behalf of a group or individual because they have personal ties to the lobbyist. Alternatively, they may not entirely agree with the bill but think it should be heard. A dramatic example involves former California state legislator Leon Ralph, who introduced a bill about dog racing on behalf of a lobbyist named George Hardie. Another legislator had promised to introduce the bill but had backed out hours before the bill introduction deadline. As Ralph recounts:

> George made a beeline from that senator's office – who's a fine man – to my office on the third floor. I was chairman of Rules. He walked in, and his eyes were big as saucers. He said, "It happened." I said, "You don't even have to tell me. I know what happened. He won't carry it, right?" He said, "No." He had had the legislation drafted with his name on. I said, "Give it to me." I took a pen and struck out that senator's name and wrote my name in and said, "I'll put it in because I think it deserves its day."[7]

Ralph emphasized that part of the reason he introduced the bill was because of his personal ties to the lobbyist: "I carried the dog racing bill as a personal favor to George Hardie, whom I had come to know after he arrived on the Sacramento scene."[8] After introducing the bill, Ralph received a death threat; he remembers "a letter arrived in my Sacramento office warning me that if I took the legislation to the committee hearing, I would be killed."[9] Several attempts were made on his life, and he received round-the-clock police protection. This instance of introducing a controversial bill on behalf of a non-legislator generated an unusual amount of (violent) pushback, but it illuminates the decision-making process behind such partnerships. The legislator reluctantly introduced a bill that was entirely the idea of the outsider to give it "its day" to be considered. Although the legislator was listed on the bill, its origins were clearly outside the legislature.

[7] https://archives.cdn.sos.ca.gov/oral-history/pdf/ralph.pdf
[8] ibid., p. 48.
[9] ibid., p. 49.

These examples demonstrate the breadth of subjects covered by bills introduced on behalf of outsiders, the motivations behind their introduction, and the drama this process can create. The rest of the chapter explores the nature of these relationships between legislators and the interest groups, companies, bureaucrats, and local governments that propose bills. In the next section I introduce the California state legislature and the unique institution that allows me to study these interactions in this state.

4.1 A PORTRAIT OF THE CALIFORNIA LEGISLATURE

California has the most polarized state legislature in the country; it is far more polarized than the US Congress (Shor and McCarty 2011). With eighty members of the Assembly who serve two-year terms and forty in the Senate who serve four-year terms, each legislator represents a large constituency. Masket (2009) argues that informal party organizations combined with the primary system drive the state's ideological polarization. From 1992 until the time of writing, Democrats have controlled the California Senate; the Assembly was under split control in the 1995–1996 session and under Republican control in only the 1997–1998 session. Trifecta control is occasionally out of reach for Democrats due to Republican control of the governor's mansion from 1992–1998 and 2004–2010.

Proposition 140 instituted stringent term limits in 1990 and limited legislators to six years in the lower chamber and eight years in the upper chamber; legislators started to term out in 1996. Voters weakened these limits in 2012 (via Proposition 28) to twelve years of service in either or both chambers. Term limits altered the state legislature's composition, turnover rates, staff retention and experience, and predicted role of outsiders.

Proposition 140 also cut the legislature's budget by 39 percent,[10] which triggered significant reductions in staff (especially senior staff) and resources (see Cain and Kousser (2004) p. 39). Yet California still has more staff than any other state legislature.[11] Many *permanent legislative staff* perform policy functions and constituency service in a number of offices. Non-partisan fiscal staffers are found in the Legislative Analyst's Office, which was created in 1941 to analyze the gubernatorial

[10] https://lao.ca.gov/LAO75

[11] www.ncsl.org/research/about-state-legislatures/staff-change-chart-1979-1988-

budget.[12] The Assembly Office of Research (created in 1966) was a source of policy expertise before it was dissolved, and the Senate Office of Research remains a source of information for legislators; it produces the bill analyses explored in this chapter.

Committee staff are described as "more professional and less partisan than personal staff;" they provide policy expertise relevant to the committee's topic area (Cain and Kousser 2004). These staff are "[a]mong the best-paid employees of the Legislature" and "specialize in specific policy areas and who advise lawmakers on legislation. They are the Legislature's experts, and their advice often shapes legislation that has major impacts on California life. The consultants, especially the veterans, are at the heart of the legislative policy community, providing institutional memory in a setting where the elected officials change constantly because of term limits."[13] The budget cuts mandated by Proposition 140 decreased the number of committee consultants from 173 in 1990 to 143 in 1995 (Cain and Kousser 2004, p. 27).

Personal staff serve individual legislators in both Sacramento and in each legislator's district office. These employees provide politically minded advice. As of 2007, "The payroll for the personal staffs of the 48 Democratic Assembly members totals $13.3 million. They average 5.5 staffers on a payroll of $277,508. Their Republican counterparts have a total payroll of $7.9 million, dividing out to 6.1 staffers and $247,407 in payroll per member."[14] Democrats also have additional staffing available via their leadership and majority status on committees. These various staffers may balance out or provide additional avenues for outsiders to contact insiders.

In the California state legislature, extra-legislative organizations or individuals that write legislation and secure a legislator to "author" the bill *may* be (but are not always required to be) listed as "sponsors." Over the time span analyzed, almost 40 percent of the bills introduced list an extra-legislative sponsor and 60 percent of the bills that become law are sponsored. In this chapter, I leverage this clear reporting institution to study groups' policy-making success and legislators' motivations for relying on group assistance. While pairing model legislation and textual reuse methods allows me to study the uptake of national groups' bills in

12 https://lao.ca.gov/LAO75

13 https://capitolweekly.net/salaries-for-legislatures-staff-top-129-million/

14 https://capitolweekly.net/legislative-staff-salaries-where-the-money-goes/

all fifty states in Chapter 5, this chapter examines the universe of group bills in more depth in a single state legislature.

This data establishes that many entities may sponsor a single piece of legislation, which differentiates these groups from the national-level organizations that proliferate model bills. Though model bills have received a considerable amount of attention, many groups are focused on the legislation in a single state. As studied in Chapter 5, the American Legislative Exchange Council (ALEC) has promulgated over 1,000 model bills throughout the country. Many of the groups that issue sponsored bills in California are interested in changing a single law or including an additional provision in the state code. Focusing on model bills may overlook particularly important instances of groups that attempt to alter the legislative structure.

This chapter highlights the intense role that non-legislators of all types (across the political spectrum, resource levels, and classifications) play in the legislative process. While prior research relies on studies of a single well-funded organization (such as ALEC) or a survey of state legislators to assess the extent to which outside groups are shaping state legislation, this work does not map out the universe of groups that are involved in the process of legislating (e.g., Hertel-Fernandez 2019).

News stories in California cover the prevalence of groups in the legislative process via this sponsorship indication. This high-quality reporting sheds light on the sponsorship process but has not decreased the use of group bills (their percentage remained stable between 2011 and 2018). Moreover, this reporting focuses on the legislature level and does not examine the *legislator-level* predictors of partnering with groups, as I do in this chapter.

The California state legislature broadly defines a bill's sponsor as the "legislator, private individual, or group who developed a piece of legislation and advocates its passage."[15] Legislators may also be sponsors, but I drop these during the processing step. A bill's author is "a member of the legislature who introduces a legislative measure."[16] The author is always a legislator while the sponsor can be a legislator or outsider. California has disclosed this information since at least the 1940s, when Anderson (1942) observed that there was a delay at the beginning of the session in the introduction of bills because groups "have not learned enough of [legislators'] abilities and interests, to make certain whom they want as

15 www.legislature.ca.gov/quicklinks/glossary.html
16 ibid.

authors of their bills" (p. 135). In addition to drafting the initial version of the bill, investigative journalists report that sponsors provide authors with talking points, memos, and testimony, and authors often allow the sponsor to "approve or reject bill changes during the committee process" (Meyers 2015). This feature of the California state legislature allows me to explore the dynamics of group–legislator interactions at the bill level.

I provide evidence that even though California state law does not require groups to be listed as sponsors, legislators follow a strong norm of disclosing outside sponsors. This institution of transparency presents an exciting opportunity to study the composition of state bill origins. For instance, in the Gwen Moore case described above, both bills involved in the sting operation clearly list the fake companies as the sponsors. My dataset also contains other controversial group sponsors. The bill analysis for A. B. 2906, which was introduced in the 2001–2002 session of the California state legislature blatantly shows: R. J. Reynolds Tobacco Company sponsored the bill.[17] While groups may hesitate to put their organization's name on bills that are likely to fail, the presence of highly controversial groups listed as sponsors provides preliminary evidence that legislators do not censor the bills listed as sponsored because of the type of group.

4.2 DATA

The data and analyses for this chapter are straightforward. First, I investigate the difference in success between outside-sponsored legislation and bills initiated internally by a legislator. This analysis allows me to justify the assumption that, on average, these outside-sponsored bills are attractive to legislators wishing to score a legislative victory. These sponsored bills can save legislators time in crafting the legislation, and sponsored bills are more likely to become law.

Next, I examine individual-level use of group bills in California to test my hypotheses about which legislators use more bills from outside sources. The data on where legislators' bills originate from in California permits additional types of analysis.

[17] The Analysis notes that "This bill is sponsored by R. J. Reynolds Tobacco Company and is intended to protect participating tobacco manufacturers from nonparticipating manufacturers" (https://tinyurl.com/yd8cjfj8 Senate Committee Analysis from June 25, 2002).

4.2.1 Relative Passage Success

My theory maintains that outsiders offer legislators appealing legislative products that can help them effectively legislate. It assumes that bills proposed by outside groups are more likely to be passed in the California legislature than those initiated by individual legislators. My bill dataset contains information on every bill introduced in the California Senate and Assembly from 1993 to 2014 from bill analyses,[18] which allows me to compare the passage rates of both types of bills. While this analysis does not answer all causal questions about the types of bills that outsiders offer, it establishes that group bills are more likely to pass and are relatively easy for legislators to introduce given the initial draft and the advocacy these groups provide.

For the bill-level analyses, the main outcome variables are dichotomous measures of bill *i*'s fate. I record bill *i*'s passage through various hurdles in the Assembly, the Senate, both houses, and whether it is enacted. In these analyses, the main variable of interest is *Group sponsorship* of the bill. This variable is dichotomous; a value of 1 indicates that the bill is listed as being sponsored by one or more groups. The California state legislature's Office of Research analyzes all bills under consideration and compiles bill analyses. Committees also compile an analysis for every bill considered. These analyses are several pages long, and contain background information, fiscal and legal implications, suggestions for improvement, lists of entities that support and oppose along with their rationales, and the bill's sponsor. Sometimes the sponsor is clearly listed at the top of the bill analysis as the source or sponsor. At other times, this information is denoted in parentheses by the group's name in the list of groups that support the bill. The text of the analysis frequently includes a sentence about (and statements from) the sponsor. Using basic text analysis tools (e.g., grep), I search each bill analysis for the source or sponsor. The bill analyses are available online from 1993 to the present (though, my data stops in 2014).

To estimate how group sponsorship affects bills' rates of passage, I first run a series of logistic regressions and then present the results from a matching analysis. These regressions of bill passage on group sponsorship are run on the 1995–2014 Assembly bill data and exclude resolutions and special session legislation; they include a set of control variables that are potentially relevant to bill passage. The Senate regressions look very

[18] I accessed and easily downloaded these documents from ftp://leginfo.public.ca.gov/pub.

TABLE 4.1 *Assembly bill progress (logistic regressions)*

	Pass committee	Pass lower	Pass upper
Group sponsored	2.20***	1.99***	1.81***
	(0.03)	(0.03)	(0.03)
Local bill	0.06***	0.04**	0.06***
	(0.01)	(0.01)	(0.01)
Urgency bill	−0.12***	−0.12***	−0.03
	(0.03)	(0.03)	(0.03)
Log bill length	1.13***	0.61***	0.73***
	(0.06)	(0.05)	(0.05)
Session fixed effect?	Yes	Yes	Yes
Observations	33,787	33,787	33,787
Log likelihood	−18,707.51	−19,611.30	−19,893.86
Akaike Inf. Crit.	37,445.01	39,252.61	39,817.72

These models report logistic regression coefficients with session fixed effects.
$p < 0.05$; $^{**}p < 0.01$; $^{***}p < 0.001$.

similar and are thus excluded, though are available upon request. Table 4.1 displays logistic regression models of passage through the committee stage, lower chamber, and upper chamber. I include a number of covariates, on the bill and bill's author, that have been shown to alter the chances of bill passage (bill level: *Urgency bill*, *Local bill*, *Bill length*, *Consent calendar*; legislator level: *Author's years of service*, *Author's distance from the chamber median*).

The results indicate that group sponsorship is a statistically and substantively significant predictor of bill passage through each of these legislative hurdles. The predicted probability of passage by an average length, local urgency bill with an outside sponsor is 73 percent, whereas a similar bill without a sponsor has a 40 percent lower probability of passing. This result is striking, and provides initial evidence that, even after controlling for a host of characteristics important to bill passage, outsider sponsorship remains an important predictor of bill enactment. Group-sponsored bills are more likely to pass through each stage compared to those without a sponsor.

Moving to final passage, I run another series of logistic regressions and include a host of relevant features of the legislation or the bill's legislative sponsor; I hold constant other features that may vary and relate to passage. Table 4.2 reports the logistic models of Assembly bill final passage (also known as chaptered bills in the California state

TABLE 4.2 *Assembly bill passage (logistic regressions)*

	Chaptered			
	(1)	(2)	(3)	(4)
Group sponsored	1.45***	1.16***	1.93***	1.77***
	(0.03)	(0.06)	(0.06)	(0.10)
Bill length	0.10***	0.06***	0.14***	0.10*
	(0.02)	(0.02)	(0.03)	(0.05)
Local bill	−0.09*	−0.06	0.06	−0.03
	(0.04)	(0.04)	(0.06)	(0.11)
Urgency bill	0.87***	1.03***	0.66***	0.60**
	(0.06)	(0.06)	(0.10)	(0.19)
Consent calendar	2.11***	—	—	—
	(0.03)			
Republican author	−0.59***	—	—	—
	(0.03)			
Lower terms	—	0.02*	—	—
		(0.01)		
Dist from house median	—	−0.42***	—	—
		(0.03)		
Group sponsor * lower terms	—	−0.00	—	—
		(0.02)		
Group sponsor * Dist from house median	—	0.39***	—	—
		(0.03)		
Support	—	—	—	1.35***
				(0.12)
Opposition	—	—	—	−1.12***
				(0.11)
Committee fixed effect?	No	No	Yes	No
Session fixed effect?	Yes	Yes	Yes	NA
Sessions included	1993–2014	1993–2009	2009–2014	2011–2012
Observations	31,500	23,562	7,659	2,700
Log likelihood	−15,228.61	−13,388.48	−4,274.39	−1,410.48
Akaike inf. crit.	30,491.22	26,808.95	8,618.77	2,834.96

Models (1), (2), and (3) report logistic regression coefficients with session fixed effects. For each model, the dependent variable is a dichotomous measure of bill chaptering.
$^{*}p < 0.05$; $^{**}p < 0.01$; $^{***}p < 0.001$.

legislature). The group sponsorship coefficient is robust to adding a number of variables that are expected to greatly influence bill passage. Model 1 includes *Consent calendar*, which indicates that the bill did not receive opposition from any legislator or group in a hearing. Even including this variable, which is intimately tied to a bill's success, does not decrease the significance of the group sponsorship variable. The author's legislator experience (*Lower terms*) and ideological distance from the chamber median (*Distance from House median*) are significant but do not detract from the substantive importance of the group sponsor coefficient (included in Model 2). Controlling for the extremity of the legislative sponsor and interacting with the presence of a sponsor is important since this might be related to the legislator's legislative success and attractiveness as a partner for outside groups. Model 3 includes committee of origin fixed effects for the 2009–2014 sessions to roughly gauge the topic of the legislation or the difficulties that bills generally face in passing through that committee. The importance of the outside group sponsor persists after including these additional variables.

It may be the case that the group sponsorship indicates something beyond general outsider support for the bill. To test whether lobbying by groups on sponsored bills explains the differential passage rate, I include indicator variables for whether the bill analyses listed group support or opposition. The bill analyses list the groups that submit letters of support or opposition. This information helps determine whether group sponsorship remains significant for bill passage after controlling for other outside forces displaying support or opposition.

For the 2011–2012 session of the lower chamber, I collected data on the number of groups that support or oppose the bill. Adding indicator variables for the presence of support and opposition does not alter the substantive results of the logistic regressions (Model 4 of Table 4.2). This finding bolsters the conclusion that group sponsorship contributes to bill passage above and beyond mere group support on a bill.

The descriptive statistics and logistic regressions indicate that sponsored bills pass at a much higher rate than those without a sponsor. However, group sponsorship is not randomly assigned among bills. Indeed, group and non-group bills are likely to differ in ways that are correlated with both group sponsorship and the probability of passage. To deal with these confounders, I use the Matching package in R to conduct one-to-one genetic matching on the 2009–2014 Assembly bill data (Henderson and Chatfield 2011; Sekhon 2011; Diamond and Sekhon 2013). This method advances the logistic regression analysis in the previous section. While the logistic regression models can carefully model the various stages of passage (committee, lower chamber, and upper chamber) and model a number of variables, the matching analysis models provide additional confidence that confounding variables are not driving the strong finding that group sponsorship is associated with passage.

In the matching analysis, the dependent variable is whether or not the bill becomes law: $Y_i(0)$ and $Y_i(1)$ are dichotomous indicators of bill i's passage with and without a group sponsor. The treatment is whether or not a group sponsors the bill. T_i represents the binary treatment indicator, which takes a value of 1 if bill i is sponsored by a group and 0 if the bill does not have a group sponsor. The covariates indicate whether the bill was a *Resolution*, a *Local bill*, an *Urgency bill*, the number of *Cosponsors* listed on the bill, and the bill's *Length*. Additional tests establish that the models are robust to unmeasured features.

Table 4.3 reports the pre- and post-matching balance statistics (standardized mean differences and the p-value for a t-test that the covariate mean is the same between sponsored and unsponsored bills). Lower mean

TABLE 4.3 *Standardized bias statistics before and after one-to-one genetic matching, for the average treatment effect*

	Before matching – std. mean diff.	Before matching – t-test p-value	After matching – std. mean diff.	After matching – t-test p-value
Assembly 2009–2010				
Resolution	−6.49	0.10	0.00	1.00
Local	17.19	0.00	0.00	1.00
Urgency	−1.19	0.75	0.00	1.00
Cosponsors	1.79	0.64	0.14	0.59
Length	8.85	0.02	0.21	0.61
Assembly 2011–2012				
Resolution	−9.50	0.03	0.00	1.00
Local	5.06	0.21	0.09	0.32
Urgency	−4.84	0.25	−0.83	0.29
Cosponsors	−4.22	0.32	−0.05	0.55
Length	8.38	0.02	0.70	0.16
Assembly 2013–2014				
Resolution	−18.01	0.00	−0.11	0.56
Local	13.76	0.00	0.00	1.00
Urgency	−12.82	0.00	−0.11	0.32
Cosponsors	−9.59	0.02	−0.11	0.40
Length	6.88	0.07	−1.60	0.48

TABLE 4.4 *Estimates from OLS and matching analyses*

	OLS (ATE)	Matching ATE	Matching ATT
Effect of group sponsor	0.44	0.39	0.39
Standard error	0.01	0.02	0.02
Covariates	✓	✓	✓

ATT = average treatment effect for the treated, ATE = average treatment effect. The standard errors in the matching analyses are Abadie-Imbens. The same controls are included as those reported in Table 4.3.

differences and larger *p*-values indicate better balance. For example, positive mean differences indicate that sponsored bills have a higher incidence of the dichotomous variables or are longer in length. Before matching, there are significant differences between sponsored and unsponsored bills. Relevant for the *Expertise Premium Hypothesis*, sponsored bills are significantly less likely to be resolutions and are longer in every session of the Assembly. While the indicator for whether a bill is a resolution is a rough proxy for expertise, it does show that legislators turn to outsiders more for substantive matters than for mere credit-claiming measures. The finding that sponsored bills are longer than unsponsored bills hints that outsiders boost the expertise contained in legislation and that legislators seek this input. The lowest post-matching *p*-value is 0.29. Matching obtains very good balance on the covariates; I use these matches to run models of the effect of group sponsorship on bill passage.

The first column of Table 4.4 reports the results from a linear probability model of bill passage on sponsorship, with the covariates. These results closely resemble those from the matching estimates. Appendix B.1 presents the results of a Rosenbaum bounds test, which provides confidence that the matching estimates are robust to hidden confounders and are reasonable estimates of the effect of group sponsorship on bill passage. Together, these models establish that group sponsorship has a statistically and substantively significant impact on bill passage, which bolsters the assumption that outsider information can help legislators achieve lawmaking goals.

4.2.2 Group-Level Data

Central normative questions about groups' involvement in the political process involve classifying them into well-resourced or poorly resourced groups. The entities that sponsor bills vary drastically. My dataset contains companies that range from the popular fast food restaurant Jack in the Box to huge energy companies such as Pacific Gas and Electric. Understanding which groups are successful at the agenda-setting stage of policymaking – and which ones successfully pass their bills into law – is essential for understanding whether certain types of groups dominate the policymaking process.

A substantial portion of the sponsors are state- or municipal-level entities or agencies. I classify the sponsoring groups according to whether they are (1) a state-level agency or local entity or (2) neither a state-level agency nor a local entity. I first determine whether the sponsor's name appears on a list of current government agencies.[19] However, this step does not capture all agencies. Since the data extends from 1993 to 2014, some of the agencies may be defunct, such as the "California Department of Financial Institutions," and thus omitted from the list. Programs within departments do not appear in this list, for example the "Small Business and Disabled Veteran Business Enterprise Certification Program." To include these cases, I go through the list of unique sponsors and identify those that should be classified as a state-level agency. I categorize municipal or local entities by the presence of phrases in the sponsor's name such as "City of," "County of," and "Irrigation District." A wide range of these municipal entities are listed as sponsors, from large cities and counties to the San Diego Coastkeeper nonprofit organization. Since the absence of common phrases to identify these entities sometimes does not accurately capture all cases of local entity sponsorship, I also go through the list of unique sponsors to identify additional municipal or local entities. The sponsors are not listed in a uniform manner on the bill analyses and the lack of complete lists of municipal entities or state-level agencies necessitates this additional step.

After identifying state- and municipal-level entities or agencies, I then hand code the remaining 4,496 entities that have sponsored a bill. Following Junk (2019), I put groups into five categories: (1) business associations and firms (*Business associations*); (2) trade unions and occupational associations (*Professional associations, unions, occupational associations*); (3) identity, religious groups, hobbies, and homeowners' groups (*Identity, religious, homeowner, hobby*); (4) public interest groups (*Public interest groups*); and (5) individual experts, think tanks, institutional

[19] www.ca.gov/agenciesall

associations, and commissions (*Think tanks, experts, commissions, institutional associations*). These categories do not exactly capture the "have" and "have not" distinction; for that, detailed information on the budget or other organizational characteristics from the group would be needed. Unfortunately, there is no reliable source of data or common metric on the relative wealth of this broad range of organizations. However, groups that fit into the categories listed above do capture different representational concerns. For example, this categorization reveals that there is a bias toward business interests over other types of groups in the sponsored bills that get introduced and passed. In other areas of politics, businesses successfully see their demands translated into public policy at greater rates than other types of entities (e.g., Yackee and Yackee 2006; Drutman 2015). Does the same apply to outsider involvement in legislating?

Further, the type of group involved in the process affects public opinion about their involvement. For example, Rosenthal (2009) recounts an exchange between a constituent and a member of the Ohio State Senate. The legislator asked if this constituent considered the AARP a special interest. The constituent, an AARP member, responded, "Not on your life... AARP isn't a special interest, it's for the public interest" (Rosenthal 2009, p. 13). This short exchange highlights the trust that some Americans may have for interest groups that they belong to or are sympathetic to versus those they view as corrupt or "special interests." Hibbing and Theiss-Morse (2004) finds that US citizens recoil against special interest involvement and think these outsiders have too much control. Rasmussen and Reher (2023) discover that involvement in later stages of the lawmaking process by a range of groups shapes the public's perceptions of the legitimacy of the process. Separating out the groups that sponsor bills and operate in the California state legislature can indicate the potential representational concerns associated with the practice.

Table 4.5 presents the number of unique groups and sponsored bills that fall into each category. For example, business associations backed 5,316 of the 28,896 sponsored bills. The group types vary by how frequently they sponsor bills. Most groups (58 percent) only sponsor a single bill. Business associations are the largest category of unique groups and comprise 29 percent of the unique groups that sponsor at least one bill.

The number of bills introduced per organization varies greatly across group types. This information reveals the range of issues that various group categories advocate in the legislature. While businesses or business associations are the largest category of organizations, on average, they

TABLE 4.5 *Group sponsors by type and number of bills sponsored*

Group type	No. of unique groups	Proportion of unique groups	No. of bills sponsored	Proportion of bills sponsored	Mean No. of bills sponsored
Business associations	1,640	0.28	5,316	0.18	3.24
Professional associations, unions, occupational associations	588	0.10	5,675	0.20	9.65
Identity, religious, homeowner, hobby	698	0.12	2,195	0.08	3.14
Public interest groups	952	0.16	3,779	0.13	3.97
Think tanks, experts, commissions	490	0.08	1,110	0.04	2.27
State agencies	254	0.04	5,316	0.18	20.93
Municipal entities	1,341	0.22	5,505	0.19	4.11

sponsor few bills. These bills tend to be narrowly focused on the business's idiosyncratic interests. Professional associations and public interest groups, such as firefighters' and teachers' organizations, represent broad constituencies and sponsor many bills that are relevant to their interests. The California Professional Firefighters' Association sponsored 210 bills from 1993 to 2014. Their website lists their legislative accomplishments to include establishing "The nation's first firefighter cancer presumption law" and erecting a memorial honoring fallen firefighters on the Capitol grounds.[20] While only 254 unique state agencies or departments sponsor bills, they sponsor the same number of bills as businesses and business associations, which constitute 28 percent of the unique organizations.

Are some types of groups more successful at shepherding the bills they sponsor into law? While securing a spot on the agenda is the first step toward legislative success, a bill must become law to have an effect. Even if the various types of groups are equally successful at securing a place on the legislative agenda, if there are differences in passage rates across group types, this may reveal that the state's pluralist system has cracks. Table 4.6 displays the percentage of bills sponsored by each type of group that is passed into law. All types of groups have high passage rates, but those for state departments and agencies are the highest. This finding may support the idea that legislators prioritize finding information during the legislative process, since these actors may provide the most expertise. It also bolsters theoretical claims that the bills provided by the bureaucracy are tailored to the state and are thus more attractive as partners to legislators – even experienced and powerful ones.

The category of bills sponsored by cities deserves special attention. These are important entities from a federalism perspective and because of their inability to contribute to campaigns. While cities and agency officials can lobby the legislature in California (Baeder 2014) – Payson (2021) shows that over 50 percent of the state's cities do so – under California's Political Reform Act, "public agency lobbyists *may not*: Contribute to or raise public funds for any candidate for elective office. Candidates also are prohibited from accepting such funds."[21] Thus, separately examining the trajectory of bills sponsored by cities versus other groups may reveal the role of information provision without the complicating consideration of campaign contributions. This analysis provides

[20] www.cpf.org/advocacy/our-legislation/historic-wins

[21] https://tinyurl.com/mvekww2

TABLE 4.6 *Percentage of bills sponsored by each category that pass into law*

Group type	Percentage of sponsored bills that pass
Business associations	60.37
Professional Associations, unions, occupational associations	55.40
Identity, religious, homeowner, hobby	60.15
Public interest groups	52.70
Think tanks, experts, commissions	61.28
State agencies	72.53
Municipal entities	65.31

some evidence that campaign contributions from these sponsoring organizations are *not* driving the finding that sponsored bills pass at a higher rate than unsponsored bills.

I conduct the matching analysis on the subset of bills that are *not* sponsored by agencies or municipal entities. Table 4.7 presents the effect sizes for the subsetted matching. Column 1 presents the original results, which lump sponsors of all types together.[22] Column 2 (Non-agency/municipal) matches bills that have at least one non-agency and non-municipal sponsor with a completely unsponsored bill. Column 3 (Only agency/municipal) presents the results for a matching analysis with bills that only have an agency or municipal sponsor listed, matched with a completely unsponsored bill. These results establish that agency or municipal sponsorship is most strongly associated with passage. However, the non-agency and non-municipal matching coefficient indicates that these bills are still significantly and substantively associated with passage. The main finding that bills are passed by entities that cannot contribute money directly to legislators reflects on the question of the social welfare effect of these bills. Information and other motivations besides money in politics appear to be at play in the provision and uptake of group bills in the California state legislature, at least for some bills.

[22] I exclude resolutions from this analysis to focus on substantive bills. The covariates are *Majority Party Status of Author*, *Local*, *Urgency*, *Cosponsors*, and *Length*.

TABLE 4.7 *Effects for the subsetted matching*

	Combined	Non-agency/ municipal	Only agency/ municipal
OLS (ATE)	0.41	0.34	0.51
	(0.02)	(0.02)	(0.02)
Matching ATE	0.41	0.37	0.51
	(0.02)	(0.03)	(0.03)
Matching ATT	0.41	0.32	0.54
	(0.02)	(0.03)	(0.03)
Covariates	✓	✓	✓

ATT = average treatment effect for the treated, ATE = average treatment effect. The standard errors in the matching analyses are Abadie-Imbens.

4.2.2.1 *Legislator-Level Data*

The previous analyses were at the bill level, to establish the differential success of group-offered bills, and the group level, to assess the expertise offered by various groups and the uptake of their legislation. In this section I examine some of the fundamental relationships posited in my theory at the individual legislator level. The previous chapter examines legislation proposed by a particular group of outsiders (bureaucrats), yet the California setting provides a more complete view of the composition of a legislator's agenda. Beyond specifying when legislators partner with the executive branch to introduce legislation, these bill sponsorship indicators can demonstrate the extent to which a legislator's agenda comes from outside groups and actors.

In the legislator component of the study, the unit of analysis is the legislator-session. This chapter examines why legislators use group-sponsored bills. It explores whether legislators alter their legislative portfolios and reliance on outsiders during their time in office and based on whether they obtain positions of power. It also examines if group bills or unsponsored bills are more successful. I find that legislators enjoy increasing success during their time in office on non-group (but not group) bills. Outsiders seem to subsidize rookie legislators to help them introduce and pass legislation. When legislators gain expertise, they substitute out of group bills and continue to experience legislative success.

To estimate the connection between legislative experience and utilization of group-sponsored bills, the main variable of interest is legislators' *Terms in office*. My theory expects less experienced legislators to use more group bills than their longer-termed counterparts because (1) they struggle to craft bills without the assistance of lobbyists and groups due to their lack of experience with the circuitous legislative process, (2) they would like to author bills that pass, and (3) group-sponsored legislation is more likely to pass than non-group-sponsored legislation. Variables about the legislator's pre- and post-term limits tenure are generated from Klarner et al. (2013) and OpenStates. *Term* indicates the term number served by legislator *i* in session *t*. I limit the set of legislators to those who were elected after term limits were introduced; I exclude legislators who served more than three terms in the Assembly because they were grandfathered in before the advent of term limits.

To measure the legislator's activity levels, I use several approaches (given the data limitations before 2009 such as lack of full digitized data on sponsorship). First, following Wawro (2001*a*) and Schiller (1995), I measure a legislator's activity as the number of bills they sponsored in a session – calculated using OpenStates (for the 2009–2014 legislators), legislative bill histories, and Lewis's database of bill descriptions (Lewis N.d.; OpenStates 2016). For each session, I sum the *Number of bills introduced* by each legislator. To measure legislators' relative success in getting the bills they introduce passed, I also calculate their *Hit rate*: the percentage of bills that the legislator introduces that become law (Frantzich 1979).

I construct several dependent variables to connect legislative effectiveness to the utilization of group bills. The legislator-level measures of the utilization of group bills are (1) the number of group bills that legislator *i* introduced during session *t* (*Number group bills*) and (2) the percent of legislator *i*'s bills that are sponsored bills (*Fraction group bills*). To compare the success of legislators' independent versus group bills, I calculate the *Sponsored bill hit rate*: the percentage of sponsored bills that become law.

4.2.3 Legislator-Level Analysis

I use simple models to test predictions about legislator characteristics and the percentage of a legislator's bills that are group bills. On average, a much higher percentage of legislators' group-sponsored bills become law compared to unsponsored (independent) bills. This indicates a possible rationale for legislators to propose group-sponsored bills. When they wish to appear successful and pass legislation, using group-drafted bills may help achieve this goal.

4.2.4 Estimating the Effect of Legislative Experience on Group Bill Use

I examine the relationship between the number of terms a legislator has served and their use of group bills, authorship of non-group bills, and success in getting type of bill passed. While other chapters use the legislator's years in office (tenure), since I focus on the lower chamber (which is limited to three terms), I use terms of service. To further explore the hypotheses, I account for factors that may alter the supply of group bills to legislators and legislators' propensity to introduce and secure their passage. As in the previous chapter, I examine the assumption of chairpersonships and leadership roles. These analyses are conducted on the 1993–2014 Assembly legislator data.

To control for legislators' *initial* differential predilections to rely on groups, I include legislator fixed effects (Ansolabehere et al. 2003). I assume these unobservable differences across legislators remain constant over time, such as prior legislative experience and pre-existing connections with groups. As I discuss in Chapter 2, legislators come to office with very different backgrounds that may translate more or less seamlessly into the legislative sphere. Compare Assembly member Mike Gatto to the Calderon brothers. Gatto authors few group bills and expresses concern for the "special-interest groups [that] draft legislation." He put out a press release to announce a "Wiki Bill" project to invite the public (rather than interest groups or companies) to draft certain types of legislation. His opposition to the practice of outsiders sponsoring bills in the legislature highlights the normative tensions that the book considers.[23] The Calderon family, by contrast, has been entrenched in California legislative politics for years and has dense networks of interest group connections.[24] I use ordinary least squares (OLS) regressions for these analyses. Since the dependent variables are counts, using probit or logit with legislator fixed effects has undesirable statistical properties (Angrist and Pischke 2008). I analyze Democrat and Republican legislators separately since Democrats have controlled the California state legislature for all but one year of the study period. Membership in the majority party is likely to influence both the supply of group bills and Republican legislators' ability to introduce and pass their bills.[25]

[23] https://tinyurl.com/3yccrea6

[24] www.laweekly.com/news/worst-legislator-in-california-part-ii-2170841

[25] Appendix B.2 reports the parallel regressions for Republican legislators. While some of the coefficients are less significant, the patterns are largely the same.

TABLE 4.8 *Assembly Democrats regressions*

	No. group bills (1)	Ratio (group/total bills introduced) (2)
Second term	-1.37^{*}	-0.02^{**}
	(0.59)	(0.01)
Third term	-2.65^{***}	-0.04^{***}
	(0.70)	(0.01)
Leader	−0.97	−0.02
	(1.31)	(0.02)
Chair	1.07	0.01
	(0.68)	(0.01)
Vote share	0.04	0.0002
	(0.04)	(0.001)
No. non-group bills	0.35^{***}	—
Introduced	(0.04)	—
Constant	4.27	0.34^{***}
	(4.08)	(0.05)
Legislator fixed effects	Yes	Yes
Observations	474	474
Legislators	205	205
R^2	0.78	0.71
Adjusted R^2	0.60	0.47

OLS regressions of number of group-sponsored bills authored by legislator *i* and the ratio of group to total number of bills authored on the number of terms in the Assembly. Legislator fixed effects included.
$^{*}p < 0.05$; $^{**}p < 0.01$; $^{***}p < 0.001$.

First, I show the models for the agenda space that group-sponsored bills take up for legislators. I then discuss the varied success of group- versus non-group-sponsored bills to demonstrate the relative success of these types of bills by legislative partner characteristics. Table 4.8 presents the results from the OLS models of sponsorship with legislator fixed effects among Democratic Assembly members. The dependent variables in these models are (1) the number of group bills that the legislator authored (*No. group bills*) and (2) the ratio of group bills to the total number of bills the legislators authored (*Ratio (group/total)*). I find that, compared to their first term, legislators in their second and third terms use fewer group bills. Legislators adjust their relative use of group and independent bills as they gain more experience.

Unlike the findings presented in Chapter 3, assuming the powerful position of committee chair does not seem to be related to the introduction of group bills. This difference highlights the appeal of different types of bills and types of expertise. Sponsored bills in California come from all types of outside forces: some may provide expert information that appeals to legislators across levels of expertise, while others provide narrower bills that do not appeal to experienced legislators. By contrast, the bureaucrats discussed in Chapter 3 provide more across-the-board insider government information that appeals to experienced legislators in positions of power and targets state-level problems.

To assess the relationship between a legislator's terms of service and their success in the legislative arena, I conduct another series of OLS regressions with legislator fixed effects (Table 4.9). The dependent variables for this analysis are (1) the percent of the group bills authored by

TABLE 4.9 *Assembly Democrats regressions*

	% Group bills became law (1)	% Non-group bills became law (2)
Second term	0.03*	0.02**
	(0.02)	(0.01)
Third term	0.04*	0.02**
	(0.02)	(0.01)
Leader	−0.08*	0.02
	(0.04)	(0.02)
Chair	0.003	0.02*
	(0.02)	(0.01)
Vote share	−0.003*	−0.0004
	(0.001)	(0.0005)
Constant	0.71***	0.10*
	(0.11)	(0.05)
Legislator fixed effects	Yes	Yes
Observations	474	474
Legislators	205	205
R^2	0.62	0.66
Adjusted R^2	0.31	0.39

OLS regressions of the percentage of group-sponsored bills authored by legislator *i* that became law and the percentage of non-group bills authored by legislator *i* that became law on the number of terms in the Assembly. Legislator fixed effects included.

*$p < 0.05$; **$p < 0.01$; ***$p < 0.001$.

legislator i that became law in session t (% *Group bills became law*) and (2) the percent of non-group bills authored by legislator i that became law in session t (% *Non-group bills became law*). The substantively and statistically significant coefficients on the term variables in Model 2 indicate that second- and third-term legislators are more successful than their first-term colleagues at getting non-group bills passed into law. These findings suggest that group bills help legislators gain legislative victories in their first term, when they are less able to pass non-group bills.

This finding is central to understanding the partnerships between outsiders and legislators. Legislative experience is significantly related to legislators' success on non-group (but not group-sponsored) bills. As the theory chapter discusses, on-the-job experience can help legislators pass bills. If they lack this experience, they may turn elsewhere for help appearing successful. Outsiders' aid in the form of supplying draft legislative text and subsequent lobbying on the bill can help offset the legislator's rookie status. Outside interests hoping to get their legislation on the agenda may therefore see first-term legislators as attractive targets and willing partners.

4.3 A LOWER BOUND ON GROUP INVOLVEMENT

This chapter investigates the extent to which outsiders are involved in crafting state-level legislation – a more overt form of interest group power on *positive* agenda setting. However, much remains unknown about the full extent of group involvement in the state legislative process. I therefore consider my findings an estimate of the lower bound of group involvement in the legislative process. For instance, I do not assess their *negative* agenda-setting role (Stokes 2020). Yet groups exert considerable efforts to prevent undesirable legislation from getting passed.[26] They lobby against bills that would not advance their interests, such as those that will impose additional restrictions or significant costs. Large companies pursue a variety of tactics to kill state-level legislation; in states with short legislative sessions, one advocate described their efforts as "running out the clock."[27] Past work consistently finds a bias toward the status quo in policymaking (e.g., Gilens 2005; Baumgartner et al. 2009).

Groups also contribute to amendments added to legislation and seek to get their preferred language into microlegislation, defined as "small

[26] https://tinyurl.com/3x4fskuu

[27] www.washingtonpost.com/technology/2023/05/03/big-tech-lobby-children-safety/

pieces of bill drafts and amendments that benefit a narrow set of interests" (McKay 2021).[28] This book treats the bill as the unit of observation, but small details may make a big difference in a bill's impact and be harder to detect.

The bill analyses in this chapter indicate that the legislature takes the points of groups that oppose bills very seriously. California's A. B. 2561 from the 2013–2014 session, sponsored by the Sustainable Economies Law Center, started as a broad bill to "remove obstacles to the practice of growing edible fruits and vegetables in urban and suburban residential neighborhoods for personal and community use or consumption."[29] In response to opposition from neighborhood and apartment associations, the author significantly amended the bill, reducing its scope to exclude multifamily dwellings. Changing the text of a bill to remove interest group opposition to increase odds of passage is a common legislative technique.

4.4 CONCLUSION

The most striking findings in the California data are the sheer volume of extra-legislative involvement in the legislative process and the differential passage rates between group- and non-group-sponsored bills. Legislators rely more heavily on group bills in their first term than in subsequent terms, which suggests that a learning process occurs that alters the relationship between groups and legislators.

While this chapter capitalizes on a unique reporting tradition in a single state, the results suggest that groups contribute extensively to the body of law within states. Legislators beyond California rely on groups for technical information. California state politics are important in their own right given the state's large population and budget (Masunaga 2015).

While neither Congress nor other states list the non-legislative sponsor of a bill as clearly as the California state legislature, qualitative evidence suggests that institutions elsewhere also rely on groups in similar ways. In the state legislature rated most similar to Congress in terms of professionalism (California's), I find that legislators heavily utilize group

[28] Using a creative set of group comments written to committees about what they wanted to see in the Affordable Care Act, made available only to the author, McKay (2021) uses text analysis to track the uptake of these requests.

[29] www.leginfo.ca.gov/pub/13-14/bill/asm/ab_2551-2600/ab_2561_cfa_20140419_2017 17_asm_comm.html

expertise (Squire 1992). If we expect legislatures with fewer resources to rely more heavily on group services, other states may depend on group bills even more (Hertel-Fernandez 2014). The next chapter examines the relationships between legislative resources and model bill uptake.

Bill passage and legislator productivity are closely related to group sponsorship and suggest legislator motivations for using this tactic. Examining the patterns of group bill utilization allows me to carefully explore group involvement in the legislative process. Mapping the participation of non-legislator entities in the legislative process is important for understanding the system of laws that influence citizens. A democratic defect may arise if elected officials must substantially rely on unelected individuals and groups to craft high-quality bills that address citizens' concerns in a timely manner.

5

Prepackaged Policy: Model Bill Use in the 50 US States

In 2019, the USA TODAY Network wrote a series of articles on model legislation that garnered considerable attention across the United States. Many local newspapers used the information to highlight bills that legislators in their state lifted from national-level organizations. When confronted about model bills, New York state legislator James Sanders defended their use: "If it's not a good bill, then you shouldn't use the model. There are plenty of good ideas throughout the U.S. and we should not spend all of our time recreating the wheel. I prefer to perfect it."[1] His take on the practice reflects the sentiment that it is not uncommon and may boost legislators' performance. Critics highlight the potential problems of letting outsiders write state legislation. Maybe it is the blatant plagiarism that reminds people of school days and raises the hackles of violating the rules of the game, or maybe it is the ability to directly see where these normally opaque bills come from, but model bills have captured the attention of scholars and the media.

Walker's 1969 canonical study of policy diffusion uses a spelling error that appears across states as a small piece of evidence of diffusion. This chapter scales this kind of investigation up by applying automated textual analysis to the study of group bills in state legislatures. Groups write model bills; under certain circumstances, state legislators introduce them and help them become laws. In this chapter, I demonstrate that using model legislation is part of a pattern of state legislators' sponsorship repertoire. By examining usage, I can determine groups' conditional influence on public policy across states.

Several organizations produce model legislation. The best known is the conservative American Legislative Exchange Commission (ALEC)

[1] https://tinyurl.com/4exx86wm

(Hertel-Fernandez 2014, 2019; Jansa et al. 2018). ALEC, a 501(c)(3) organization founded in 1973, aims to "advance the fundamental principles of free-market enterprise, limited government, and federalism at the state level."[2] Its membership comprises over 2,000 state legislators as well as private sector representatives and corporations. The State Innovation Exchange (SiX), previously the American Legislative and Issue Campaign Exchange (ALICE, a word play on being the opposite of ALEC), organized as a liberal alternative to ALEC in 2012. Wisconsin Democratic state representative Mark Pocan likened SiX to a "barking Chihuahua compared to an 800-pound gorilla" (Smith 2012). Unlike ALEC, SiX has no corporate backers and does not host yearly policy conferences. In this chapter I use textual analysis (based on plagiarism detection technology) of model legislation – a group's ideal policy – from these groups and a range of others to determine the extent of group influence on introduced bills. This tactic of tracing laws is increasingly used in political science research assessing the spread of legislative text (e.g., Hinkle 2015; Wilkerson et al. 2015; Linder et al. 2020).

This outsider tactic differs somewhat from those examined in Chapters 3 and 4. Instead of "shopping" the model bills around to find legislators willing to introduce them, any legislator with access to the model bill can (in theory) introduce a version of it. Of course, these groups do sometimes approach specific legislators to request the bill introduction, but the text is available for any interested legislator to take parts or all of it. This dynamic changes the relationship between the outsider and the legislator. Model bills may provide political information in the form of text, but they are not tailored to the state's needs.

As in previous chapters, this chapter highlights the importance of institutions in the context of group input within legislatures. It uses a consistent measure across all fifty states to address these connections. I link institutions that vary across states (e.g., staff resources, term limits) and expertise across legislators to group influence to illuminate the process by which groups shape legislative outcomes.

5.1 GROUP SELECTION

Prior research on model bills has focused on those created by a single successful group, ALEC. My study of model legislation examines a range of groups that have produced at least one model bill (Table 5.1). I identified

[2] www.c-span.org/organization/american-legislative-exchange-council/19223/

TABLE 5.1 *Groups that produce model legislation that are included in the study and the number of model bills included*

Organization	No. of model bills	Organization	No. of model bills
ALEC	1,041	State Innovation Exchange (SiX) (formerly ALICE)	202
American Association of Motor Vehicle Administrators	22	National Alliance for Model State Drug Laws	14
Tenth Amendment Center	14	AUL	13
Innocence Project	11	Alliance for School Choice	10
American Bar Association	9	Institute for Justice	7
Born Free USA	5	Good Jobs First	5
National Consumer Law Center	5	SEMA	4
American Public Policy Alliance	3	HumanRights	3
American Planning Association	3	Bill of Rights Defense Committee	2
National Hispanic Caucus of State Legislators	2	National Court Reporters Association	2
OffNow	2	Personal Watercraft Industry Association	2
Cato Institute	2	Prison Policy Initiative	2
Animal Legal Defense Fund	1	American Association of Colleges for Teacher Education	1
ChangeLabSolutions	1	Association of Fish and Wildlife Agencies	1
Association of Inspectors General	1	Alcohol Justice	1
Autistic Self Advocacy Association	1	Benefit Corp	1
Bike League	1	American University Center for Democracy and Election Management	1
Center for Internet and Society	1	Compact for America	1
Constitution Project	1	Discovery Institute	1
Electronics TakeBack Coalition	1	Polaris Project	1
ProEnglish	1	Project on Student Debt	1
Protection of Conscience Project	1	Recreational Off-Highway Vehicle Association	1
Safe Access Now	1	Smart Growth America	1
Upstream	1	Wireless Infrastructure Association	1
Multistate Tax Commission	1	National Alliance for Public Charter Schools	1
National Association of Insurance Commissioners	1	National Association of Sports Officials	1
National Center for Victims of Crime	1	National Council for Interior Design Qualification	1
National Council on Disability	1	National Criminal Justice Reference Service	1
National Juvenile Defender Center	1	National Partnership for Women and Families	1

the set of groups and their model bills from Google searches of "model bill," "model legislation," and "model statute." While this selection of groups is not generated from a random sample of a comprehensive list of national-level groups (as Strolovitch (2008) does), my approach provides insights into how often state legislatures use model legislation. While many groups disseminate model legislation, the sheer volume of groups included in comprehensive lists would obscure the use of this tactic in a random sample. Including model bills from several groups allows me to assess the relative effectiveness of interest groups and assuage concerns related to only looking at model legislation produced by broad ideological groups, which receive publicity due to their successes.

Even if it would be ideal and possible to collect a random sample or a more cohesive set of groups or model bills, my method generates a wide-ranging set of groups and types of model bills. In some of the following analyses, I classify the findings into three main groups (the main liberal group, the main conservative group, and the remainder of the groups) to assess whether legislatures and legislators use model bills consistently *across* groups.

5.2 DATA

Identifying the origins of state legislation requires three huge datasets and significant computational power. Unlike the previous chapters, which use clear indicators that bills have originated outside of the legislature, groups typically do not list all the states that introduce their bills or the exact pieces of legislation that are derived from their models.

My first and primary data source is the text of the state legislation. Bills are the heart of states' policies, and the resulting statutory law constrains or empowers state actors. Unfortunately, the raw text of these bills is not readily available since states do not use a common format for storing bills. Recent sources of state-level legislative data make this endeavor more systematic and cleaner. Second, the text of groups' model bills provides the point of comparison for state bills. Finally, to assess the theoretical expectations, I add covariates about the state, individual legislative sponsor, political environment, and the institution in which bill was introduced. In the following sections, I detail these datasets since they allow me to analyze which states introduce and pass model bills (and thus group-preferred legislation).

5.2.1 State Bills

It is difficult to gather the full text of state bills across a wide range of years for several reasons ranging from a lack of data transparency in the states to mundane technical problems with PDFs that are not converted into text (via OCR). LexisNexis is a main source of state-level bill text data (e.g., used in Hertel-Fernandez (2019)), but it is not publicly available or affordable for most academics or the public. I therefore compiled cleaned state bill text. This dataset represents one of the book's main contributions; future work can better explore the nature of lawmaking in states.

To create the corpus of state bills, I collected all bills introduced in states between 2009 and 2020. LegiScan provides an API that allows researchers to pull the encoded text of bills. I processed these texts to ensure they are consistent across states.[3] The dataset contains 1,176,985 introduced bills and 333,338 passed bills from all fifty states. Appendix Table C.2 presents the number of bills and bill versions per state contained in my database.[4]

5.2.2 Model Bills

I gathered model legislation from fifty-nine groups that propose state-level models (listed in Table 5.1). The groups vary ideologically. ALEC is the largest conservative group and SiX is the most prolific liberal group. From each group's website, I scraped all publicized model bills (n = 1,427). Some groups have several model bills, but most (58 percent) only publicize one. The text of ALEC model legislation comes from two different sources. ALEC began posting its model legislation on its website in March 2013 (Celock 2013). I scraped the 619 bills that were available on this website as of September 20, 2013. Yet the organization previously promoted additional bills that were not available on this website. State legislators still have access to these model bills via extant "bluebooks" and Dropbox folders. In addition, model bills available to ALEC state legislators were leaked to the Center for Media Democracy in 2011

3 Where possible, I removed the deleted text from the bills, often indicated by tags such as <deleted> </deleted>. Because the original bill text was provided in PDF or HTML format, I also had to remove page numbers, headers and footers, and dates.

4 Appendix C.1 compares the number of bills per state in the dataset to a *Congressional Quarterly* listing of the number of bills introduced in a state session to ensure that LegiScan includes a complete list of bills.

and published on ALECexposed.org in July 2011.[5] I downloaded all the model bills available on this site and deleted duplicates (same title and summary) from those on the official ALEC site. I added 422 unique bills from this leaked set. The dataset contains a total of 1,041 model bills from ALEC and 386 from other groups. These numbers show that ALEC is the most prolific of model law producers, but the other groups are important to consider.

5.3 SIMILARITY MEASURE: DETERMINING THE ORIGINS OF STATE BILLS

After collecting and processing the state bills and model bills, the next step is to identify state bills that use model bill language. I calculate pairwise comparisons between each state bill and each model bill. The 1,427 model bills and 1,176,985 bill versions yield 1,678,206,995 pairwise comparisons (1,176,985 × 1,427). Therefore, I must automate the process of identifying similarities between each pair.

Wilkerson et al. (2015) and Casas et al. (2020) apply computationally intense Smith–Waterman algorithms to assess the origins of policy in the US Congress. This complex empirical approach is needed to trace the full pathways of legislative text. Yet previous studies demonstrate that straightforward metrics can reliably detect plagiarism and are easier to interpret (Lyon et al. 2001; Clough and Stevenson 2011). I am therefore able to employ a simpler approach to identify state bills that substantively resemble model bills. This section details my method.

Sponsors of state legislation can use model bills in at least three ways (1) use the entire model bill text verbatim (making only minimal changes such as the state's name), (2) use exact copies of paragraphs or sections from the model, or (3) extract sentences or phrases. I define a "match" between a state bill and a model bill as a pair that contains "significant" overlap in non-boilerplate language on the basis that the sponsor would not have come up with this language without the aid of model legislation (or looking at another source that used the model).

To measure the overlap between model bills and state bills, I determine the percentage of five-word strings of adjacent words that intersect between them. Based on spaces, the process first separates the text into sequential five-word strings on a rolling basis. For example, if the entire document is "shall verify the employment eligibility of the employee

[5] www.democracynow.org/2011/7/15/alec_exposed_state_legislative_bills_drafted

through the everify program," the program would generate the seven following five-word strings:

(1) shall verify the employment eligibility
(2) verify the employment eligibility of
(3) the employment eligibility of the
(4) employment eligibility of the employee
(5) eligibility of the employee through
(6) of the employee through the
(7) employee through the everify program

This method of splitting documents has several advantages over other approaches. For instance, it takes word order into account (as opposed to the cosine similarity measure), which is important since I do not want to include false-positive matches that could arise if bills were on similar topics. Based on the length of the documents and prior work in this area (Broder 1998; Lyon et al. 2001), I tested strings of three, five, eight, and thirteen words and decided to use the five-word strings.

The next step is to compare the documents. The size of the corpuses and the computational intensity of calculating these comparisons limits which methods I can use. I employ a simple, but effective and previously used *ratio-of-matches* metric. This measure divides the intersection of the two sets of five-word strings per document by the total number of unique five-word sequences across both documents. This metric determines the extent to which subsequent state bills use prior model bill text.

I must then determine the threshold of similarity at which a state bill is considered to draw significantly on a model bill. Figure 5.1 plots the distribution of similarity values over 0.04. I cut the data at 0.04 because there are so many comparisons at or around 0 that the distribution is barely visible if all values are included. I employ a cut-off rule whereby pairs that fall below 0.1 on the similarity score are rated as *not* model bills, and state bills that have a match with a model bill over 0.1 are counted as originating from a model bill. After looking through a random sample of 100 bills with scores of less than 20 percent, I determined that matches below 10 percent capture boilerplate language rather than state legislature reuse of model legislation, while matches above the 10 percent threshold reflect the use of substantive portions of the model. Therefore, I coded the pairs with less than 10 percent overlap as 0 and retained the percentages for pairs with 10 percent or more overlap.

When deciding on this threshold, I considered the case of students plagiarizing a paper. If long strings of text without attribution are copied

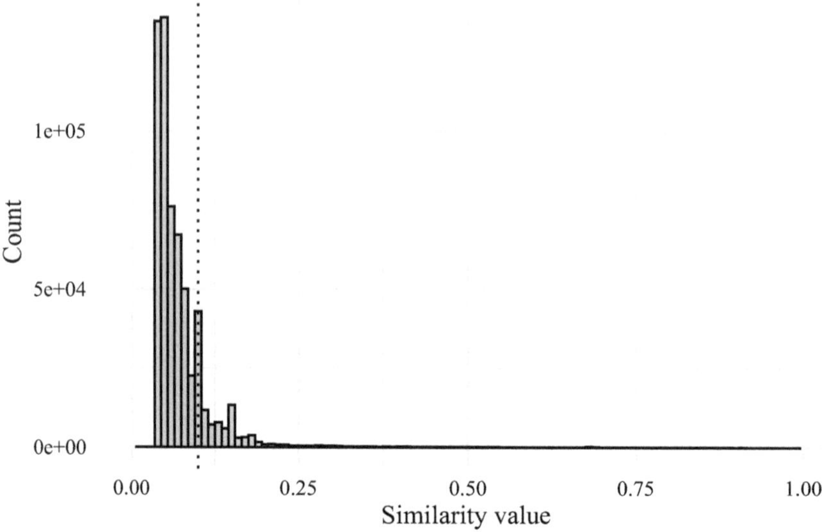

FIGURE 5.1 Distribution of comparison similarity values over 0.04. Dashed line denotes the 0.1 threshold used in the main analyses.

from other sources, a sizable chunk of overlapping text would be enough to cast doubt on the originality of the text. According to Editage (a website that helps researchers with publications), less than 15 percent overlap in words "is acceptable by the journals and a similarity of 25% is considered as high percentage of plagiarism. But even in case of 15% similarity, if the matching text is one continuous block of borrowed material, it will be considered as plagiarized text of significant concern."[6] While I am not equating legislators using model bills with students plagiarizing, the same notions of detecting overlapping text apply to both scenarios. To provide more confidence that the state bill derives from the model bill, I drop the matches if the state bill was introduced before the model bill.

In summary, the steps of the process are as follows:

(1) Tokenize the document into five-word strings.
(2) Compare every model bill to every state bill.
(3) Determine threshold.

[6] www.editage.com/insights/what-is-the-acceptable-percentage-of-plagiarism-report. Also see https://tinyurl.com/4svxbhxj

5.4 ANALYSIS

I then use these similarity scores for each model bill–state bill pair to examine the crux of my theoretical inquiries on the predicted relationships between individual and institutional capacity and use of outsider input in all fifty states. Similar to the analyses on the use of bureaucrats' bills, I conduct legislature- and legislator-level analyses. At the legislature level, I can compare the relationship between legislative resources/constraints and model bill use across all states. The data also includes a huge range of individual legislators across these states and a large volume to explore the relationship between experience and introducing model bills. Before getting to the patterns across legislatures and legislators, I first examine the success of the groups, especially ALEC.

5.4.1 Which Groups Are Successful?

The analyses indicate that ALEC is the most successful group by a large margin and produces by far the most model bills; SiX and the Tenth Amendment Center follow. Across all years and states in my data, ALEC model bills were introduced 4,937 times and passed 804 times, for a success rate of 16 percent. Only 8 percent of SiX's 2,062 introduced bills passed into law. As Figure 5.2 shows, ALEC has introduced fewer model bills over time but has maintained a relatively steady passage rate, with a slight drop in the 2019–2020 sessions. The most popular ALEC bills are about education, health care, and immigration. Many of the commonly used SiX bills are also about education or schools and health care, but unlike ALEC, popular SiX bills also include those about the criminal justice system, family corporation policies, and inequality. Groups widely differ in their ability to get model legislation introduced and passed in state legislatures. Ideological groups are the most successful. The information they provide is carefully crafted ideologically approved legislation.

5.4.2 Descriptive Maps of Model Bill Utilization

At the state level, I am first descriptively interested in the sheer volume of model bills introduced in each state. Figures 5.3 and 5.4 display the percentage of introduced and passed bills that are model bills, respectively. Because some states limit the number of bills each legislator may introduce during a session, and due to other reasons for variation, the

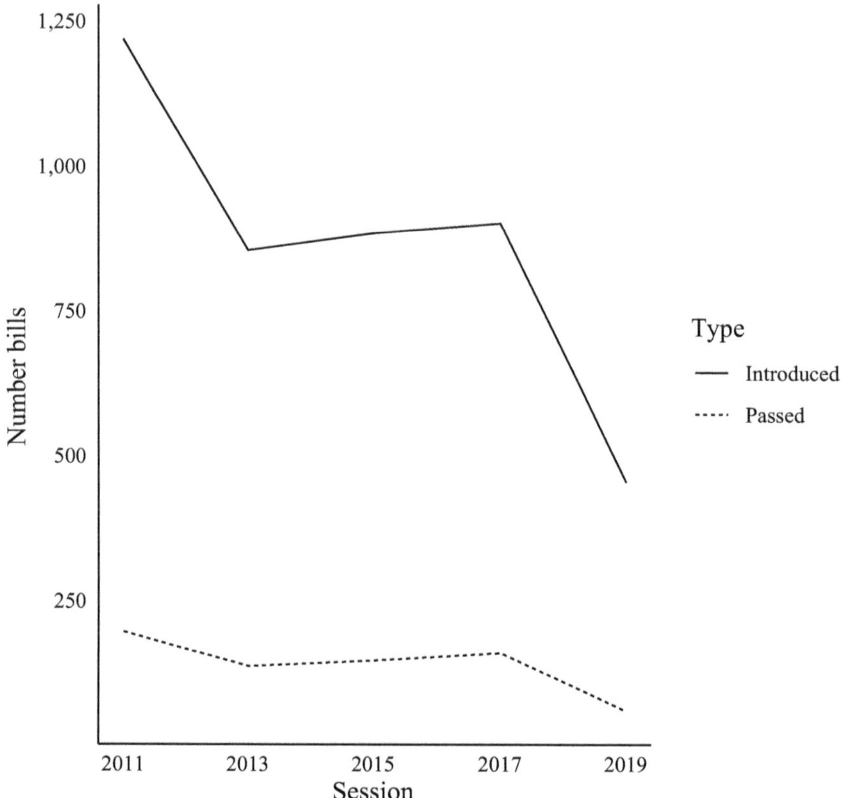

FIGURE 5.2 Introduction and passage of ALEC model bills over time.

number of introduced bills varies drastically across states. I therefore use proportions to assess each state's *utilization* of model bills. The proportion of the legislative agenda and statutory law that comes from interest groups in the form of model bills varies across states. Overall, a maximum of 3 percent of introduced and passed bills come from model bills. This finding underscores the need to have a more complete picture of the bills provided by interest groups. I use the variation across states in the use and success of model bills to study the correlates of interest group lawmaking. Figures 5.3 and 5.4 indicate where this tactic is successful at the various legislative stages. For example, model bills form a relatively high proportion of Oklahoma's agenda and statutory law, while in New Mexico they are more successful at the introduction stage than at the passage stage. The next section explores the reasons for these differences.

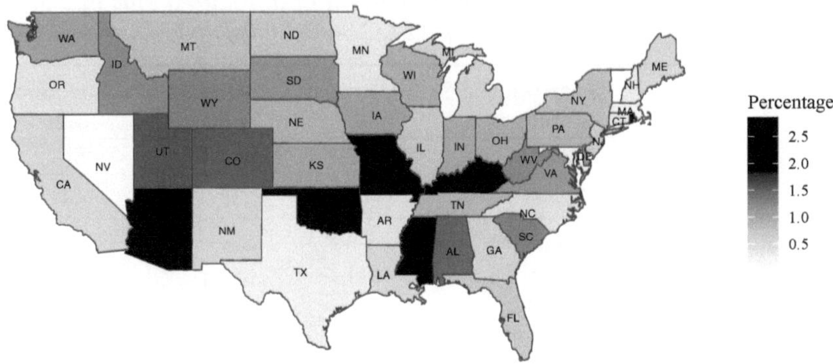

FIGURE 5.3 Average percentage of *introduced* bills derived from model bills across states, 2009–2019.

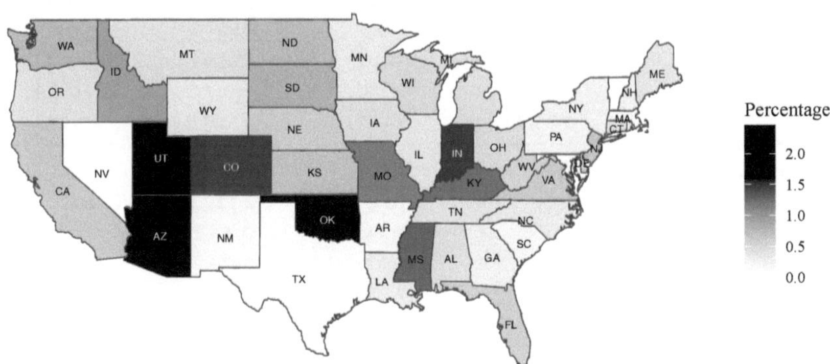

FIGURE 5.4 Average percentage of *passed* bills derived from model bills across states, 2009–2019.

5.5 ANALYSIS: LEGISLATURE-LEVEL RESULTS

This section examines the correlates associated with the state-level uptake of model legislation, while the next section explores the individual-level predictors of model bill use. Table 5.2 presents the results of the ordinary least squares (OLS) models of which states *introduce* model bills. Column 1 reports the percentage of introduced bills that are model bills, and Columns 2–4 break this down by the source of the model bill (ALEC, non-ALEC, or SiX). Grouping the model bills in this way helps me investigate whether the study of ALEC model bills is driving my results about the connection between legislative capacity and model

TABLE 5.2 *Regression models of the percent of introduced bills that are model bills, ALEC model bills, non-ALEC model bills, and SiX model bills*

	% Introduced bills	% Introduced bills (ALEC)	% Introduced bills (Non-ALEC)	% Introduced bills (SiX)
	(1)	(2)	(3)	(4)
Republican legislature	0.22**	0.15**	0.07	−0.02
	(0.07)	(0.05)	(0.04)	(0.02)
Split legislature	0.21	0.13	0.05	−0.0003
	(0.11)	(0.07)	(0.07)	(0.03)
Log session length	0.15	0.10	0.12*	0.04
	(0.08)	(0.05)	(0.05)	(0.03)
Log salary	0.04	0.02	0.03	0.01
	(0.04)	(0.02)	(0.02)	(0.01)
Log expenditures	−0.19***	−0.10***	−0.09**	−0.01
	(0.05)	(0.03)	(0.03)	(0.01)
Term limits	0.15*	0.07	0.06	0.07**
	(0.07)	(0.04)	(0.04)	(0.02)
Constant	0.71	0.19	−0.13	−0.13
	(0.41)	(0.27)	(0.25)	(0.13)
Session fixed effects	Yes	Yes	Yes	Yes
Observations	402	402	402	402
R^2	0.08	0.14	0.12	0.08
Adjusted R^2	0.07	0.11	0.09	0.04
Residual std. error	0.64 (df = 395)	0.39 (df = 385)	0.37 (df = 385)	0.19 (df = 385)

$^{*}p < 0.05$; $^{**}p < 0.01$; $^{***}p < 0.001$.

bill use. I do not use state fixed effects because term limits do not vary during the study period.[7]

These results establish that state partisanship clearly matters for states' use of model bills, which fits with the relative popularity of ALEC (a conservative group) compared to other groups and prior research on model bill use (Hertel-Fernandez 2019). The portion of introduced bills that are model bills is higher in legislatures controlled by the Republican Party. There is a separation between Democrats and Republicans in the

[7] In Appendix C.3, I remove the term limits variable and add state and year fixed effects to isolate the effect of changes in legislative capacity and partisan variables. Several other studies also analyze state-level data in this way (e.g., Cook and Fortunato 2022). This method captures within-state changes in legislative capacity on model bill use, which brings the study closer to the ideal of causal analysis.

introduction of model bills. This pattern is driven by the prevalence of ALEC model bills; there is no liberal counterpart to ALEC to appeal to Democrats.

The results are relatively constant across the various types of model bills. Each column of Table 5.2 reveals a negative relationship between logged legislative expenditures and the percentage of a state's legislative agenda that is dedicated to model bills. This finding is in line with my predictions about the relationship between legislative capacity (measured as expenditures) and turning to outside groups for legislative ideas or text. The results indicate differences across the components of the legislative professionalism score. Logged *session length* is positively related to the composition of the legislative agenda proposed by these outsiders. Yet logged *salary* is not significantly related to the outcomes. Hoffman and Lyons (2020) survey legislators on how they spend their time and find that "higher salary is robustly associated with legislators spending more time on fundraising" but that it "is also robustly associated with less time spent on legislative activities and has no clear relation to time spent on constituent services." This finding helps explain the divergent findings across the components of legislative professionalism. Legislative expenditures best capture capacity as it relates to the legislature's ability to generate internal knowledge stores.

In line with the *Legislative Constraints Hypothesis*, term limits appear to greatly affect the composition of state legislation. They are significantly and positively related to the percentage of introduced bills that are model bills. Term limits can constrain the legislature's ability to develop expertise to counter input from outside groups. Instead of protecting the institution from entrenched interests, term limits' impact on overall capacity seems to increase the role of outsiders.

Examining the composition of statutory law that comes from model bills reveals a different picture. While institutional features of the legislature shape the *legislative agenda*, the capacity and constraints on the legislature have less of an impact on *the bills that get passed*. Table 5.3 presents the *% Passed bills* that are model bills per state-session. While party remains significant, none of the constraints or capacity measures significantly predicts the composition of the passed legislation that originates in model bills. This finding might be hopeful from a normative perspective of constraining outsiders. Perhaps the legislatures, regardless of their institutional capacity or constraints, are vetting model bills enough that differences do not arise when the actual statutes are under examination.

TABLE 5.3 *Regression models of the percent of passed bills that are model bills*

	% of passed bills
Republican legislature	0.28
	(0.16)
Split legislature	0.68**
	(0.24)
Log session length	0.02
	(0.18)
Log salary	0.07
	(0.08)
Log expenditures	−0.07
	(0.10)
Term limits	0.06
	(0.15)
Constant	−0.08
	(0.92)
Session fixed effects	Yes
Observations	402
R^2	0.04
Adjusted R^2	0.003
Residual std. error	1.32 (df = 385)

*$p < 0.05$; **$p < 0.01$; ***$p < 0.001$.

5.6 ANALYSIS: LEGISLATOR-LEVEL RESULTS

Legislative capacity and chamber structures vary drastically by state. Individual legislators also range from new and inexperienced to experts on various topics due to experience in the relevant profession, education, or time in the legislature. I expect that less experienced legislators are more likely to partner with interest groups by introducing model bills. Unlike bills from departments or agencies, model bills are generally "info-drops" (in Hall and Deardorff's (2006) language). Thus, legislators with less experience (measured as how long they have served in the state legislature) will be especially willing and eager to introduce these bills. I analyze data on individual legislator-level decisions to sponsor model bills to examine this hypothesis.

These analyses examine the determinants of model legislation sponsorship. The unit of analysis is the state legislator in session t. The dependent variable is the total number of model bills introduced with legislator i listed as a sponsor in session t. The outcome variable can assume a value of 0 (if legislator *i* sponsors no model bills in session *t*) or the number of model bills introduced (if legislator *i* sponsors one or more model bills in session *t*). This analysis captures the extent to which a legislator draws on model bills at the stage of bill introduction.

Tenure denotes an individual legislator's years of legislative service to indicate their level of experience. Despite providing evidence of on-the-job exposure to lawmaking, tenure is only one component of the legislator's experience that could help determine their reliance on groups and lawmaking. i Miquel and Snyder Jr (2006) find that effectiveness (as evaluated by fellow legislators, lobbyists, and journalists) varies across legislators even among those with the same length of tenure. They find that effectiveness in the first term of office predicts holding future leadership positions in the legislature. Other features of a legislator's background are likely to be relevant to their ability to generate independent legislation, proclivity to utilize model legislation, and connections with groups. While I could ideally include factors such as a legislator's career background, educational experience, or general skill at legislating, this information is difficult to obtain for all fifty states. The chapters that focus on bureaucratic partnerships (Chapter 3) and California state legislators (Chapter 4) add additional variables on the legislator-level and legislator fixed effects to assess these relationships more carefully. I include a *Republican* party indicator given the inclusion and prevalence of ALEC. To control for each legislator's overall productivity, all models include their # *Introduced* bills in a session.

I also capture the setting in which the individual legislator operates by including the chamber-level variables that I describe in the previous section (resources and constraints) – whether the legislature is *Term limited*, *Log session length*, *Log salary*, *Log expenditures*, and *Senate* to indicate upper chamber membership. These factors are important because the capacity of the overall legislature and constraints on the membership as a whole affect how individuals will interact with outsiders in lawmaking.

Table 5.4 presents the results of the OLS regression models of (1) the total number of model bills introduced, (2) ALEC model bills, (3) non-ALEC model bills, and (4) SiX model bills. These results reveal which individual legislator characteristics are associated with introducing more model bills. The *Tenure* variable links to the theoretical prediction that legislators with less experience will rely more heavily on some types of group legislative aid. While this variable is significantly related to the number of all model bills introduced, ALEC model bills introduced, and non-ALEC model bills introduced, I do not observe a large decrease in

TABLE 5.4 *Effect of legislator- and legislature-level characteristics on model bill introductions*

	All Models	ALEC	Non-ALEC	SiX
# Intro	0.01***	0.004***	0.005***	0.003***
	(0.0001)	(0.0001)	(0.0000)	(0.0000)
Republican	0.37***	0.35***	0.01	−0.06***
	(0.01)	(0.01)	(0.01)	(0.004)
Tenure	−0.003**	−0.002*	−0.002*	−0.0003
	(0.001)	(0.001)	(0.001)	(0.0004)
Term limited	0.03	0.04***	−0.01	0.001
	(0.02)	(0.01)	(0.01)	(0.01)
Log session length	0.21***	0.11***	0.09***	0.03***
	(0.02)	(0.01)	(0.01)	(0.01)
Log salary	0.02*	0.02***	−0.003	0.001
	(0.01)	(0.01)	(0.005)	(0.002)
Log expenditures	−0.07***	−0.05***	−0.02**	0.01**
	(0.01)	(0.01)	(0.01)	(0.003)
Senate	0.07***	0.03**	0.05***	0.004
	(0.01)	(0.01)	(0.01)	(0.005)
Constant	−1.18***	−0.62***	−0.56***	−0.27***
	(0.09)	(0.06)	(0.05)	(0.03)
Observations	52,218	52,218	52,218	52,218
R^2	0.26	0.16	0.20	0.20
Adjusted R^2	0.26	0.16	0.20	0.20
Residual std. error (df = 52,199)	1.51	1.04	0.94	0.50

$^{*}p < 0.05$; $^{**}p < 0.01$; $^{***}p < 0.001$.

the number of model bills predicted to be introduced for each additional year of service in the legislature. This small effect size is likely because in most sessions, legislators are not introducing model bills from any of these specific groups. Also, while this may not seem like many bills, some model bills significantly affect state policy and policymaking discussions in the state and beyond. The pattern is informative, but the size is less indicative than other chapters because I do not have the full set of model bills that a legislator introduces. Early-career legislators need more help to navigate the complicated legislative environment and learn about the process of legislating. This finding mirrors those presented in Chapter 4. Experienced legislators may be less likely to use some types of outsider input at the agenda-setting stage of lawmaking.

When examining the legislature-level variables, most of the same patterns emerge as in the previous regressions of the overall volume of model bills in the legislature. *Log expenditures* is negatively associated with all model bill introductions, ALEC model bill introductions, and non-ALEC model bill introductions. At the legislator-session level, the amount of money dedicated to the state legislature's functioning is importantly related to legislators' reliance on model bills. However, for the number of SiX model bills a legislator introduces in a session, the direction of the relationship flips. This difference in results indicates the importance of studying a range of groups when evaluating the nature of the relationship between group input and resources. Across the board, the models establish a positive relationship between *Log session length* and model bill introductions. As in the previous state-session level, the other metrics of professionalism appear to operate differently than expenditures when it comes to looking outside the legislature for input. Indeed, perhaps there is more time to introduce more model bills in longer sessions. The effects for *Term limits* and *Log salary* are concentrated in the introduction of all model bills and only ALEC model bills. Overall, modeling the number of various types of model bills that individual legislators introduce per session reveals strong and important relationships between state institutions, but these are conditional upon the type of group that produces the model bill.

Legislative institutions and legislator experience affect how many model bills a legislator introduces. As legislators gain experience and have *some* legislative institutions to substitute for outsiders, they become less likely to use model bills. This simple conclusion highlights the central institutional and individual features that protect against outside influences on state-level policymaking.

5.7 CONCLUSION

This study of model legislation examines the conditions under which groups influence the policy process. I test these predictions using a comprehensive dataset of state and model bill text. Using a matching method based on plagiarism detection, I identify legislatures' uptake of model legislation language. By connecting institutions (such as legislative resources and term limits) that vary across states and levels of expertise (that vary across legislators) to group influence, I shed light on the process by which groups influence legislative outcomes.

This research contributes to the study of interest group influence and legislative politics. Weak or ambiguous measures of group influence stymie researchers' ability to reach solid conclusions about the extent to which groups succeed in the legislative arena. My measure of model legislation uptake provides a clear test of a theory of the interactions between groups and legislatures. This chapter employs more of a detective approach to figuring out which bills originate from outsiders, including California's "sponsored bills" and bills proposed by state-level departments. Model bills are more hidden; the effort required to determine which bills come from outsiders highlights the nature of much work that outside groups conduct in the states. Model bills are also different because they are not directly provided to legislators: Lawmakers can obtain the text themselves and use as they please. Legislators face uncertainty about the relationship between the policies they craft and the political and policy outcomes. Expertise offered by groups in the form of model legislation may help reduce this ambiguity.

In focusing on ALEC, other studies of model legislation utilization do not capture a huge portion of outside groups' involvement in bill drafting in state legislatures. Tracking which states introduce these bills requires access to the text of model legislation and bills introduced/passed. This identification strategy requires these organizations to be transparent. Moreover, many of the bills crafted by organizations, lobbying firms, or corporations are targeted at a single state. Lobbying firms tout their ability and expertise in drafting legislation, but do not disseminate these legislative products as model legislation. Chapters 3 and 4 complement this investigation into model bills.

By exploring a wide-ranging set of groups that produce model legislation, my work advances prior studies of model legislation uptake. While ALEC is an influential organization that merits considerable research, my study explores the broader picture of where legislation originates from. ALEC's influence makes it important to study in work like Hertel-Fernandez (2019), but it is also a special case for researchers interested in when and where legislators partner with interest groups more broadly. Certain types of legislators may not partner with ALEC due to its conservative leanings, but would with some other groups. This chapter's finding that ALEC is by far the most successful at getting model legislation into state legislatures demonstrates the need to study other forms of outside influence to assess how resources and expertise shape these relationships. Moreover, I find varying patterns of relationships between resources and model bill use across different types of model bills. These disparate findings highlight the need to study multiple groups when assessing outsider input and legislative capacity and constraints.

This chapter highlights the importance of institutions in the context of group influence within legislatures. While the federal legislature retains higher staff levels than those of the states, the trend in Congress to cut government capacity may increasingly make this research relevant to federal-level lawmaking.[8] Looking to the states to predict the consequences of reducing the resources available to members of Congress may shed light on the future of group influence on national legislation.

[8] See https://tinyurl.com/bdhnxvrx

6

Complexity and Deliberation by Design

When Gladys Sargent first began lobbying the California legislature in the early 1950s, she didn't understand the art of the legislative deal. As a committed animal rights activist, Sargent brought bills she had helped write to lawmakers with high hopes and moral conviction. But once those bills went through the legislative wringer, they didn't always return in the same form or with the same intent. She recounts that the legislature "sometimes amended our bills without letting me know. I'd work for a bill and maybe it was changed, maybe not the same bill. But I didn't realize I should work with the aides while they were writing up the bills, the Legislative Counsel, as well as the legislator."[1] She recalled that as she waited in the front office, "other people were coming in another door (the powerful lobbyists). It took me a while to know my way around."[2] These memories reflect how subsequent policy power extends beyond bill introduction. Sargent learned that the battle is not won when a bill gets introduced, and that the revisions it is subjected to reflect the power of the legislative outsider. Her account suggests that subsequent control of lobbyists' legislation is a key aspect of authority. She no doubt learned the ins and outs of protecting legislation: She continued lobbying until her death in 1996 at age 96.[3]

So far, the book has established that legislatures and legislators partner with outsiders like Sargent in systematically different ways depending on the resources, constraints, and power available to them. But what

[1] https://archives.cdn.sos.ca.gov/oral-history/pdf/sargent.pdf

[2] ibid.

[3] www.sfgate.com/news/article/OBITUARY-Gladys-Sargent-2964247.php

happens next? In this chapter, I investigate whether bills written by outsiders are systematically different from those that are not. I also explore whether the deliberative legislative process is actually deliberative. The empirical approaches I present in this chapter to assess the democratic implications of allowing outsiders to write legislation focus on the *process*. While there are many different lenses through which to examine the implications of outsider involvement in legislating, I concentrate on the deliberation surrounding this legislation. The care with which the legislature examines the products brought by outsiders (who may have narrow interests) provides insights into the role that these groups play in legislating – and if legislators are abdicating some of their representational duties by relying so heavily on outsiders for legislative text. Lawmakers' ability to check the bills that are drafted by outsiders and the extent to which legislators change these externally generated bills capture important considerations surrounding democratic deliberation in the legislative process.

In this chapter, I probe legislators' ability to vet legislation proposed by outsiders. I start by discussing the quality of state law and various ways to approach the connection between legislation and statehouse democracy. I then evaluate the role of groups. Are bills offered by outsiders more comprehensible to generalist legislators than those generated by legislators? I approach this question in a few different ways. While I do not equate the complexity of the legislation with its quality, this metric can help capture the ability of legislators (and other actors who may be constrained by the legislation in the future or state courts interpreting the law) to understand what the outsiders propose. In this chapter I examine the text of proposed bills. In the next chapter, I focus on public opinion regarding representation and reliance on outsiders.

According to Fenno (1973), producing high-quality policy is a main goal of legislators; the concept is normatively central to the study of legislation. Yet what counts as high-quality legislation or policy, and how can it be empirically captured? In the current polarized US policy environment, people may view a policy as high quality only if they agree with it. Legislative quality, and how legislation furthers or hinders democratic representation, can be examined from at least three angles. The first is its contribution to social welfare – whether it improves outcomes like reducing crime or increasing economic growth – though such valence goals often involve tradeoffs that complicate their assessment. The second concerns the legislation's ability to function as intended; even well-meaning bills may fail to produce the desired policy outcomes due to vague language or implementation challenges. Finally, legislative quality can be judged by how well it aligns with constituent preferences. While some studies find strong links between public opinion and state policy, others note more limited responsiveness, often shaped by factors such as legislative professionalism (Erikson et al. 1993; Lax and Phillips 2012; Caughey and Warshaw 2022).

This chapter explores the role of *process* in constructing the legislation and how this affects legislative quality. While this dimension differs from the aforementioned conceptions of quality, it captures the legitimacy of legislation. Mansbridge (2007) describes the deliberative democratic perspective as "the better the quality of deliberation in legislatures and throughout civil society, the more legitimate the eventual laws; in addition, the better the quality of aggregative processes, the more legitimate the eventual laws." Across bills, time, and institutions, the process through which laws are considered matters not only for outcomes, but also acceptance of (and inclusion in) the process. The legislature's full consideration and discussion of potential laws can fix mistakes or loopholes that may lower the quality of the legislation. Even if citizens disagree with the final legislative product, they may be more willing to accept it if they feel it was generated by a democratic process.

The 2004 session of the Oklahoma state legislature provides an example of how an outsider's involvement in the political machinations can reduce democratic accountability and produce unintended policy outcomes. The state's Agriculture Department promoted a bill that "would pave the way for the unfunded transfer environmental regulation of the swine, cattle and poultry industries to the Agriculture Department."[4] Six versions of this bill were offered during the session. Given all of the changes to the bill and the last-minute nature of the final version, the process and final bill were criticized. The article notes that this lack of attention from the media and the other interests is especially unusual on the topic, since generally "any mention of legislation pertaining to hog or poultry farms drew scores of Oklahomans to the Capitol, some from as far away as the Panhandle." This case demonstrates the implications of studying the legislative attention surrounding outsider-provided bills.

6.1 WHERE DO OUTSIDERS WRITING LEGISLATION FIT IN?

This chapter explores two metrics that capture the details of lawmaking. The first measures the relative complexity and semantic features of the

[4] https://tinyurl.com/muhf8b5s

laws that outsiders propose. The second is the extent to which outsiders' bills change, since this reflects the degree of examination of legislation and deliberation surrounding the input. While both measures examine the legislative process, rather than the quality of the resulting legislation or representation, they capture the systematic differences across bills proposed by outsiders. This information can provide insights into the legislature's ability to check outsiders' work throughout the legislative process.

In Robert Carro's extensive biography of powerful New York political operative Robert Moses, Carro notes that:

> bill drafting was called by Albany insiders 'the black art of politics.' An expert bill-drafter had to know thousands of precedents, so that he could pick out the one that, embodied in the bill he was working on, would make the bill legal, or so that by careful wording he could avoid bringing the new act within the purview of an old one that might make it illegal. He had to know a myriad ways of confirming or denying power by the written word. He had to know how to lull the opposition by concealing the real content of a bill (Caro 1974, p. 141).

The book recounts instances of Moses using his bill-drafting skills, while in the governor's office, to obscure components that the legislature would not agree to had they understood them. Capturing the extent to which outsider bills obscure the true intent of the legislation or the difficulties legislators face in evaluating outsiders' policies furthers our understanding of their role in the quality of legislating.

If outsiders exercised a tight grip over the full legislative process, their bills would be passed with few changes. The oral histories presented in Chapter 2 convey the sentiment that the legislature serves as a check on outsiders' proposals by weeding out "bad" or overextending rent-seeking bills. The legislature's ability to do so may depend on the time and resources available to it. (Bressman and Gluck 2014, p. 743) assess how the Legislative Counsel drafts laws for Members of Congress and caution that members' personal staff lack sufficient experience to interpret the text and ensure that the "Legislative Counsel accurately translates their deals." A respondent to their survey compared the task to "translating the Bible" (Bressman and Gluck 2014, p. 743). The following sections detail how these concepts and metrics connect to the theory about legislative reliance on outsiders, conditional upon legislative resources.

6.1.1 Thinking about Complexity

Edwin Dirck, Democratic State Senator in Missouri from 1977 to 1992, recounted how he reworked a bill on campaign finance ethics. He cut the idea to the core elements by reducing the bill from over 100 pages to two and a half.

I decided to draft a new bill, because we were deadlocked. It took, I think, after they got it typed up, two and half pages. Before that it was like a hundred and some odd pages. In essence what it said was that every nickel you receive you shall report; how you got it, where it come from, and how you spent it. And if you don't do these things, you're guilty of a felony, and you'll go to jail… But I got back and I got the bill typed; I filed it as the committee met that morning. I filed it as a conference committee substitute. Well, hell, I just blew the tops out of all the lawyers. And by God I had enough votes to pass it, if I had pressed it. But I was trying to show them how ridiculous we were getting, with all the little "ands" "ors" and "buts" and so forth that we had in there. *And how the whole damn thing was drafted you had to be a lawyer to read it. And then the lawyers couldn't read it, the same way. They all read it, but different ways.* And so we busted that thing down just about half the size it was, that day. I know that one of my Republican friends from the House, Representative Bud Barnes (who by the way is very strong on the heritage of Missouri) and he really complimented me on that bill. He said, "by God Eddy, it's the best thing that's come up since we've been in conference." But he and I looked at it pretty much the same way. You know, you report what you get, you report what you spend, where you got it, how you got it, how you spent it (what bar). That's all it needs to be. (Emphasis added.)[5]

This anecdote highlights the importance of legislators' ability to understand the bills they consider, and how difficult this can be. Dirck's sentiment also demonstrates that simply worded legislation helps legislators interpret it in a common way. As representative John Conyers (D-MI) articulated, "What good is reading the bill if it's a thousand pages and you don't have two days and two lawyers to find out what it means."[6] He maintains that understanding complex bills is practically impossible due to the multiple ways in which the text can be interpreted.

I argue that the presence of outsiders alters the complexity of state legislation, which is an important part of legislating. As the examples above show, it is more difficult for legislators to process complex bills and anticipate their outcomes. If outsiders manipulate the complexity of the bills to make the provisions less comprehensible to lawmakers, this could interfere with the democratic process. Even worse, outsiders could intentionally hide rent-seeking provisions in complicated bills.

5 Edwin L. Dirck, Sr., Will Sarvis, February 23, 1996, Transcript, and The Oral History Program of the State Historical Society of Missouri, Politics in Missouri Oral History Project.

6 www.politico.com/story/2009/09/read-the-bill-it-might-not-help-026846

Their complexity could be used to conceal their true intent. Complexity can also be somewhat innocuous when outsiders are involved. For example, some policy areas might require more descriptive legislation while others may be more technical. Therefore, if bureaucrats or other outsiders tend to request bills in particular policy areas, the composition of these bills might differ. The nature of legislating and the text of bills highlights the need to account for differences in policy areas.

Other scholars examine the complexity or readability of various political documents. Black et al. (2016) assess "how easily a member of the public could pick up [a Supreme Court] opinion, read it, and understand it." This chapter similarly uses multiple measures of bill complexity to assess the ability of generalist legislators to understand the bills they are tasked with improving and voting on. Other political science scholars have used these measures to assess the complexity of state bills (Hansen and Jansa 2021), elite speeches (Spirling 2016), and presidential speeches (Benoit et al. 2019). Potter (2017) uses various complexity metrics to explore how the bureaucracy obfuscates when crafting *regulations*. Potter (2017) argues that more complex rules "deter[s] oversight (or at least make it more costly) by making it difficult for laypeople to ascertain the true consequences of a policy proposal." I take the same approach to studying legislators' ability to determine the true intent of outsider legislation.

Overly complex legislation also generates representational concerns among constituents. *Federalist 62* decries this possibility, saying, "It will be of little avail to the people, that the laws are made by men of their own choice, if the laws be so voluminous that they cannot be read, or so incoherent that they cannot be understood" and argues that this complexity and instability advantage businesses and the wealthy (Madison 1788*b*). Constituents will struggle to hold legislators and the legislature as a whole accountable if they cannot understand the laws under consideration. If outsiders provide laws that the people do not understand (especially if they are more complex than those generated internally), citizens might not be able to hold legislators accountable for their partnerships with outsiders.

6.1.2 Thinking about Changes in the Legislative Process

Differences in the initial legislation that outsiders propose, as well as the alterations the bills undergo during their (sometimes circuitous) legislative journey are essential for understanding outsiders' control and power in the legislative process. In discussing legislative compromise, Fred Krupp, president of the Environmental Defense Fund, said "I could sit in my office and write a perfect bill, but it wouldn't be one that could become law in the United States."[7] The details, quality, and sometimes very nature of a bill can change drastically during the democratic process. This section examines what these adjustments can mean for power within versus outside legislatures.

Legislative actors carefully oversee the changes that bills undergo as they progress through the increasingly complex lawmaking process.[8] The lawmaking process in the United States has become increasingly complex and the "textbook legislative process" fails to capture the complexities of the changes that legislative vehicles undergo (Sinclair 1991). I use modifications in the text of legislative vehicles to ascertain the relative power of outsiders in their proffered bills.

Bills change, via amendments, while under consideration in various legislative bodies for a variety of reasons. Legislators may add or delete text to clarify the intent and execution of a policy or to fix drafting mistakes (Lewallen 2016). Interest groups, agencies, the executive, or constituents may appeal to legislators to amend the bill, and legislators may respond to these demands because of the merits of the argument or to please a constituency that is important for their re-election. In other instances, the legislative vehicle may be altered by removing objectionable portions or adding sections that benefit specific legislators or groups to make it more likely to pass. Amendments may be offered that are unlikely to be passed as a position-taking device.[9] Weingast (1989) attributes increasing amending activity in the US House to supporters of legislation countering amendments offered by the opposition with amendments of their own. Though their existence and frequency are contested, "killer amendments" may be added to make a bill unpalatable (Wilkerson 1999; Jenkins and Munger 2003; Finocchiaro and Jenkins 2008). The gruesome-sounding "gut-and-amend" tactic involves deleting the entire text of a bill and replacing it with a new bill, under the same number, sometimes completely altering its subject or intent.[10] Each of

7 https://tinyurl.com/3t2nsu5w

8 A large literature explores amendment rules; see, for example, Cox and McCubbins (2005) and Sinclair (1994).

9 For example, a Louisiana state legislator introduced a sexist amendment (to specify a weight limit on strippers) as a "joke" and to call attention to legislative overreach (www.wnd.com/2016/05/bill-amendment-aimed-to-limit-stripper-weight/).

10 For example, A. B. 1188 from the 2015–2016 session of the California state legislature was introduced as a bill about gambling. After it reached the Assembly floor, the entire

these types of changes can alter the subject of the bill or keep its underlying meaning constant while altering its ideological bent or removing objectionable portions. While the amendment process may be used for a number of reasons that can affect the distribution of power differently, the underlying outcome of changing the content of the original legislation is easily measured via simple textual analysis. I use the extent to which the proposer's policy is altered to study the strategic interaction between the outsider and the legislature.

How does having an outsider as the initiator shape the ultimate changes that these bills undergo? I argue that the extent to which the proposer's policy is altered is an important way of determining the power of the outsiders and the vetting that their preferred bills receive in deliberative bodies. Legislative Counsel staffers revealed in a survey that they have less freedom to change the text of bills drafted by the White House, agencies, or outsiders such as lobbyists than those "drafted inside Congress" (Bressman and Gluck (2014) p. 758). Retaining direction over a bill's amendments and the extent of changes made to it is essential for the legislative product and the effect on the state and outsider. I assess the bill text to determine if outsiders' bills remain more intact than non-outsider bills.

6.2 DATA AND ANALYSIS

I analyze the corpus of state bills (from the states where the corresponding sponsorship data is available) gathered from LegiScan introduced in Chapter 5. I clean the text from each bill to remove the preamble and footer to help capture the complexity of the legislative text and the changes across multiple versions.

I examine the textual features of bureaucratic bills across multiple states and sponsored bills in California. I exclude model bills from this analysis because of the way I capture these bills. Since I classify model bills as such if the text is above a threshold of similarity, the bill often includes text that cannot be attributed to the model bill. Since the measures are at the bill level, they depend on classifying the entire bill as an outsider bill.

In the following sections, I first present the textual complexity analyses and then discuss how I measure the extent of changes to the bills' text. In

text was deleted and replaced with new statutory language lifting a ban on kangaroo products (Noyes 2015).

each section, I start by analyzing the data from the bureaucracy and then move to the California sponsorship information.

6.2.1 Textual Complexity

From the bill text corpus, I generate a number of variables. First, and most central to the chapter, I include variables related to bill complexity or specificity. While textual measures cannot capture intricacies such as bill drafting ability, simple metrics can indicate how different legislators sponsor bills. State legislative drafting manuals instruct legislators, their staffers, and bill drafting offices on how to craft legislation. For example, South Dakota's guide instructs that "the use of short, simple sentences is best. Using complex sentences often requires excessive punctuation which can be confusing and lead to possible misinterpretation." It also advises that "The wording of legislation should be precise, clear, and concise. Avoid both conversational and legalistic expressions. Use shorter, simpler words if there is a choice."[11]

The first dependent variable to capture complexity is the *Flesch-Kincaid Readability Score*, which gauges the bill's overall "readability" to estimate the level of education (expressed as the US grade level) someone would need to understand it (Flesch and Gould 1949; Kincaid et al. 1975; Benoit et al. 2019). This score is calculated using a numerical conversion of the average sentence length and average number of syllables per word, as represented by the following Eq. 6.1:

$$0.39 \times \left(\frac{\textit{Number of words}}{\textit{Number of sentences}}\right) + 11.8 \times \left(\frac{\textit{Number of syllables}}{\textit{Number of words}}\right) - 15.59 \tag{6.1}$$

While this metric evaluates the use of "shorter" words as the South Dakota drafting guide urges, it does not evaluate the relative simplicity or commonness of the words included in a bill (Benoit et al. 2019). These other components are important for assessing relative differences across bills by sponsor gender and should be incorporated using techniques developed by Benoit et al. (2019). The ideal measure of complexity would incorporate coding of the bills by people or entities who are constrained by interpreting the laws. For now, I apply this measure given its previous use in political science and its uniformity across bills. Other measures

[11] https://sdlegislature.gov/docs/referencematerials/draftingmanual.pdf

capture the logged number of words, the number of dollar amounts, the number of numbers, and the number of sections in each bill.

Several other variables capture the semantic features of the legislation. The *Logged number of words* is a proxy measure of the detail included in the legislation. I also count the *Number of dollar amounts* that appear in each bill to gauge its financial complexity. This measure could identify budget bills or financial legislation. However, controlling for topic alleviates this concern. The *Number of numbers* in a bill evaluates its specificity. Bills with more numbers likely provide more detail and precision. The *Number of sections* indicates the breadth of the legal code that the bill seeks to change; sections are the building blocks of bills and generally cover a single topic or area of specific law. These simple metrics help me gauge baseline differences and contextual interactions between outsider bill provision and bill complexity.

6.2.1.1 Bill Topic

A bill's subject matter likely impacts its composition. For example, some policy areas might require more descriptive legislation, while others involve more technical language. Therefore, if bureaucrats or other outsiders tend to request bills in certain policy areas, the composition of their bills might differ. To investigate this possibility, I classify bills into topical categories using the structural topic model (STM) package in R (Roberts et al. 2019; Roberts et al. 2014). STM can use information about the document, in this case the state where the bill was introduced, to add more detail and precision to the model. I chose thirty-five topics based on the substantive and statistical interpretations. I label each topic based on the top words associated with it. Resolutions are the most common topic in this bill dataset.

A quick check of the mean complexity scores across topics provides a simple face validity check of the complexity scores across bill topics (see Appendix Table D.1). I expect that resolutions are generally less complex than bills in other topics, and anticipate that bills which include "fiscal" contain many more numbers and dollars. This short test indicates that the topics and metrics of complexity are detecting important differences between bills.

6.2.2 Complexity in Bureaucratic Bills

I employ a series of ordinary least squares (OLS) regressions to model the various metrics of bill complexity. Table 6.1 starts with a sparse model:

TABLE 6.1 *Regressions of departmental sponsor on metrics of complexity*

	Flesch Kincaid	Log no. words	No. dollars	No. sections	No. numbers
	(1)	(2)	(3)	(4)	(5)
Departmental	0.15	0.09***	−3.63***	1.32***	−8.20
	(0.08)	(0.02)	(0.64)	(0.17)	(7.98)
Constant	20.02***	5.76***	1.45	2.70***	104.48***
	(0.11)	(0.03)	(0.94)	(0.25)	(11.68)
State fixed effects	Yes	Yes	Yes	Yes	Yes
Topic fixed effects	Yes	Yes	Yes	Yes	Yes
Observations	149,329	150,823	150,823	150,823	150,823
R^2	0.002	0.01	0.05	0.03	0.05
Adjusted R^2	0.001	0.01	0.05	0.03	0.05

*$p < 0.05$; **$p < 0.01$; ***$p < 0.001$.

It only includes bureaucratic sponsor. Table 6.2 adds features of the state legislature. For both regressions, the tables present predictors of (1) the *Flesch Kincaid reading score*, (2) *Logged no. words*, (3) *No. Dollars* in the bill, (4) *No. Sections* in the bill, and (5) *No. of Numbers* in the bill. Fixed effects for bill topic (for Tables 6.1 and 6.2) and state (for Table 6.1) are included.

Even after controlling for bill topic via topic fixed effects, important structural and complexity differences remain between bills offered by bureaucrats (aka departmental bills) versus those that are not. Departmental bills score higher on the Flesch Kincaid score compared to non-departmental bills, indicating more complex documents. Since topic fixed effects are included, I compare bills in the same topic area and find that departmental bills are systematically longer, more complex, and have more sections than non-departmental bills. Departmental bills also have fewer dollar signs, which might reflect the finding from Chapter 3 that these bills cost less than their non-departmental counterparts. Overall, these findings demonstrate that departmental bills are written differently than those that originate elsewhere. The Flesch Kincaid scores indicate that these bills may be more technical or formal. These differences can affect the legislature's ability to understand the bill and adequately check its contents without the expertise of the department that drafted the legislation.

Next I explore the structural features of the legislature that may interact with the complexity of legislation, which I establish in previous

TABLE 6.2 *Regressions of departmental sponsor and state capacity on metrics of complexity*

	Dependent variable				
	Flesch Kincaid	Log no. words	No. dollars	No. sections	No. numbers
	(1)	(2)	(3)	(4)	(5)
Departmental	0.52**	0.18***	−0.21	1.90***	27.65
	(0.17)	(0.04)	(1.27)	(0.34)	(15.77)
Low prof.	0.11	0.05**	−3.81***	0.14	15.15
	(0.08)	(0.02)	(0.64)	(0.17)	(7.99)
Medium prof.	0.05	0.14***	1.85***	1.68***	67.13***
	(0.04)	(0.01)	(0.32)	(0.09)	(4.04)
Departmental × low prof.	−0.89**	−0.30***	4.55*	−0.66	66.18*
	(0.28)	(0.06)	(2.12)	(0.57)	(26.37)
Departmental × medium prof.	−0.42*	−0.06	−5.64***	0.43	−34.31
	(0.20)	(0.04)	(1.50)	(0.41)	(18.72)
Constant	19.99***	5.74***	1.55	4.23***	59.15***
	(0.11)	(0.02)	(0.85)	(0.23)	(10.53)
State fixed effects	No	No	No	No	No
Topic fixed effects	Yes	Yes	Yes	Yes	Yes
Observations	149,329	150,823	150,823	150,823	150,823
R^2	0.002	0.01	0.05	0.01	0.05
Adjusted R^2	0.001	0.005	0.05	0.01	0.05

$^{*}p < 0.05$; $^{**}p < 0.01$; $^{***}p < 0.001$.

chapters relates to the uptake of departmental bills. Table 6.2 reports the regressions of the various readability measures and departmental sponsorship and adds the legislature professionalism levels and interactions with departmental bill sponsorship. Figure 6.1 plots the interaction terms. The main effects of departmental sponsorship remain largely the same, but the significance on the coefficient for the relationship between departmental bills and the number of dollar signs in the bill disappears and the departmental bills are significantly related to the number of numbers in the bill. For easier interpretation, I classify states as having low (ID, MT, ND, and SD), medium (MD, NC, NV, OR, and WA), or high (CA and NY) levels of professionalism. In those with low professionalism, departmental bills have a 0.668 point lower Flesch Kincaid score than non-departmental bills in high professionalism states. This indicates that departmental bills in the former are written in simpler language than

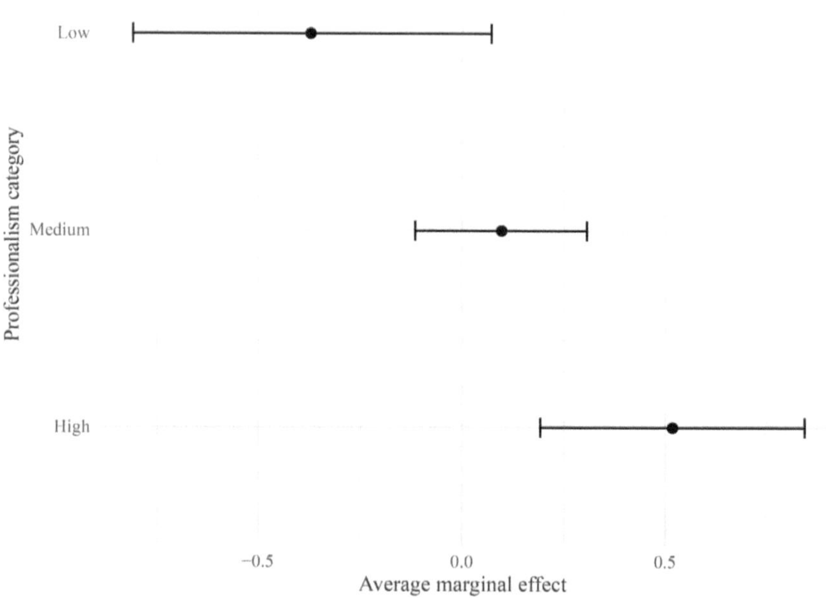

FIGURE 6.1 Marginal effects plot of departmental bills and legislative professionalism for Flesch Kincaid scores.

those in the latter. This finding indicates that departments in states with lower professionalism might tailor their bills to the legislative context (or deal with less complex material). The bureaucracy in such states may need to communicate more with legislators with fewer staff or less time to dedicate to the job. Departmental outsiders do not appear to ramp up the complexity in low-capacity states to mislead the legislature.

6.2.3 Complexity in California Sponsored Bills

This section employs a similar approach to explore the relative complexity of group-sponsored bills in California's legislature. I use the indicator of group sponsorship from Chapter 3 to compare the complexity of bills drafted by outsiders. Unlike the previous section, this data combines different types of outsiders. For instance, expert tax organizations are included with ideological groups as sponsoring legislation. Since important differences may emerge between these types that have normative

TABLE 6.3 *Regressions of outside sponsor on metrics of complexity in California.*

	Flesch Kincaid	Log no. words	No. dollars	No. sections	No. numbers
	(1)	(2)	(3)	(4)	(5)
Group sponsor	0.21	0.06	−0.18	0.66***	−24.36
	(0.18)	(0.03)	(0.35)	(0.20)	(22.46)
Local bill	−0.44*	−0.19***	0.50	−0.87***	26.59
	(0.18)	(0.03)	(0.36)	(0.20)	(22.53)
Urgency bill	−0.90**	−0.03	2.70***	0.72*	152.50***
	(0.29)	(0.05)	(0.57)	(0.31)	(36.02)
Resolution	−2.90***	−0.18**	−1.03	−2.66***	−58.65
	(0.31)	(0.06)	(0.60)	(0.33)	(38.24)
Cosponsors	0.01	0.001	-0.01	0.002	−0.33
	(0.01)	(0.001)	(0.01)	(0.01)	(0.88)
Constant	24.84***	5.96***	1.44***	3.63***	69.26**
	(0.20)	(0.04)	(0.39)	(0.22)	(24.65)
Session fixed effects	Yes	Yes	Yes	Yes	Yes
Observations	14,127	14,206	14,206	14,206	14,206
R^2	0.05	0.01	0.002	0.01	0.002
Adjusted R^2	0.05	0.005	0.002	0.01	0.001

*$p < 0.05$; **$p < 0.01$; ***$p < 0.001$.

implications for evaluating complexity, Table 6.4 separates businesses and business organizations following the coding presented in Chapter 4.

Table 6.3 presents the OLS regressions of group sponsorship and the various complexity measures. The controls relate to the various features of the bill that might be related to its complexity. For example, resolutions have significantly lower Flesch Kincaid scores, on average, than non-resolutions. The group-sponsored bills do not stand out like departmental sponsored bills. Group-sponsored bills are longer and have more sections than non-group-sponsored bills, but do not have significantly different Flesch Kincaid scores. Since this composite measure of group sponsor includes all types of sponsors, this lack of difference may be due to heterogeneity across group types. I investigate this possibility in the next set of analyses.

Are bills drafted by business groups more complicated? A normative concern with this kind of outsider involvement is that groups that represent business interests or individual businesses advocate bills that seek to write into law special privileges that are not welfare enhancing for the state as a whole (recall the Taser International example). It may be harder to conceal the true intent of bills from these types of outsiders. According to former long-term legislative staffer Scott Lilly, "The legislative process is made up of people who are artisans at being able to craft language that looks innocuous [but isn't]."[12] Businesses may therefore be more likely to provide complicated "artisanal" language that has hidden benefits for small swaths of the economy.

Table 6.4 explores this possibility by separating out business organizations and businesses from the rest of the sponsoring organizations. I run the same regressions as above with additional categories indicating whether the bill has a business or non-business sponsor. The excluded

TABLE 6.4 *Regressions of outside sponsor on complexity metrics in California*

	Flesch Kincaid	Log no. words	No. dollars	No. sections	No. numbers
	(1)	(2)	(3)	(4)	(5)
Non-business sponsor	0.19	0.05	−0.15	0.85***	−20.54
	(0.19)	(0.04)	(0.38)	(0.21)	(24.12)
Business sponsor	0.65*	0.14*	−0.19	−0.10	−44.56
	(0.33)	(0.06)	(0.64)	(0.35)	(40.44)
Local bill	−0.42*	−0.19***	0.50	−0.88***	25.93
	(0.18)	(0.03)	(0.36)	(0.20)	(22.55)
Urgency bill	−0.91**	−0.04	2.70***	0.74*	153.36***
	(0.29)	(0.05)	(0.57)	(0.31)	(36.04)
Resolution	−2.90***	−0.18**	−1.02	−2.66***	−58.53
	(0.31)	(0.06)	(0.60)	(0.33)	(38.23)
Cosponsors	0.01	0.001	−0.01	0.002	−0.34
	(0.01)	(0.001)	(0.01)	(0.01)	(0.88)
Constant	24.81***	5.96***	1.44***	3.63***	70.68**
	(0.20)	(0.04)	(0.39)	(0.22)	(24.75)
Session fixed effects	Yes	Yes	Yes	Yes	Yes
Observations	14,127	14,206	14,206	14,206	14,206
R^2	0.05	0.01	0.002	0.01	0.002
Adjusted R^2	0.05	0.005	0.002	0.01	0.001

Outside sponsors are classified as business or non-business.
$^{*}p < 0.05$; $^{**}p < 0.01$; $^{***}p < 0.001$.

[12] www.politico.com/story/2009/09/read-the-bill-it-might-not-help-026846

category is no sponsor. The findings are somewhat mixed, but the Flesch Kincaid scores indicate that bills with business sponsors are significantly less "readable" than those with no sponsor. Non-business sponsors also write different bills compared to unsponsored bills, with more words and more sections, but no significant difference in Flesch Kincaid scores. This finding provides some evidence that businesses write different bills than other types of groups and unsponsored bills, and that these differences manifest in more complicated (and potentially difficult to process) bills.

6.3 CHANGING THE BILL

As another way of assessing whether bills proposed by outsiders go through a different process, I introduce the measure of the extent to which bills are altered throughout the lawmaking process. I employ the same measure that was introduced in Chapter 5 to gauge the extent of change in bill language across versions. It indicates the amount of text shared between every two versions of a bill; this is the ratio of matches that captures how much subsequent versions of the bill draw from earlier versions (0 = less similar; 1 = more similar). Higher scores indicate that the bill changed less. Table 6.5 reports the years and states for which this information is available; in LegiScan, Idaho and New York do not have the versions of the bills needed for the comparisons.

I limit the comparisons to the first (introduced) and final (passed) version. If other comparisons were included in the analysis, this would hide

TABLE 6.5 *Years of joint bill version text and bureaucratic bill data availability per state*

State	Years available
California	2009–2014
Idaho	—
Maryland	2009–2014
Montana	2009–2014
North Carolina	2009–2014
North Dakota	2009–2014
Nevada	2009–2014
New York	—
Oregon	2009–2014
South Dakota	2009–2014
Washington	2009–2014

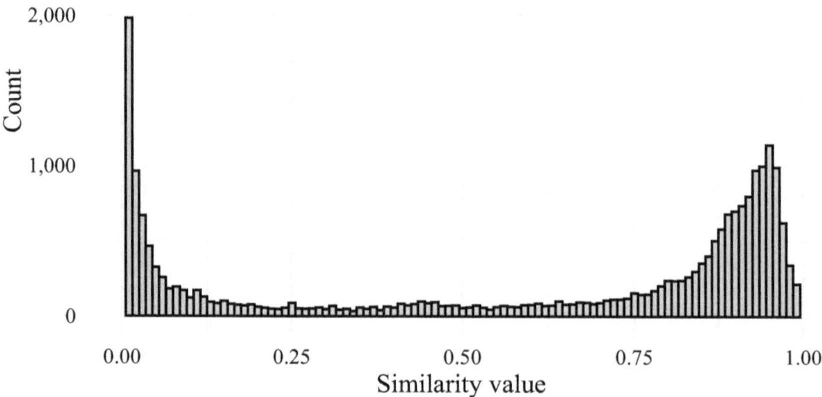

FIGURE 6.2 Distribution of the comparison similarity values between versions of the bills, 2009–2014.

the extent to which the full legislature examines or alters bills. For example, if the state legislature amends a bill, this generates another version of it. This version can be amended many more times before a final version is agreed upon, and these amendments may reflect minor changes. While this scope limits the analysis to bills that pass into law, it narrows the focus to those that bind the state actors. These texts will have the full force of law and alter or expand the actions state businesses, people, and agencies. Figure 6.2 displays a histogram of the similarity values between versions of the bills between 2009 and 2014 in the nine states for which bureaucratic bill indicators are available (see Table 6.5). The figure depicts a bimodal distribution of similarity: The vast majority of bills that eventually pass either change drastically (near 0, the low end of the similarity value) or remain largely unchanged (near 1).

This metric is not the only way to capture changes in legislation. Ideally, we could assess the extent and significance of the modifications. While this metric is a shortcut to determine the level of deliberation, it does reveal the relative consideration of bills to each other. The number of times a bill is amended may also capture the extent to which the sponsor's bill has been altered. Martin and Vanberg (2014) use the "total number of (sub-) articles altered in the bill plus the number of (sub)articles added or deleted" to gauge how much a draft measure changes (p. 985). I argue that my automated textual measure more completely captures the extent to which a bill has undergone revisions since it is a continuous measure and the calculations can be automated over a large number of bills. A single amendment could either drastically alter the bill or change it slightly (e.g., fixing a grammatical mistake or word choice). The percentage of words in the bill that have been changed between two versions accordingly weighs the extent to which the bills have been altered. Additionally, the consolidation of amendments, engrossing (the incorporation of amendments), and institutions surrounding amendments may differ in important ways across states, whereas the textual measure is a consistent measurement across states. To measure the relationship between the number of amendments and the percentage of the bill's text that changes, I calculate the correlation between these two measures in the California state legislature. The number of amendments and the percentage similarity between introduced and chaptered versions correlate at −0.32. The number of amendments added and the percentage of bills that are changed are weakly correlated. I proceed using the textual measure, given the previously mentioned advantages.

6.3.1 Bill Change in Bureaucratic Bills

In this section, I present the results from OLS regressions of the presence of a departmental sponsor and the similarity of a bill between its first and final versions. To account for differences across states and types of bills, I include state and topic fixed effects. I control for the length of the first version of the bill, *Logged no. words*, since this may be importantly related to the refinements it undergoes during the legislative process. Table 6.6 reports these results.

This analysis demonstrates that bills with a departmental sponsor change less than those without a departmental sponsor listed, which demonstrates these actors' power within the legislative process. This finding provides evidence that the legislature does not vet these bills as thoroughly as it does other types of bills. The difference could indicate that the bills are getting checked less or that they are of higher quality and need fewer changes. Or it could be the case that fewer additions are made as concessions to other legislators because these bills are less controversial. While a number of mechanisms could be behind this interesting difference, it does show that the bureaucracy gets more of what it wants during the legislative process than similar bills not requested by

TABLE 6.6 *Regression of bill similarity between versions and departmental sponsor*

	Similarity
Departmental sponsor	0.04***
	(0.01)
Log no. words	0.01***
	(0.001)
Constant	0.51***
	(0.01)
State fixed effects	Yes
Topic fixed effects	Yes
Observations	25,638
R^2	0.40
Adjusted R^2	0.40

*$p < 0.05$; **$p < 0.01$; ***$p < 0.001$.

these outsiders. This finding indicates that the legislature is not appropriating (or is unable to appropriate) the expertise and work that these bureaucrats put into drafting legislation. In other words, the finding that the bills offered by bureaucrats remain relatively unchanged suggests that the legislature is not exploiting the expertise offered by the bill.

Next, I explore the role of legislative professionalism in this relationship. Table 6.7 includes professionalism categories and interactions with departmental sponsorship. For bills in legislatures with a medium degree of professionalism, being sponsored by a department results in a 0.064-unit decrease in similarity compared to bills from highly professional legislatures that are also sponsored by a department. This is an unexpected result, because departmental bills face higher levels of scrutiny in medium professional legislatures compared to highly professional legislatures. Since this result is based on the nine states for which the bill change data is available, it is not as robust as a fifty-state study. The main effect on departmental sponsor remains significant even after controlling for these legislature-level features. Departmental bills retain their initial form and language more, on average, than those without a departmental sponsor.

6.3.2 Bill Change in California Sponsored Bills

Since I have more detail on bills in the California legislature, I include more control variables to account for differences across sponsored and

TABLE 6.7 *Regression of bill similarity between versions and departmental sponsor*

	Dependent variable
	Similarity
Departmental sponsor	0.04*
	(0.02)
Log no. words	0.003*
	(0.002)
Low professionalism	0.24***
	(0.01)
Medium professionalism	−0.12***
	(0.01)
Departmental × low prof.	0.001
	(0.02)
Departmental × medium prof.	−0.06***
	(0.02)
Constant	0.53***
	(0.02)
State fixed effects	No
Topic fixed effects	Yes
Observations	25,638
R^2	0.17
Adjusted R^2	0.17

Regression includes professionalism levels and interactions.
$^{*}p < 0.05$; $^{**}p < 0.01$; $^{***}p < 0.001$.

unsponsored bills that may explain proclivities to alter the bill during the legislative process. These variables are described in detail in Chapter 4. Urgency bills may be more important pieces of legislation, and thus receive more discussion and scrutiny. Resolutions might change less because they are not substantively altering law and are less important. The indicator variable *Group sponsor* includes group sponsors of all types.

Table 6.8 reports the regression results. Similar to the results for departmental sponsors, group-sponsored bills in California change less than unsponsored bills. Even controlling for other features of the legislation that seem closely related to the changes the bills will deferentially undergo, the coefficient on *Group sponsor* remains significant. While a 0.057 increase in similarity may seem small, the similarity score ranges between 0 and 1. Moreover, even small changes to bills can meaningfully

TABLE 6.8 *Regression of bill similarity between versions and group sponsor in the California state legislature*

	Similarity
Group sponsor	0.06***
	(0.01)
Urgency bill	−0.14***
	(0.02)
Local bill	−0.02
	(0.01)
Resolution	0.35***
	(0.01)
Constant	0.52***
	(0.01)
Observations	4,104
R^2	0.14
Adjusted R^2	0.14

*$p < 0.05$; **$p < 0.01$; ***$p < 0.001$.

alter their intent or remove portions that are important to the outside sponsor. This finding suggests that the California state legislature is not heavily altering outsider bills after they are introduced.

As in the section on bill complexity, I want to see if the differences between sponsored and unsponsored bills are driven by bills written by businesses or business associations. I include a categorical indicator for if the bill was sponsored by a non-business group, a business group, or unsponsored. The results presented in Table 6.9 establish that business entities are not driving the results reported above. Bills sponsored by business groups tend to undergo *fewer* changes than unsponsored bills during the legislative process, but the effect is less pronounced compared to non-business sponsors. As a whole, these findings on bill similarity across versions indicate that the California legislature does not radically alter bills proposed by outsiders. I argue that examining the trajectory of legislative vehicles is important for understanding outside actors' degree of control over final policy outcomes.

TABLE 6.9 *Regression of bill similarity between versions and group sponsor in the California state legislature with business sponsor classification*

	Similarity
Non-business sponsor	0.06***
	(0.01)
Business sponsor	0.04*
	(0.02)
Urgency bill	−0.14***
	(0.02)
Local bill	−0.02
	(0.01)
Resolution	0.35***
	(0.01)
Constant	0.52***
	(0.01)
Observations	4,104
R^2	0.14
Adjusted R^2	0.14

$^{*}p < 0.05$; $^{**}p < 0.01$; $^{***}p < 0.001$.

6.4 LIMITATIONS AND CONCLUSION

Additional outsider or partnering legislative sponsor characteristics may be important to consider. For example, Woon (2008) argues that the "legislators with higher agenda positions will moderate their proposals to a greater extent than legislators with low agenda positions, and that legislators with low agenda positions will tend to propose bills that reflect position taking" (p. 201). Woon (2008) finds that committee leaders and majority-party sponsors moderate their bills. This work suggests that powerful legislators may anticipate the centripetal pull of the legislative process and alter their sponsored bills prior to introducing them. Groups and bureaucrats may strategically also modify their proposals depending on their goals for the legislation.

While the previous empirical chapters provide evidence that groups and bureaucrats are very involved in crafting the laws that govern US states, what do these findings mean for the people of these states? This chapter and the remainder of the book shifts its substantive focus away from mapping the extent of outsiders' involvement and variation in usage across states and legislators to probe the implications of the bills these outsiders produce. Given the constraints placed on state legislatures – low resources, lack of federal action, high expectations – what does this high level of input from outsiders in the legislative process mean for democracy in the states?

Measuring and comparing bills offered by outsiders of different stripes to those generated internally within the legislature reveals important and meaningful differences in complexity and scrutiny. The results demonstrate that bills from bureaucrats and business outsiders in California are markedly different from unsponsored bills. Bills proposed by bureaucrats or groups are more complex than unsponsored bills. This simple finding suggests that outsiders write different types of bills, which can complicate the process for legislators seeking to read and process bills quickly. It can also introduce hidden rent-seeking provisions and make the body of law more complicated in the state; these differences may affect the construction of the code books in the state. Furthermore, the bills from these outsiders change less during the legislative process than unsponsored bills. This difference implies that group bills are receiving less scrutiny from the legislative body than other types of bills. While bills from outsiders may be unproblematic, constituents deserve guarantees that these outsiders are getting checked by the legislative body tasked with legislating.

The fundamental question about what the legislature or legislator would do in the absence of outsider input remains. Using this input can free up a legislator's time to conduct other forms of representation like providing constituency service (Harden 2016). From the perspective of the legislature, outsider bills can alter the overall production of legislation that addresses issues that are important to the state. This overall question of quality is elusive. In this chapter I take a first step toward establishing that the supply of bills from outsiders differs from those developed internally (or via unmapped sources). These differences can alter the ability of legislators (and those bound to abide by the laws) to understand the legislation. Importantly, the smaller changes made to these outsiders' bills call into question the legislator's assurances that outsiders do not get a blank check from the legislature. In the next chapter I study constituents' opinions on this input. This angle of democratic accountability advances arguments about what this tactic and reliance mean for legislative accountability.

7

The Electoral Connection: Democratic Implications of Outsider Involvement

This chapter shifts from examining the text and sources of legislation to public preferences. Ordinary citizens seem to want it all when it comes to policymaking. Lindblom captured the public's angst about the policymaking process in 1980: "On the one hand, people want policy to be informed and well analyzed. On the other hand, they want policymaking to be democratic, hence necessarily political." How can low-resourced legislators craft high-quality legislation that is also democratically crafted and considered? While interest groups and their influence are frequently reviled, the public may accept the need for their input.

When people learn about the role that interest groups play in the legislative drafting process, it can have implications on public opinion. Hibbing et al. (2021) finds that "people's satisfaction with processes affects election outcomes, legislative successes, compliance with laws, and even overall democratic health." Politicians' actions fundamentally affect public trust, which serves as a check on their conduct (Heterington 2005). While legislative processes often occur behind closed doors, sometimes the tactics are revealed and generate a public reaction. For example, the series of news stories about model bills in the Associated Press discussed in Chapter 5 garnered attention and illuminated normally opaque state policymaking processes. The opinions that people form about these actions and the politicians engaging in them can affect what happens to the bills within the legislature as well as the health of democracy.

This chapter explores how turning to outsiders influences public opinion. Chapter 1 discusses the social welfare implications of relying on outsiders, and this survey experiment examines how the people affected by the laws view the process. Another way to assess this normative question would be to compare the direct outcomes of laws that groups and bureaucrats advocate to those drafted internally. Dorrell and Jansa (2022) provide an excellent example of assessing the social welfare implications of legislating. They investigate whether using model bills on "organ donation legislation, e-cigarette/vaping bans for minors and anti-bullying legislation" increases or decreases the uptake of the relevant programs. They assess the degree to which these policies copy model legislation and find that bills that more closely resemble the models generate less policy success. While I laud this approach to determining if *specific bills* have the intended effect depending on their levels of reuse, I examine whether the political *system* is better off with model/group/bureaucratic bills. Only looking at specific policy areas is an important step toward answering this question, but cannot determine whether the presence of group bills may crowd out legislation that would advance state interests. I examine a slice of the normative implications by focusing on public opinion about this involvement, but I argue that public opinion is important given the electoral connection and centrality to democratic accountability.

The book's empirical chapters provide evidence that groups, individuals, and bureaucrats are very involved in crafting US state legislation. This chapter examines how such outside involvement affects the people governed by these laws. Does the public assess policy and politicians differently when the policies come from outside the legislature? Do voters evaluate legislators and policy more favorably when the legislator crafts a bill with or without input from outsiders?

Plenty of news articles hint at the impropriety (or even explicitly decry) the involvement of lobbyists, corporations, or industry groups in drafting legislation. These articles call out both federal- and state-level legislators and follow a common trope. First, the journalist, an academic, a citizen, or an opposing interest group or legislator expresses outrage or at least questions the ethics behind the outsider's involvement and its implications for democracy. The sassy *Huffington Post* headline "Elected Legislators Continue To Occasionally Assist Bank Lobbyists in Drafting Legislation" exemplifies this writing.[1] Next, another commentator postulates the merits of involving these outsiders in the process of drafting legislation. These articles demonstrate that people have an interest in the inner workings of their legislatures and the blatant examples of group involvement shock the senses of a public that recoils from indications of

[1] www.huffpost.com/entry/bank-lobbyists-draft-legislation_n_3332901

plagiarism. This chapter merges such coverage with prior findings that citizens generally do not care what their state representatives are up to and find the policymaking process a bore. I draw on these news articles as inspiration for my survey experiment.

Since policymaking does not occur in a vacuum, it is difficult to separate the causal effects of interest group input, partisanship, and expertise on public opinion. To causally identify how group involvement in legislating affects the perceived legitimacy of policies and politicians, I use a survey experiment that randomly exposes respondents to bill source and expertise treatments and asks them to assess the policy and lawmaker. This survey has a clean design; it generates estimates of the "costs" for politicians of engaging with outsiders on drafting legislation. I argue that the findings also apply to how people read about state legislative policymaking, should they choose to do so (or even have the opportunity given the lacuna of statehouse reporters), and other matters.

On the one hand, citizens may not care how legislators generate legislation or legislative ideas. Americans know little about national politics (Campbell et al. 1960; Carpini and Keeter 1996) and even less about state politics. Rogers (2017) finds that "little constrains state legislators' behavior" because constituents do not pay attention to them. However, other studies conclude that state policy is generally responsive to public opinion. In experimental work, Butler and Nickerson (2011) report that state legislators adjust their behavior after learning about constituents' opinions, suggesting they seek to be responsive. However, Broockman and Skovron (2018) determine that state legislators systematically assume constituents' policy views are further to the right than they are. Moreover, people may not need to know very much about the details of policymaking or policies to have strong opinions about how the process *should* work. They may also have visceral reactions to plagiarism of policy; stories that mention outright copying may trigger ideas about fairness. Partisan considerations may outweigh potential concerns about the democratic accountability of turning to outsiders. Process concerns about the role that groups play in legislating may trouble some groups of voters or potential voters. In turn, public opinion about process may indirectly influence legislative action.

Polls find that lobbyists are reviled (Drutman 2015; Pew Research Center 2019). This distrust may translate into skepticism of legislation and politicians attached to the groups they represent. News stories about interest group involvement in the legislative process, especially when legislators seem to know little about the bills they are putting their names on, make constituents skeptical of their input.

Even if voters distrust group involvement in the legislative process and would prefer legislators to write bills independently, the net effect of the involvement may still be positive. Legislators may be better able to represent constituents by using model legislation, groups' preferred bills, or bureaucrats' ideas. These templates may produce higher-quality policy because of the expertise offered by these actors. Moreover, the groups represent some constituents' desires. Thus, by enacting the groups' preferred policies, legislators can efficiently translate policy demands into legislation. Prepackaged bills can free up valuable time for legislators to pursue other policies or constituency service.

Special interests groups describe their involvement as constituency service. In a *Washington Post* article that discusses lobbyist involvement in federal medical malpractice legislation, the chairman and chief executive of the company that spearheaded the legislative push argues that the involvement of groups bolsters the legislature's representative function: "I don't think any of us would want to live in a society where all laws are imposed by regulators, a judge, a congress, a president. . .We live in a society where the laws meet the needs of those they are meant to govern. Ideally, it should be a collaborative process in the context of the overall national interest."[2] In response to this article, the Physician Insurers Association of America responded that this interaction represents "legislators consulting with their constituencies about proposed legislation, concerned stakeholders providing their feedback, and those concerns being appropriately considered and addressed."[3]

However, group bills may not reflect the interests of the legislators' constituents (Gilens and Page 2005; Kimball et al. 2012). Even if bills provided by interest groups or bureaucrats increase public policy's responsiveness or alignment with public opinion, we may still be concerned that a specific piece of legislation could unfairly advance the interests of the group introducing the bill.

While the alignment between outside bills and what the public wants from their state-level representatives is beyond the scope of the book, this chapter assesses the alignment between legislators' actions and constituents' *process* preferences. If the survey results demonstrate that

[2] https://tinyurl.com/5yw8d4cs

[3] https://web.archive.org/web/20250325050542/; https://tinyurl.com/26d4dyzm

voters are not bothered by extra-legislative involvement in crafting legislation, we may conclude that citizens do not regard it as a normative concern. However, if the results show that the respondents prefer policies and politicians that do not rely on outsiders to craft legislation, this suggests outsiders can shape peoples' experiences with the policymaking process even outside of policy concerns. Moreover, it may indicate that legislators are not responsive to constituents' desires when considering this type of legislation. Given that the previous chapters establish that there is substantial involvement from interest groups and bureaucrats, if the survey concludes that people prefer legislators to act without outside help, we may be troubled by the widespread reliance on outsider input. Exploring source considerations and what potential voters think about outsider involvement yields insights into the democratic accountability of groups writing bills.

7.1 PRIOR WORK ON PROCESS CONCERNS

Canonical work by Hibbing and Theiss-Morse (2001) studies approval of the lawmaking process and establishes that people prefer not to see the nuts and bolts of policymaking. Especially relevant to my study, Hibbing, and Theiss-Morse (2002) conclude that people prefer "to defer to non elected actors, such as independent experts or a bureaucratic elite, to promote a level of efficiency and effectiveness within the government that self-serving elected officials cannot provide" (p. 141). In a fascinating law review, Feinstein (2024) experimentally studies agency decision-making. Feinstein (2024) focuses instead on the *rulemaking* process, and finds experimental support "for the century-old, seemingly shopworn idea that empowering politically insulated, expert decision-makers legitimizes agencies." While these expert decision-makers are strongly supported in some areas, bringing them into the legislative process may alter the perception that bureaucrats are insulated technocrats. Indeed, the very act of getting involved in the legislative process may make bureaucrats seem less apolitical. Differences in the types of outsiders may lead observers to have divergent views of outside bills and politicians who push bureaucrats' vs. interest group bills. These differences may help explain why powerful legislators and those with more resources partner with bureaucrats.

Recent studies update Hibbing and Theiss-Morse (2001) to assess commitment to democratic norms (VanderMolen 2017; Bloeser et al. 2024). Work by Laurel Harbridge-Yong and co-authors concentrates on the link between cooperation, coordination, decision-making, and legislative approval (Harbridge-Yong and Paris 2021). Other work by Harbridge et al. (2014) finds that bipartisan processes do not win out over partisan concerns in public evaluations of policy. Turning to the role of outsiders, Rasmussen and Reher (2023) conduct some closely related experiments to those in this chapter, but explore a stage of the policy-making process in which people generally know that interest groups play a role – parliamentary hearings. They "examine when and why (unequal) involvement of different types of interest groups in a formal, closed form of policy consultation, specifically – hearings in national parliaments – affects citizens' perceptions of the legitimacy of the policy-making process" (Rasmussen and Reher 2023).

While some research in this area studies public opinion on legislative action depending on strategy, much of the work that explores the link between process and opinion focuses on the executive branch. Several studies examine the connection between executive orders and public opinion (Reeves and Rogowski 2018; Christenson and Kriner 2019, 2020; Reeves and Rogowski 2020; Lowande and Rogowski 2021). Some of these studies establish that there is no connection between how a policy is implemented during a crisis; that is, whether it is enacted by congressional action or unilateral executive decree (Lowande and Rogowski 2021). Yet, other work finds that public opinion is the main constraint on unilateral executive action (Christenson and Kriner 2020). Though state legislators operate in a different information environment than executives, activated opinions may still constrain state politicians. My study explores varying levels of support for legislators and policies when the legislation draws on outside sources; I investigate the role of interest groups as a source of variation in support for policy and politicians.

The literature on "source cues" focuses on ballot initiatives (Lupia 1994). People generally know that interest groups (or at least unelected officials) sponsor or write the text of ballot initiatives; in fact, that is the point of the initiative process. Since the people elect legislators to legislate, we may expect to find lower approval for outsider involvement in legislatures compared to studies of the initiative process. D.ür (2019) determines that approval of these measures depends more on the policy argument than the source. I explore how information about the source of legislation affects their view of the process, the legislation, and the politician.

All else equal, people may prefer that interest groups and bureaucrats remain out of the legislative process. Yet because state legislators operate in an information-constrained environment, constituents may be open to the merits of using outsiders' expertise. People do not like legislative gridlock (Flynn and Harbridge 2016). If they see outsiders as a way to prevent gridlock and improve productivity, this may temper their distrust of outsiders. The experimental manipulations can help us explore the policymaking process when other components are held constant.

7.1.1 Partisan Concerns

Most people are partisans. Voters view and assess policies and politicians through the lens of party identification. Process concerns about where legislators are getting their ideas and the text of bills from will thus likely operate through a partisan lens (Jones 2013; Broockman et al. 2023). However, Coppock (2022) finds that information about other types of group cues can be persuasive.

Partisanship shapes how the public views nearly every political process – even on issues previously viewed as "fundamental predispositions like racial attitudes" (Engelhardt 2020). Perhaps unsurprising after the COVID pandemic, but with interesting findings pre-pandemic, Krupenkin (2021) finds that "presidential co-partisans are 4–10 percentage points more likely to vaccinate than presidential out-partisans" during the Bush and Obama administrations. When investigating how the public will view bills and politicians that rely on outsiders, the co-partisan status of the legislator sponsoring the bill should be taken into account.

7.2 EXPECTATIONS

I expect the survey respondents' preferences regarding the bill and legislator to differ depending on the source, expertise, and partisan alignment of the bill's sponsor. These pre-registered (AsPredicted #241265) hypotheses follow from the literature on constituent public opinion. The results have implications for the perspectives of constituents thinking about outsiders' involvement in the legislative process. The most basic aspect of analyzing what the public thinks is assessing the role of outsiders. I expect public opinion to decrease when an interest group is involved. The public is generally skeptical of interest groups' role in policymaking; it monitors outsiders for rent-seeking behavior. This leads to the first hypothesis:

Source hypothesis: When an interest group writes the legislation, the public will express less support (for the legislator and the policy) than when an interest group is not identified as the source.

The public might be skeptical of interest group influence, but if the benefits can be made clear (such as the value of their expertise), voters may not punish the legislator for partnering with the group. The next hypothesis is thus:

Expertise advantage hypothesis: When the group writing the legislation is identified as having expertise, the public will express more support (for the legislator and the policy) than when no expertise is identified.

Finally, given the importance of partisanship in organizing political thought, I include a third prediction, which requires significant power for the interaction:

Partisan override hypothesis: When an interest group writes the legislation, outpartisans (from the bill sponsor) will express a greater decrease in support than copartisans.

7.3 SURVEY DESIGN

I fielded this survey in the summer of 2025 using CloudResearch's Connect platform. Respondents answered standard demographic questions and a question about sources of state legislation before reading a hypothetical news story about a piece of legislation. The vast majority (1,898 of 2,000) of recruited respondents passed the attention check and were included in the results. Appendix E.1 presents the descriptive breakdown of the respondents, which indicates that the sample leans Democratic. The experimental manipulations involve source cues, expertise cues, and partisan cues.

Each respondent was randomly assigned to read two vignettes, one for each study. In the first study, respondents were randomly assigned to one of six experimental conditions. Table 7.1 reports the combinations. Control group respondents read a newspaper clipping about a bill introduced in the state legislature that was sponsored by a state senator. Respondents in two of the groups received additional information about the bill's source – either an influential interest group or the state's Department of Education. Respondents in the remaining groups received information on the high level of expertise provided by the group or Department of Education. Because knowledge of state legislative behavior is generally low, partisanship may override other legislative cues by serving as a powerful heuristic, so it was excluded from the first study.

In the second study, I introduced an additional randomization that ascribes partisanship to the legislator in the vignette, for a total of

TABLE 7.1 *Full factorial treatment combinations*

	Sponsor party[1]	Bill source	Expertise cue
1	Democrat	None	No
2	Democrat	None	Yes
3	Democrat	Interest group	No
4	Democrat	Interest group	Yes
5	Democrat	Bureaucrat	No
6	Democrat	Bureaucrat	Yes
7	Republican	None	No
8	Republican	None	Yes
9	Republican	Interest group	No
10	Republican	Interest group	Yes
11	Republican	Bureaucrat	No
12	Republican	Bureaucrat	Yes

[1] Only included in Study 2.

12 treatment groups. This allows me to estimate the effects of source and expertise cues when partisanship is not known as well as when it is known. After reading the short newspaper clip, reproduced below, respondents were asked about their level of support for or opposition to the legislation and the legislator who introduced it.

The hypothetical vignette was designed to mimic a real local news story about a bill being considered in a state legislature; the source and outsider's expertise levels were randomized. The phrases in parentheses were included or excluded based on the respondent's treatment assignment:

> The state legislature is currently considering S.B. 151, a bill on education [that was written by the state Department of Education/that was written by an influential interest group]. This bill seeks to change education policy in the state. [Republican/Democratic][4] State senator Alexander, a legislator on the Budget Committee, sponsored the bill. The bill would expand pre-kindergarten programs across the state and change the materials covered in these programs. Supporters say that the bill will advance the interests of children in the state and boost overall educational achievement. [The [interest group/Department of Education], which wrote the bill, has an extensive staff with expertise on the topic and experience drafting legislation.]

This newspaper clip reflects real coverage of state legislative action that mentions where the legislator got the idea. Long wait times and disorganization at the Department of Motor Vehicles (DMV) in North Carolina

[4] Only included in Study 2.

have prompted reorganization and loud calls for change in the agency. Articles about the legislative response to the issues mention how the DMV requests some of the changes. For example, a 2025 proposal to eliminate some requirements mentions the input from the agency: "If passed, driving log requirements would also be eliminated. That comes after a request from the NC Department of Motor Vehicles, according to bill sponsor Rep. David Willis, R-Union."[5] The media covers the input that legislators receive from outsiders and what type of help they provide. This type of coverage hints that the public is interested in the role that outsiders play.

7.4 PUBLIC PERCEPTIONS ABOUT BILL SOURCES

The survey first asks respondents where they think state legislators get their ideas. I was curious about whether they already knew that groups and bureaucrats write the bills or whether they thought legislators come up with their own ideas and draft the bills themselves. Perhaps these expectations vary by state legislative characteristics. The survey asked: "When legislators get ideas or text for legislation, what percentage do you think they draw from the following sources?" They were asked to choose amounts on sliding scales that add up to 100 percent of the legislation. The options were: interest groups (including corporations), bureaucrats, constituents, or legislator's own ideas. Figure 7.1 displays the mean percentage of legislation that respondents think comes from each source. The previous chapters establish that figuring out the "true" percentage of state law that originates in these sources is nearly impossible. Thus, comparing perceptions to the truth is not the goal. Yet, this exercise does reveal that respondents view the legislative process with appropriate skepticism and guess that legislators are not generating *all* of their own ideas for bills. Instead, it illustrates that constituents are aware that legislators are generating legislative text from a variety of sources. However, survey respondents probably overestimate the percentage of bills that comes from constituents.

While not a one-to-one comparison since the respondents are drawn from all fifty states, the data from California in Chapter 4 provides the best comparison between the percentage of bills that comes from each source and what respondents guess is the percentage. For example, the

[5] www.wral.com/news/state/nc-bill-speed-up-teen-licensing-dmv-delays-april-2025/

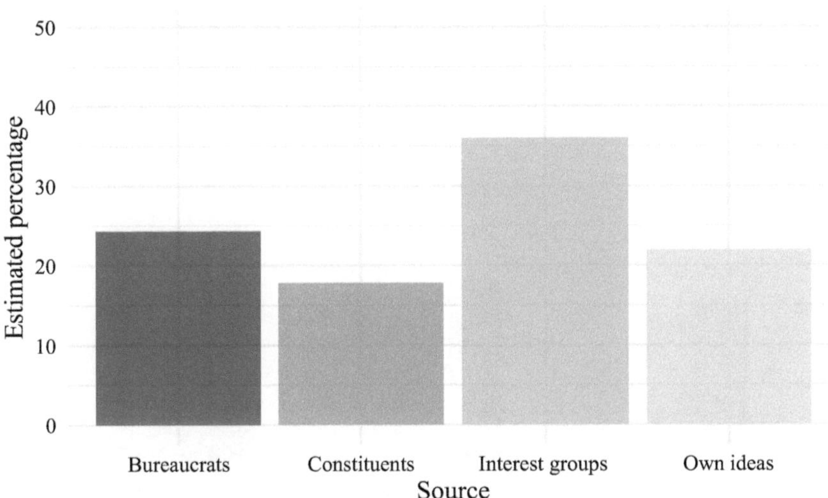

FIGURE 7.1 Average perceived percentage of bills that survey respondents estimate per source of legislation.

categorization of the bill sources in the California state legislature estimates that about 18 percent come from state agencies. On average, the survey respondents guessed that 24 percent come from agencies and that interest groups are the most common source of bills (36 percent of bills). Constituents ranked last as a perceived source of legislation. These numbers indicate that constituents recognize that legislators do not draft legislation without outside input.

These perceptions may vary across the type of legislature in the respondents' state. The previous chapters establish that state legislators have different relationships with outsiders and rely on them more when they have fewer resources. However, the survey respondents do not appear to pick up on those conditional relationships. Figure 7.2 charts the mean percentage of bills by source per legislative professionalism categories. These categories are from the National Conference of State Legislatures, which classifies state legislatures as having low, medium, or high levels of professionalism.[6] Given constituents' low knowledge of their state legislatures, it may be unsurprising that they do not differentiate across different types of legislatures.

Next, the survey experiment randomized the source of the legislation and the source's expertise. After reading the newspaper article,

[6] www.ncsl.org/about-state-legislatures/full-and-part-time-legislatures

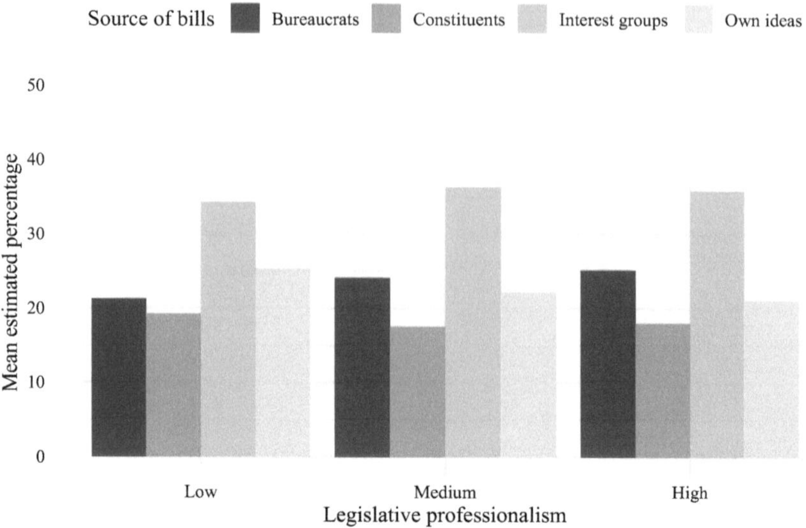

FIGURE 7.2 Average perceived percentage of bills that survey respondents estimate per given source of legislation by legislative professionalism categories.

respondents were asked about their support for the legislation and the bill's sponsor. They were also asked about their views on the legitimacy of the lawmaking process and whether the legislator made the decision that is best for the state's citizens. I use these treatment conditions and outcome questions to assess multiple hypotheses about preferences for expertise and source. For the outcome variables, I scale the responses from 0 (strongly oppose) to 1 (strongly support). The corresponding questions are: "How much would you support or oppose this legislation?" "To what extent do you agree or disagree, if at all, that the lawmaking process through which this bill was introduced is legitimate?" and "To what extent do you agree or disagree, if at all, that the legislator made the decision that is best for the citizens of the state?" Figure 7.3 plots the treatment effects of the sources of legislation and expertise.

The main interest is how the experimental treatment about the source and expertise affects support for the legislation or the legislator who sponsors the bill. Figure 7.3 illustrates that the legitimacy and evaluation that the legislator acted in the best interest of the public drops when respondents are told that an interest group provided the bill.[7] Thinking

[7] I use 83.5 percent confidence intervals since the hypotheses compare differences in the means of two groups (Maghsoodloo and Huang 2010).

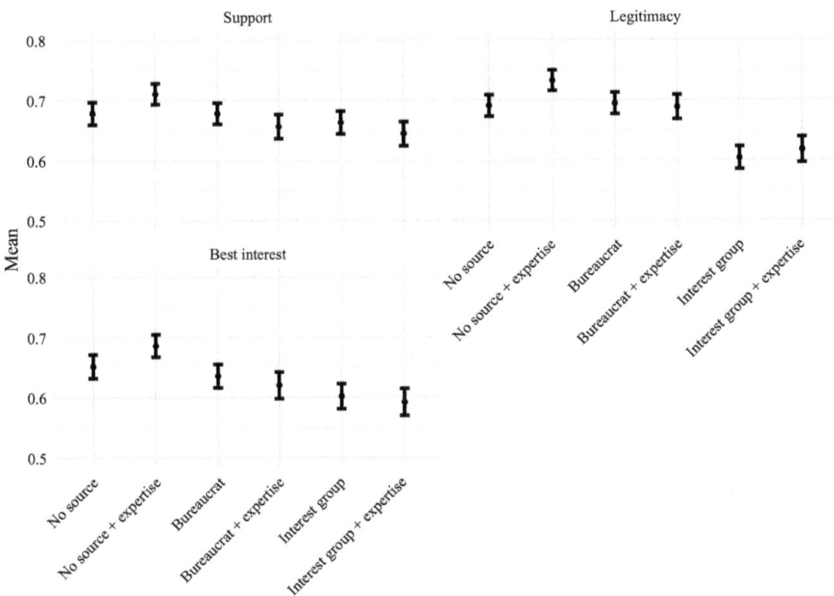

FIGURE 7.3 Treatment effects on evaluations of the process and policy. Points denote mean scores on a 0–1 scale; error bars represent 83.5 percent confidence intervals.

about the ratings of the legitimacy of the lawmaking process, bills identified as provided by bureaucrats were indistinguishable from the control condition with no source ($p = 0.85$). Yet in line with the pre-analysis predictions, bills from interest groups significantly reduced the perceived legitimacy compared to the control ($p < 0.001$). In contravention of the Expertise hypothesis, adding an expertise cue did not significantly change legitimacy ratings within either the bureaucrat ($p = 0.76$) or interest group ($p = 0.48$) conditions. On average, bureaucrat-provided bills were rated as more legitimate than interest group-provided bills ($p < 0.001$). Finally, bills from interest groups significantly reduced perceptions that the legislator was acting in the best interest of the state's citizens compared to the control ($p = 0.02$). Relative to the control of no source of legislation given, the interest group source decreased evaluations of legitimacy in the process and evaluations that the legislator acted in the best interest of the people. The expertise cue about the outside source did *not* affect evaluations. This lack of treatment effect may reflect general skepticism toward expertise in the population or indicate that the public views expertise as a way to inject self-interest into the legislative process.

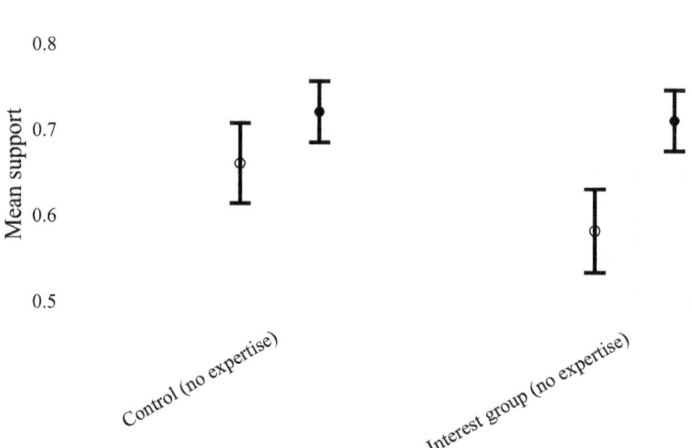

FIGURE 7.4 Effect of interest group sponsorship on support for the bill, by respondent party match with the sponsor. Points denote mean support on a 0–1 scale; error bars represent 83.5 percent confidence intervals.

Further evaluations of the role of expertise in public evaluations of outsiders in the legislative process could help us understand the tradeoffs that legislators face.

Figure 7.4 examines the effect of party alignment between the sponsor and respondent in these evaluations. For simplicity, I examine support for the bill as the dependent variable. In the control condition (no expertise cue), copartisans of the bill's sponsor expressed higher support for the legislation (0.73) than outpartisans (0.66). Introducing an interest group outside source (no expertise cue) reduced support for both groups, but the decline was notably larger among outpartisans. For outpartisans, mean support fell by roughly 0.08 points to about 0.62, whereas for copartisans, support dropped only slightly – by about 0.01 points. This pattern is consistent with the Partisan override hypothesis that interest group sponsorship depresses support more strongly among outpartisans than among copartisans, though the difference in penalties was not statistically significant.

7.5 CONCLUSION

Public opinion can influence policy and the policymaking process. Though people may be uninformed about policymaking processes, especially at the state level, they may still have strong opinions once they are informed. This potential for activation may shape the conditions under which politicians turn to outsiders (and what type of help they seek) and activate tradeoffs associated with relying on group bills. This chapter explores the connection between outsider input and constituent evaluations of legislatures and legislators.

The normative implications of relying on outsiders for legislative text are nuanced. Those who care about democratic outcomes may wish to see less input from outsiders who have a vested (and potentially self-interested) need for a law. Understanding how constituents perceive this input can help us learn about how they are being represented in these quintessential representative bodies. Voters' opinions may constrain legislators – or at least make them more likely to think before they unabashedly rely on outsiders for the full text of legislation.

Further investigations into the secretive nature of the partnerships may reveal other normative observations about the process. For instance, do constituents care about the source if legislators keep their input a secret? The secretive nature of the role of outsiders may further weaken public opinion about the legitimacy of the policy process.

Experimentally assessing legislators' opinions about legislation offered by outsiders would be a worthwhile extension. Perhaps they would avoid introducing a group bill in the abstract, but could be convinced if there are time pressures. This type of experimental manipulation could help me assess the book's core theory about capacity, time constraints, and the appeal of outside aid.

While the survey described in this chapter assesses people's satisfaction with the process, politicians, and policy resulting from using group bills, it cannot help us understand the system-wide effects of their use. Other studies could examine the system-wide correlation between the use of outsiders' bills and representation. Do states that use more such bills score lower on representation metrics than other, similarly situated states? I avoid this approach because of the other factors at play that are shown to be relevant to both representation and legislative capacity.

This chapter's exploration of constituent attitudes about outsider help in drafting legislation helps assess a normative concern about this interaction. Further, the survey experiment allows me to concentrate on the relationship between interest group input and feelings without the usual messiness of the legislative process. Even if it is benign or helpful, interest group input erodes the legitimacy of the legislative process.

8

Conclusion: Democracy in the States

While the public may dislike the role of lobbyists in the legislature and have strong opinions about the ways to lessen the pervasive influence, these "fixes" do not always have the intended effect. In fact, sometimes they can backfire. Term limits being example number one. In California, voters enacted Proposition 140 to impose not only term limits but also significantly "[l]imits expenditures of Legislature for compensation and operating costs and equipment, to specified amount."[1] As I show throughout this book, decreased staffers and resources to the legislature is associated with increasing the role of outsiders.

This book shows that expertise and resources available to the legislature matter for the interaction between legislators, bureaucrats, and outside groups in shaping statutory law. While it is difficult to make definitive claims about whether bills from non-legislators and their aid on legislation are net positive or negative for society, determining the bounds of this activity matter for the functioning of democracy in these legislative institutions. Since legislators are not eager to share credit for their work, I turn to several settings and sources of data to triangulate the reliance on this source of information across legislators and legislatures.

Using newly available data and computationally intensive methods, this book can further the field of interest group and state politics. Examining the legislative output via the bill texts, I pin down the nature, extent, and distribution of group influence. By connecting institutions, such as staff resources and term limits, that vary across states and expertise

[1] https://tinyurl.com/3t4ejjk4

across legislators to group influence, we can illuminate the process by which groups come to influence legislative outcomes.

Since the full universe of legislative origins is unknown, I bring several datasets to bear on questions of group influence. The first chapter focuses on a specific type of outsider: the state bureaucrat. In order to understand separation of powers within states, I show that we need to bring in the role of the state bureaucracy in crafting state legislation. Bureaucrats shape the state legislative agenda and statutory law. Instead of passively accepting their directives, I show that bureaucrats help shape their power. Across states, legislatures rely more heavily on bureaucrats when they are resource constrained or constrained by term limits. Partisan factors are also at play. However, on the individual level, legislators introduce more bills provided by bureaucrats when they gain power. Bureaucrats are such attractive partners because of the expert bills that they bring to the table that they can secure powerful partners within the legislature.

Since the departmental bills only come from one type of outsider and they do not include the full universe of group bills, the previous study can only help us determine some variation and determining the extent to which groups alter the legislative agenda in the states is left to the next analysis. By collecting data from a unique state reporting institution in California, I can get a sense of how much state legislation (albeit in a single state) draws from outside sources of all types. This data also gives detailed findings on when legislators use group bills. When legislators gain experience, they use fewer group bills. This chapter leverages variation across legislators and finds outsiders can help fill in for experience.

The first builds on prior work and interest in "model bills." By combining the text of the interest groups' preferred bills with the state legislation, I can assess where interest groups are successful. Using a matching method based on plagiarism detection, I identify uptake of model legislation language. While a low percentage of introduced and passed bills come from model bills, the patterns of use by partisanship of the legislature and capacity of the legislature to generate expertise are informative about the role of internal legislative capacity and reliance on outsiders. In this study, I leverage the variation across the 50 states to study the correlates of model bill use.

While Congress has high staff levels relative to state legislatures, the trend in Congress to cut government capacity may make this state-level look at outsiders more relevant for Congressional implications. Looking to the states to predict the consequences of reducing resources available to members of Congress may shed light on the opaquer national legislation process. In their own right, state legislatures create policies and politics that shape every facet of life. This book finds out the entities that are behind the bills that start out this policymaking process.

Despite low knowledge about state politics, people have preferences over how policy is made in the legislative institutions. To explore the role of outsiders in mediating this relationship, given the large role that these groups and bureaucrats play, I introduce a survey experiment. This involvement may matter for democratic health in important ways that are beyond the strict economic or separation of powers concerns. The final empirical chapter allows me to disentangle if, when, and why people care about groups and other outsiders writing state legislation. When the public learns that interest groups write legislation, they rate the process and legislators as less legitimate – even when told those groups provide expertise – highlighting a democratic tension between outside influence and public views of the legislature.

8.1 EVEN CONGRESS

Even in Congress, where legislators receive a sizable budget, information and expertise are valued commodities. If members of Congress can be understood as an "enterprise" in which members act as CEOs of their firms of staffers and resources, state legislators can be thought of as garnering support from beyond the institution, relying on not only the slim staff allotted to the state legislature, but also the outsiders eager to get their interests represented (Salisbury and Shepsle 1981). While scholarship on Congress studies the strategic choices legislators make with staffing decisions, the more relevant choice for state legislators is to look outside the legislature for information or rely on the limited and mercurial sources of internal information. In the US House of Representatives, "House rules forbid members from employing more than the maximum 18 full-time equivalents, plus up to four part-time equivalents" (Crosson et al. 2021, p. 748). On the federal level, Crosson et al. (2020) find that legislators with more and experienced staff are more effective.

Despite the high capacity of Congress relative to state legislatures, the resources this body has to carry out the high-level functions and policymaking demands are still limited (Reynolds 2020). In interviews with the Senate Judiciary Committee, Nourse and Schacter (2002) find that "the sentiment was uniform that lobbyists can have a strong influence on statutory text and that this is not a rare event but, instead, a normal part of the drafting process" (p. 610). A *New York Times* analysis uncovers that seventy of the eighty-five lines of a financial regulation bill came from Citigroup recommendations (Lipton and Protess 2013). Ansolabehere et al. (2010) come to the simple conclusion that groups "have substantial influence in setting the legislative agenda and in helping craft specific language in legislation" (p. 531). As Baumgartner et al. (2009) write: "There is evidence that organizational advocates are often successful in getting Congress to make policy decisions that are informed by research and the technical expertise that they provide." While a theory of institutional variation and use of outsiders' bills may not anticipate a high degree of outside influence in Congress, the competing demands on the time of federal legislators make the time pressures of these legislators extreme.

8.2 GROUPS BILLS AS CONSTITUENCY SERVICE

What are the social welfare implications of this role of the outsider? As I show in several ways throughout the book, we can think about this question in a variety of ways. We can assess if these bills look different from non-group bills in terms of passage, vote tallies, or cost to the state. While these are vital components of the implications for representation in the states, understanding what the representatives themselves think about the bills can help us understand the relationship. In some of the instances where organized groups push bills, legislators clearly believe that they are conducting consistency service by virtue of introducing the legislation into their legislature. A long-time journalist in Sacramento discusses an interaction with former Assembly member Tom Bane.[2]

> Somebody'd asked him about a bill. And he said, "I didn't even read it." [Assemblyman John F.] Foran was another one. He said, "I didn't even read it. You'll have to ask the lobbyist. I don't know what's in it." And they have said that. Bane took offense, and he called me and said, "Let me tell you something. When I came up here, the savings and loans couldn't do anything The banks had it all. And in my twenty years (or however many years) I've gotten them to be able to loan and this and this. Certainly, when I give a dinner, the savings and loans buy tickets to it. Absolutely. I'm their guy here. I have done more for them. And they're in my district, and it's for my district. It's not against my district. It's a home industry for me. That's it. Sure, I'm a savings and loan guy. Of course that lobbyist writes those bills. There's nothing wrong with that." So, this was said in his office across a desk, and me with a pad. And so, how are you going to argue

[2] https://archives.cdn.sos.ca.gov/oral-history/pdf/oh-wrightson-james.pdf, p. 194

that? I mean, what's sinister [about that]? It's true, and you publish it. This guy's a savings and loans guy. But what do you care, if you're in his district, if he's working his district okay? You don't care.

This exchange demonstrates the role of outside bill "sponsors" in California. The legislator admits to not even reading the bill text provided by the banks. This lack of a minimal check on outside influence makes it difficult to argue that the bills are mere subsidies and instead strong crutches for legislators. Further, Representative Bane gives the reason behind his lack of oversight as the lack of committee staff at that time. Finally, it displays the defensive nature of the legislator's view of this interaction and his claim that this bill would help his district; it is a district issue, and thus falls well within his ideals of what a legislator should do.

In another oral history, former legislator Raymond Seeley discusses a particular bill about geothermal resources that he introduced but did not have strong feelings toward. He goes on to generalize that legislators would often introduce bills at the request of a group or entity in their district because it was an issue important to the district. This quote also further backs up the argument that at least a portion of these bills would not have been considered absent the outsider's provision of the text. Seeley recounts that: "A.B. 890 is another one on geothermal resources. This has to do with regulating the land. I remember this. This wasn't introduced from my pressure. It was brought to me to carry because it involved my district. That's true of a lot of bills. Absolutely. You were carrying it for a reason that was an interest of your district."[3]

Interest groups represent people and businesses within these state legislators' districts. The bills that these groups push are sometimes in the interest of these constituents. Through this pathway, group bills may help legislators represent the people they are tasked with representing. The legislators themselves certainly see the bills as this type of good governance aid, at least at times.

8.2.1 Remaining Areas of Exploration

This book does not examine several areas of the policymaking process in which groups or bureaucrats surely are intimately involved. I do not study the role that groups or bureaucrats play in the amendment process. The decision to model involvement by capturing if the *bill* comes

[3] https://archives.cdn.sos.ca.gov/oral-history/pdf/seeley.pdf

from the outsider is intentional. This meaningful unit of analysis within legislatures is substantial and discrete. Of course, major amendments or changes to bills can also be central for policy and negotiating for passage. As mentioned in previous chapters, outsiders have a hand in altering the text of their bills and others throughout the legislative process to get the bill closer to passage. This form of involvement in state legislatures is worthy of future research.

This book also leaves for future research the study of negative agenda-setting by groups in the states. I do not capture the negative agenda-setting power that groups exert in state legislatures in this book. However, this is surely an important component of outside interests' power in the states. Perhaps an even more principal component of business groups' plan to exert influence in the state legislatures because of a commonly held belief that they wish to maintain the status quo. Additionally, killing a bill may be a less noticeable form of influence than positive agenda-setting and blatant rent seeking. In a legislative history, former state legislator Anthony Beilenson discusses California's Governmental Organization Committee which was "known often as the 'graveyard committee,' to which bills were sent that lobbyists wanted killed."[4] Chapter 4 shows the relative success of outsiders' bills in California, but this positive power of outsiders to get what they want is but one face of power.

8.2.2 Other Pathways

The book treats bureaucrats' bills and interest group bills as separate. However, bureaucrats and groups are connected in a variety of ways that make this black-line distinction potentially an oversimplification. For one, we know that bureaucrats and groups are linked via the revolving door. While we don't know patterns of the revolving door as much on the state-level, from the federal level, we know that these interactions are frequent and powerful. Bills may flow from interest groups to bureaucrats or vice versa. On the federal level, we know that *most* lobbying happens after the passage of legislation (You 2017). While we do not have a similar type of analysis to You (2017) on the state level, we know that interest groups lobby state-level bureaucracies (Bradley 2014).

[4] https://archives.cdn.sos.ca.gov/oral-history/pdf/oh-beilenson-anthony-v1.pdf, p. 24

8.3 NEW TECHNOLOGY AND BILL DRAFTING

The recent phenomenon of open artificial intelligence platforms that are simple to use deserves mention in a book about state capacity and bill drafting. State lawmakers are both interested in regulating (or preventing regulation on) the new technology but also *using* it in their own jobs by writing legislation.[5] Could ChatGPT replace interest groups and bureaucrats as sources of bills? I don't think so. While the text of the legislation itself is helpful and a part of the puzzle, the big point of the bills is the expertise offered within the texts. Legislators face uncertainty about the relationship between the policies that they craft and political and policy outcomes. Expertise offered by groups in the form of legislation helps reduce this variance. As I show, expertise and resources shape the relationships between groups, bureaucrats, and the legislature.

8.4 RECOMMENDATIONS

This section may be more aptly entitled recommendations against recommendations. Calls for giving more resources to state legislators in the form of more staffers, better-salaried staffers, or their own salaries are abundant in the scholarly literature and popular punditry. However, the case of California shows that even in a well-funded and highly professional legislature, the involvement of groups abounds.

An *Atlantic* article heralds Future Now as the left-wing alternative to ALEC. Former New York state senator, Daniel Squadron co-founded the group and walks through the logic and appeal of model legislation: "The idea that state legislatures are under-resourced, that state legislators are part-time, and there's just not enough state legislative staff, and therefore you need some national partnership in order for in-state lawmakers to figure out what's best for their state – there's nothing wrong with that. What's wrong with that is when the partnership has an insidious, secretive, corrupt goal."[6] This mission sounds similar to subsidy-based stories about why state legislators need to look outside the typical legislative capacity routes for information. Future Now's solution to the normative troubles of this involvement is to post all of their model bills online, so that the public can track which states have considered and passed their model laws. Is this a sanguine view of the legislative process? First, we may be concerned that those paying attention are those with outsized

5 https://abovethelaw.com/2023/04/chatgpt-draws-state-lawmakers-attention-to-ai/

6 https://tinyurl.com/2dm2vb73

money and influence in the first place. Also, transparency as a panacea seems like a weak argument (Kirkland and Harden 2022).

Perhaps one policy solution would be for groups that represent the poor or intersectionally disadvantaged to write legislation and fight for it within the state legislatures. Of course, this is a simplified proposal. If those proposals cost the state more money or are tricky to sell to constituents or voters, then it would be difficult to make them as attractive as the proposals offered by companies. Not to mention that the groups without corporate backers would struggle to come up with the resources to hire high-quality staffers to draft these model bills. However, changing the range of the conversation via the proposed bills may be the first step to representation of these groups.

This book pushes researchers to explore the black box of what goes into lawmaking beyond the legislature. I show that outsiders are not only significant players in this game, but also contingent upon legislative resources and legislator characteristics. Divided government, term limits, and legislative expenditures especially matter for the balance of power between insiders and outsiders in the lawmaking process. State lawmaking shows an inherent tension between capitalizing on outsider expertise and conflicting motivations across the players. The ability of legislators to check and engage independently with creating the laws that determine state outcomes is determined by internal capacity and constraints on the legislature.

APPENDICES

Appendix A

Appendix Chapter 3

A.1 THE PLURAL EXECUTIVE

Some states have plural executives, these interesting institutions are outside the scope of the analysis in the chapter, since one of the main assumptions is about the partisan alignment between the governor and the agency, which is broken by the separate election of these executives. However, I want to note that these bureaucrats also provide bills to the legislature and are important outside actors. For example, in North Carolina, the colorful former Secretary of State Rufus Edmisten talks about successfully securing his preferred legislation into the state legislature. "It's '92 and we're going along and then I had made some bad choices – I got everything I wanted past the legislature. Every single thing that I went for, I got done" and when the interviewer asks about this process, Edmisten casually emphasizes that "Oh, yeah. We got all kinds of legislation passed to do different things. I was so perfect for the job. I had been attorney general, candidate for governor, etc."[1] Edmisten recalls his experience in a range of positions as helpful for lobbying the state legislature.

The separate election of the top spots of state bureaucracies creates separation of powers dynamics that do not exist on the federal level (Berry and Gersen 2008; Seifter 2019). Indeed, state legislatures frequently alter the structure of the state executive branch because of partisan politics or scandal (Seifter 2019). While I could speculate that this legislative manipulation of the executive branch levels of independence

[1] www.senate.gov/artandhistory/history/resources/pdf/Edmisten3.pdf

are to get more information from the bureaucracy, this is an area of the literature that is underdeveloped. These separately elected agencies also provide legislation to the legislature, but they do not exist within the normal framework of divided government, so I exclude agencies that do not have a head appointed by the governor from many of the analyses in this chapter.

A.2 AGENCY BILL INDICATOR DATA PER STATE

TABLE A.1 *Agency bill indicators per state available*

State	Data
California	The "sponsor" of the bill is defined as the "legislator, private individual, or group who developed a piece of legislation and advocates its passage." Sponsors can include state agencies. Sponsorship information per bill comes from this FTP site: www.leginfo.ca.gov/FTProtocol.html. I scrape this sponsorship information per bill, and then identify the bill as an agency bill if the only listed sponsor is an agency.
Maryland	There is an option to list "Administration" or "Departmental" bills per session on the legislature's website (e.g., for the 2006 session, see https://mgaleg.maryland.gov/mgawebsite/). Departmental bills are sponsored by the chairperson of the relevant committee. For example, the Chairman of Environmental Matters sponsored HB 92 in 2002 (the MD Egg Law).
Montana	Lists if a bill is "By Request Of." For example, this page shows the table that is presented per bill that is "By Request Of": http://bills.legmt.gov. I limit the agency bills to those that are not at the request of the governor, the legislative council, or a committee.
North Carolina	The legislature indicates bills requested by state agencies with and "-AB" at the end of the short title for the bill (as determined via email correspondence with North Carolina Representative Chuck McGrady).
North Dakota	Clearly lists if the bill was introduced at the request of a state department or agency at the top of the bill's page. For example, Representative Sveen introduced H. B. 1103 in the 1997 legislative session at the request of the Department of Transportation (shown at https://ndlegis.gov/api/assembly/55-1997/regular/bill-text/HQOI0100.pdf).

(*continued*)

TABLE A.1 (*continued*)

State	Data
Nevada	The group or department that the bill was introduced for is indicated by "ON BEHALF OF" at the top of the introduced bill text. When an executive branch entity wishes to have a bill introduced on their behalf, they fill out this form: www.leg.state.nv.us/Session/75th2009/BDRForms/ExecutiveBranchBDR2009_Enabled.pdf
New York	Legislature denotes agency bills in the sponsor listing. "(At the request of . . .)" appears following the sponsor or list of sponsors. I scrape all of the bills from the State Assembly's legislative page (https://nyassembly.gov/leg/?sh=advanced), and subsequently scrape for the phrase "At the request of" from the text of these bills. I exclude "J" and "K" bills, which are memorializing bills and are not introduced at the request of departments.
Idaho	If the contact person on the Statement of Purpose/Fiscal Note attached to each bill is a state agency, then the bill is agency legislation (determined via email correspondence with Gideon Tolman, Idaho Financial Management Analyst in the Division of Financial Management for the Executive Office of the Idaho Governor). I scrape all the Statement of Purpose documents and search for the office or agency (pre-2009 sessions). If this contact is state agency, then the bill is classified as an agency bill.
Oregon	Every bill in the Oregon state legislature lists if it was introduced "At the request of:". For example, https://apps.oregonlegislature.gov/liz/2007R1/Measures/Overview/HB2143 shows a bill that was requested by Attorney General Hardy Myers for the Department of Justice.
South Dakota	South Dakota requires that "all executive agencies are required to prefile any legislation that they wish to have considered" (https://mylrc.sdlegislature.gov/api/Documents/171806.pdf). Agency legislation is indicated by the line "at the request of" following the bill's sponsor.
Washington	The Washington state legislature reports lists of the bills introduced in each legislative session (https://app.leg.wa.gov/bi). These lists have "Flags," one of which is for if the bill is a Departmental bill or a Governor bill.

A.3 AGENCY BILLS OVER TIME

A much lower percentage of introduced bills in North Carolina and New York come from agencies compared to the other states. The Washington and Maryland state legislatures fall in the mid range of 5–10 percent of their introduced bills coming from agencies. The California and Idaho state legislatures see the highest percentages of their introduced bills originating in agencies, clocking in at about 15 percent of bills coming from their state agencies.

There is also within-state variation in terms of the proportion of bills drawn from agencies. In some states, these fluctuations do not correspond with changes in the party composition of the state government. For example, departmental bills in Idaho drop to a low, as a percentage of the legislative agenda, in 2001. South Dakota also sees a sharp drop in departmental bills in 2011, but as with Idaho, these changes do not correspond with divided government. Oregon sees a decline in the percentage of bills introduced that are departmental in 2011, when the Democrats lose their unified control of the branches and the state House is divided.

Several observations are notable from looking at the percentage of departmental and non-departmental bills that are chaptered across sessions of each state legislature. First, there is a significant gap in the passage rates between departmental and non-departmental bills. Departmental bills pass at higher rates compared to non-departmental bills. This observation holds across all legislatures and sessions for which the data is available. For some states, this gap is more pronounced. For example, the gap in passage rates between departmental and non-departmental bills in the Maryland state legislature stays consistently high at an average of 39.5 percent difference between the percentage of departmental bills chaptered and percentage of non-departmental bills chaptered. Whereas, the Idaho state legislature has a much lower 9.3 percent difference in passage rates between these types of bills. Additionally, for most states, the passage rate of non-departmental bills stays relatively constant over time, whereas there is more variability across time in terms of the percentage of departmental bills that pass. In the Idaho state legislature, only 11.0 percent of departmental bills passed in the 2011–2012 session of the state legislature, compared to 22.8 percent of departmental bills that pass in the 1993–1994 session of the state legislature (a 11.8 percent gap). Compare this to the non-departmental bill passage rate also in Idaho, which was at a minimum of 6.1 percent in the 1999–2000 session and a maximum of 8.4 percent in the 1993–1994 session (a 2.3 percent gap).

Not only a significant portion of the legislative *agenda*, but also of the *law* created by state legislatures originates in the state bureaucracy. In several legislative sessions of the California, Idaho, and Washington state legislatures, almost a full quarter of the session law comes from bureaucrats. Even at the lowest point over the nearly twenty-five year time period, around 12 percent of passed legislation were agency bills. Indeed, this provides compelling evidence that in the Washington state legislature, a semi-professional legislature, a significant portion of their law comes from bureaucrats. The South Dakota session law originates in departments at an even higher rate; the percentage of law that originates in state agencies hovers around a striking 45 percent in this state. Departmental bills form a large portion of the bills that are eventually chaptered into law in the Idaho state legislature. A low of 10.6 percent of chaptered bills are departmental bills in the 2001 state legislature, but departmental bills comprise 21.5 percent of chaptered bills in the 2004 legislative session. Overall, these plots are the most revealing evidence that bills originating from the bureaucracy form a large portion of the state law and govern bureaucracy action.

A.4 EFFECT ON PRE-TREATMENT OUTCOMES

Following Fouirnaies (2018), I estimate whether being a committee chair in session s is related to the sponsorship of agency bills in sessions before s. In other words, I want to show that the future role of committee chair does not have a significant relationship with agency sponsorship in previous sessions when the legislator was not chair. That is indeed what the results presented in Table A.2 show. Before the legislator assumes the position of committee chair, there is not a significant relationship between future chairpersonship and sponsorship of departmental bills.

TABLE A.2 *Future committee chairpersonship and number of departmental bills introduced*

	(1)	(2)	(3)	(4)
Chair	0.456**	—	—	—
	(0.160)			
Chair_{s-1}	—	−0.254	—	—
		(0.138)		
Chair_{s-2}	—	—	−0.155	—
			(0.187)	
Chair_{s-3}	—	—	—	0.285
				(0.292)
Governor copartisan	0.509***	0.495***	0.491***	0.490***
	(0.136)	(0.136)	(0.136)	(0.136)
In chamber majority	0.490*	0.632**	0.680**	0.685**
	(0.223)	(0.222)	(0.220)	(0.218)
Leader	−0.159	−0.223	−0.244	−0.248
	(0.244)	(0.237)	(0.234)	(0.235)
Log no. introduced	1.489***	1.535***	1.529***	1.541***
	(0.136)	(0.142)	(0.144)	(0.142)
Legislator fixed effects	✓	✓	✓	✓
Chamber-session-state Fixed effects	✓	✓	✓	✓
Observations	2,980	2,980	2,980	2,980
Legislators	1,162	1,162	1,162	1,162

*$p < 0.05$; **$p < 0.01$; ***$p < 0.001$.

A.5 FUNCTIONAL CATEGORIES IN ASAP SURVEY

Page 365 of the ASAP code book contains the listing of categories that the agencies are in and some examples of the agencies in each category. That table is reproduced here:

TABLE A.3 *ASAP functional category codes and example agencies per category*

Functional category	Example agencies
Elected Officials	Treasurer, Secretary of State, and Attorney General
Staff-Fiscal	Revenue, Administration, and Comptroller
Staff-Non Fiscal	Personnel, Planning, and Information Systems
Income Security & Social Services	Aging, Unemployment Insurance, and Welfare
Education	Education, Higher Education, and Special Education
Health	Health, Mental Health, and Agency Medical Services
Natural Resources	Fish and Wildlife, Natural Resources, and Soil Conservation
Environment and Energy	Environmental Protection, Solid Waste Management, and Energy
Economic Development	Commerce, Economic Development, and Lottery
Criminal Justice	Corrections, Juvenile Rehabilitation, and Parole and Probation
Regulatory	Banking, Food and Drugs, and Securities
Transportation	Highways, Mass Transportation, and Motor Vehicle Registration
Other	Emergency Management, Libraries, and Public Works

Appendix B

Appendix Chapter 4

B.1 ROSENBAUM BOUNDS TEST

While the balance on covariates between sponsored and unsponsored bills improves drastically after matching, the results may be misleading if unobserved covariates remain after matching. I conduct a Rosenbaum bounds test to evaluate the sensitivity of the matching estimate to unobservable differences between sponsored bill and unsponsored bills (Rosenbaum 2002). Group bills and non-group bills may be different in unobserved or unmeasured covariates. In this setting, hidden bias is the extent to which sponsored bills would have to be more likely to pass compared to unsponsored bills to bias the matching analysis estimates. Perhaps group bills differ in intrinsic quality which is unmeasured. The Rosenbaum bounds test how large this hidden bias would have to be before altering the substantive interpretation of the matching estimate. The researcher changes the sensitivity parameter, Γ, which represents the log odds of receiving treatment. The Rosenbaum bounds indicate that the results become insignificant when $\Gamma > 1.8$, $\Gamma > 2.2$, and $\Gamma > 2.2$ for the 2009–2010, 2011–2012, and 2013–2014 Assembly data, respectively.[1] These parameters indicate that for the 2009–2010 Assembly, one of the observations in a matched pair of bills could be 1.8 times as likely to have received treatment without eliminating the observed estimate of treatment. These Γ values are quite robust (Keele 2010). This sensitivity analysis provides confidence that the matching estimates are robust to hidden confounders and are reasonable estimates of the effect of group sponsorship on bill passage.

[1] Using the hlsens function from the rbounds package which gives the Hodges-Lehmman point estimate for the sign rank test (Keele 2010).

B.2 REGRESSIONS FOR REPUBLICANS

TABLE B.1 *Assembly Republicans Regressions*

	No. group bills	**Ratio (group/total bills introduced)**
	(1)	(2)
Second term	−0.002	0.016*
	(0.026)	(0.007)
Third term	0.010	0.017*
	(0.031)	(0.008)
Leader	0.004	−0.004
	(0.051)	(0.013)
Chair	−0.016	0.043**
	(0.050)	(0.013)
Constant	0.655***	0.090**
	(0.129)	(0.034)
Legislator fixed effects	*Yes*	*Yes*
Observations	320	320
Legislators	142	142
Observations	314	320
R^2	0.581	0.652
Adjusted R^2	0.228	0.363

OLS regressions of number of group sponsored bills authored by legislator *i* and the ratio of group to total number of bills authored on the number of terms in the Assembly. Legislator fixed effects included.

$^{*}p < 0.05$; $^{**}p < 0.01$; $^{***}p < 0.001$.

TABLE B.2 *Assembly Republican Regressions*

	% group bills became law	% non-group bills became law
	(1)	(2)
Second term	−0.002	0.016*
	(0.026)	(0.007)
Third term	0.010	0.017*
	(0.031)	(0.008)
Leader	0.004	−0.004
	(0.051)	(0.013)
Chair	−0.016	0.043**
	(0.050)	(0.013)
Constant	0.655***	0.090**
	(0.129)	(0.034)
Legislator fixed effects	*Yes*	*Yes*
Observations	320	320
Legislators	142	142
Observations	314	320
R^2	0.581	0.652
Adjusted R^2	0.228	0.363

OLS regressions of percentage of group sponsored bills authored by legislator *i* that become law and the percentage of non-group bills authored by legislator *i* that become law on the number of terms in the Assembly. Legislator fixed effects included.
$^{*}p < 0.05$; $^{**}p < 0.01$; $^{***}p < 0.001$.

Appendix C

Appendix Chapter 5

C.1 NUMBER OF BILLS

C.1.1 Comparison of Number of Bills in 2013

To ensure that the number of bills that we have from the LegiScan dataset corresponds with the number of bills introduced in other states, I compare the dataset to Congressional Quarterly's listing of the number of bills introduced in 2013.[1]

[1] https://info.cq.com/resources/states-six-times-more-productive-than-congress/

TABLE C.1 *Comparison of the number of bills between LegiScan bill dataset and CQ listing*

State	CQ #	LegiScan #	Difference	state	CQ #	LegiScan #	Difference
AK	747	746	1	MT	3,251	1,201	2,050[2]
AL	1,850	1,845	5	NC	2,162	2,162	0
AR	2,662	2,662	0	ND	920	920	0
AZ	1,254	1,254	0	NE	1,825	1,825	0
CA	4,800	4,795	5	NH	1,554	1,685	−131[3]
CO	711	620	91	NJ	8,382	8,383	1[4]
CT	3,091	2,872	219	NM	1,656	1,656	0
DE	920	905	15	NV	1,127	1,136	−9
FL	1,898	1,901	−3	NY	18,123	17,988	135
GA	4,935	4,934	1	OH	1,226	1,225	1
HI	6,730	3,676	3,054[5]	OK	5,152	5,102	−50[6]
IA	3,012	3,011	1	OR	2,685	2,686	−1
ID	624	624	0	PA	5,594	5,591	3
IL	13,172	13,355	−183	RI	4,914	4,914	0[7]
IN	1,601	1,601	0	SC	3,793	3,781	12
KS	1,637	1,299	338[8]	SD	652	648	4
KY	1,228	1,228	0	TN	7,703	7,703	0
LA	1,744	1,761	−17	TX	11,721	10,374	1,347[9]
MA	6,972	6,946	26	UT	757	1,038	−281
MD	2,618	2,618	0	VA	5,449	3,006	2,443
ME	1,949	1,917	32	VT	1,778	1,773	5
MI	4,114	4,112	2	WA	3,699	3,457	242
MN	6,735	6,735	0	WI	1,892	1,888	4
MO	1,682	1,654	28	WV	2,252	2,252	0
MS	3,152	3,153	−1	WY	429	429	0

2 From the Book of States, 1,201 bills and resolutions were introduced in MT in 2013.
3 2013 and 2014.
4 2012.
5 The number from LegiScan is the same as that in www.capitol.hawaii.gov/advreports/main.aspx.
6 2014.
7 2013 and 2014.
8 From the Book of States, 1,288 bills and resolutions were introduced in KS in 2013 and 2014.
9 From the Texas state legislature website (https://capitol.texas.gov/Reports/General.aspx), 10,630 bills were introduced in the 2013 regular session.

C.1.2 Total Number of Bills in Dataset

TABLE C.2 *Total number of bills in LegiScan dataset*

State	Introduced	Passed	State	Introduced	Passed
AK	4,327	1,039	MD	26,836	7,143
AL	19,349	8,879	ME	11,608	4,416
AR	12,990	7,759	MI	24,494	7,519
AZ	13,669	3,672	MN	42,987	1,370
CA	28,600	11,672	MO	20,950	1,324
CO	7,340	3,990	MS	32,269	7,097
CT	22,422	2,451	MT	7,404	3,262
DE	5,416	2,421	NC	13,860	3,459
FL	26,996	2,108	ND	5,729	3,336
GA	28,310	19,238	NE	8,988	3,700
HI	51,303	4,508	NH	10,613	3,349
IA	15,927	1,698	NJ	47,042	2,549
ID	6,171	3,519	NM	13,327	2,400
IL	75,810	23,075	NV	6,693	3,613
IN	13,687	3,778	NY	106,978	8,441
KS	8,124	2,196	OH	12,387	6,693
KY	12,050	4,262	OK	38,399	7,843
LA	23,030	14,144	OR	15,406	4,813
MA	42,149	2,855	PA	31,910	8,845
RI	22,889	9,086	SC	20,908	9,517
SD	5,718	2,466	TN	50,132	26,551
TX	68,991	34,071	UT	10,023	4,580
VA	33,068	17,422	VT	8,992	3,669
WA	21,816	4,100	WI	11,257	1,893
WV	23,935	4,150	WY	3,706	1,397

C.2 CHANGE THRESHOLDS: SENSITIVITY ANALYSIS

TABLE C.3 *Fifteen percent threshold: Regression models of percent of introduced bills and percent of passed bills*

	Dependent variable: (1)	Dependent variable: (2)
Republican legislature	0.217***	0.250***
	(0.074)	(0.080)
Split legislature	0.212*	0.153
	(0.112)	(0.123)
Log session length	0.149*	0.027
	(0.083)	(0.090)
Log salary	0.044	0.067*
	(0.036)	(0.039)
Log expenditures	−0.186***	−0.093*
	(0.047)	(0.051)
Term limits	0.146**	0.157**
	(0.072)	(0.079)
Constant	0.715*	0.389
	(0.412)	(0.449)
Observations	402	401
R^2	0.083	0.057
Adjusted R^2	0.069	0.042
Residual std. error	0.637 (df = 395)	0.694 (df = 394)
F statistic	5.986*** (df = 6; 395)	3.943*** (df = 6; 394)

*$p < 0.1$; **$p < 0.05$; ***$p < 0.01$.

C.3 SESSION AND STATE FIXED EFFECTS

TABLE C.4 *Regression models of percent of introduced bills that are model bills, ALEC model bills, non-ALEC model bills, and SiX model bills*

	Dependent variable: (1)	Dependent variable: (2)	Dependent variable: (3)	Dependent variable: (4)
Republican legislature	−0.038	−0.010	−0.029	−0.022
	(0.114)	(0.075)	(0.068)	(0.035)
Split legislature	−0.028	−0.015	−0.013	−0.050
	(0.110)	(0.073)	(0.066)	(0.034)
Log session length	0.151	0.107	0.044	0.010
	(0.106)	(0.070)	(0.064)	(0.033)
Log salary	−0.111	−0.022	−0.089*	−0.059**
	(0.076)	(0.050)	(0.045)	(0.023)
Log expenditures	−0.375*	−0.285**	−0.090	−0.105
	(0.219)	(0.144)	(0.131)	(0.067)
Constant	2.883	1.830	1.053	1.109**
	(1.827)	(1.201)	(1.090)	(0.561)
State fixed effects	Yes	Yes	Yes	Yes
Session fixed effects	Yes	Yes	Yes	Yes
Observations	402	402	402	402
R^2	0.587	0.544	0.562	0.560
Adjusted R^2	0.510	0.459	0.480	0.478
Residual std. error (df = 338)	0.462	0.304	0.276	0.142
F statistic (df = 63; 338)	7.629***	6.391***	6.880***	6.837***

Fixed effects for state and session added and term limits variable removed.
*$p < 0.1$; **$p < 0.05$; ***$p < 0.01$.

Appendix D

Appendix Chapter 6

D.1 TOPIC MODEL

As a simple validity check on the complexity measures, I calculate the average complexity metric scores for bills within each topic – Table D.1. I identify the maximum topic identified with each bill. I expect that, especially, resolutions would have fewer dollars and numbers compared to other topics. This is the case and that a topic like "fiscal" has a much higher number of numbers and dollars.

FIGURE D.1 Top twenty topics by prevalence in the corpus of legislation. The words presented in the plot are the top words that contribute to that topic.

TABLE D.1 *Mean complexity scores per topic*

Topic	No. dollars	No. numbers	Flesch Kincaid	Log no. words
Agriculture	2.05	60.55	20.32	5.78
Land boundaries	3.86	192.08	20.28	5.78
Census	0.06	7488.50	20.40	5.71
Child welfare	0.67	101.26	20.47	5.81
Corporations	1.89	109.88	20.58	5.83
Courts	1.57	72.11	20.48	5.82
Crime	2.33	120.60	20.51	5.81
Departmental	0.98	75.34	20.50	5.80
Departmental programs	0.87	48.44	20.50	5.80
Drugs	1.73	136.05	20.51	5.78
Education	2.06	81.17	20.45	5.80
Elections	0.68	75.41	20.37	5.81
Employees	2.46	111.47	20.71	5.82
Energy	2.14	79.23	20.70	5.82
Environmental	2.07	82.32	20.42	5.81
Fiscal	27.40	312.87	20.47	5.80
Health care	1.82	105.09	20.50	5.83
Process	46.70	1217.93	20.17	5.83
Insurance regulation	2.27	106.69	20.64	5.84
Legal structure	0.17	14.47	19.79	5.60
Legislative organization	0.28	21.13	20.25	5.73
Licensure	4.14	95.48	20.45	5.82
Local government	1.94	103.93	20.59	5.84
Lottery	4.10	134.82	20.45	5.86
Medical licensing	0.75	80.17	20.48	5.79
Political campaigns	6.29	106.39	20.64	5.86
Process	0.86	24.44	20.53	5.63
Public funds	5.50	83.69	20.06	5.70
Public records	0.51	54.20	20.55	5.80
Resolutions	0.25	13.64	20.60	5.74
Sales	2.84	108.82	20.46	5.83
School	4.08	133.16	20.44	5.83
Statutory organization	0.52	36.86	20.28	5.69
Taxes	7.51	149.51	20.49	5.83
Transportation	2.29	73.49	20.48	5.79

Appendix E

Appendix Chapter 7

E.1 SURVEY SAMPLE DESCRIPTIVE STATISTICS

TABLE E.1 *Survey sample descriptive statistics*

Characteristic	Percentage Respondents
Age	
18–24	7.8%
25–34	28.5%
35–44	28.7%
45–54	16.8%
55–64	11.6%
65–74	5.9%
75–84	0.8%
Education	
Less than high school diploma	0.5%
High school graduate (including GED)	9.8%
Some college but no degree	20.0%
Associate's degree in college (2-year)	10.8%
Bachelor's degree in college (4-year)	41.6%
Master's degree	13.5%
Professional degree (JD, MD, etc.)	2.2%
Doctoral degree	1.6%
Gender	
Female	49.6%
Male	50.0%
Non-binary / third gender	0.2%
Other (please specify)	0.1%
Prefer not to say	0.1%
Partisanship	
Democrat	49.9%
Independent	26.3%
No preference	2.3%
Republican	21.5%

Bibliography

Abney, Glenn. 1988. "Lobbying by the insiders: Parallels of state agencies and interest groups." *Public Administration Review* 48(5):911–917

Acs, Alex. 2015. "Which statute to implement? Strategic timing by regulatory agencies." *Journal of Public Administration Research and Theory* 26(3):493–506.

Anderson, Hobson Dewey. 1942. *California State Government*. Stanford University Press.

Angrist, Joshua D. and Jörn-Steffen Pischke. 2008. *Mostly Harmless Econometrics: An Empiricist's Companion*. Princeton University Press.

Ansolabehere, Stephen, Benjamin Ginsberg, Kenneth Shepsle, and Theodore Lowi. 2010. *American Government: Power and Purpose*. W. W. Norton.

Ansolabehere, Stephen, John M. De Figueiredo, and James M. Snyder. 2003. "Why is there so little money in US politics?" *The Journal of Economic Perspectives* 17(1):105–130.

Baeder, Ben. 2014. "Who pays the most for California government lobbying in Sacramento? Government." *Los Angeles Daily News*, https://tinyurl.com/mwtbk4xx.

Ban, Pamela, Yeon Park Ju, and Hye Young You. 2024. *Hearings on the Hill: The Politics of Informing Congress*. Cambridge University Press.

Baumgartner, Frank R. and Beth L. Leech. 1998. *Basic Interests: The Importance of Groups in Politics and in Political Science*. Princeton University Press.

Baumgartner, Frank R., Jeffrey M. Berry, Marie Hojnacki, Beth L. Leech, and David C. Kimball. 2009. *Lobbying and Policy Change: Who Wins, Who Loses, and Why*. University of Chicago Press.

Benoit, Kenneth, Kevin Munger, and Arthur Spirling. 2019. "Measuring and explaining political sophistication through textual complexity." *American Journal of Political Science* 63(2):491–508.

Berkman, Michael B. 1993. "Former state legislators in the U.S. House of Representatives: Institutional and policy mastery." *Legislative Studies Quarterly* 18(1):77–104.

Berkowitz, Daniel and George A. Krause. 2018. "How bureaucratic leadership shapes policy outcomes: Partisan politics and affluent citizens' incomes in the American states." *Journal of Public Policy* 40(2):305–328.

Berry, Christopher R. and Jacob E. Gersen. 2008. "The unbundled executive." *University of Chicago Law Review,* 75(4):1385–1434.

Berry, Jeffrey M. 1989. *The Interest Group Society*. 2nd ed. Scott, Foresman and Company.

Black, Ryan C., Ryan J. Owens, Justin Wedeking, and Patrick C. Wohlfarth. 2016. *U.S. Supreme Court Opinions and Their Audiences*. Cambridge University Press.

Bloeser, Andrew J., Tarah Williams, Candaisy Crawford, and Brian M. Harward. 2024. "Are stealth Democrats really committed to democracy? Process preferences revisited." *Perspectives on Politics* 22(1):116–130.

Boushey, Graeme T. and Robert J. McGrath. 2016. "Experts, amateurs, and bureaucratic influence in the American states." *Journal of Public Administration Research and Theory* 27(1):85–103.

Bowen, Daniel C. and Zachary Greene. 2014. "Should we measure professionalism with an index? A note on theory and practice in state legislative professionalism research." *State Politics and Policy Quarterly* 14(3): 277–296.

Bradley, Katharine W. V. 2014. Who Lobbies the Lobbyists? Bureaucratic Influence on State Medicaid Legislation. PhD thesis, University of Michigan, https://tinyurl.com/3apz3z2p.

Bradley, Katharine W. V. and Jake Haselswerdt. 2016. "Who lobbies the lobbyists? State Medicaid bureaucrats' engagement in the legislative process." *Journal of Public Policy* 38(1):83–111.

Bressman, Lisa Schultz and Abbe R. Gluck. 2014. "Statutory interpretation from the inside – An empirical study of congressional drafting, delegation, and the canons: Part II." *Stanford Law Review* 66:725.

Broder, Andrei Z. 1998. Filtering near-duplicate documents. In Annual Symposium on Combinatorial Pattern Matching, pp. 1–10. Springer, 2000.

Broockman, David E. and Christopher Skovron. 2018. "Bias in perceptions of public opinion among political elites." *American Political Science Review* 112(3):542–563.

Broockman, David E., Joshua L. Kalla, and Sean J. Westwood. 2023. "Does affective polarization undermine democratic norms or accountability? Maybe not." *American Journal of Political Science* 67(3):808–828.

Butler, Daniel M. and David W. Nickerson. 2011. "Can learning constituency opinion affect how legislators vote? Results from a field experiment." *Quarterly Journal of Political Science* 6(1):55–83.

Cain, Bruce E. and Thad Kousser. 2004. *Adapting to Term Limits: Recent Experiences and New Directions*. Public Policy Institute of California San Francisco, CA.

Campbell, Angus, Philip E. Converse, Warren E. Miller, and Donald E. Stokes. 1960. *The American Voter*. University of Chicago Press.

Carey, John M., Richard G. Niemi, and Lynda W. Powell. 2000. *Term Limits in State Legislatures*. University of Michigan Press.

Carey, John M., Richard G. Niemi, Lynda W. Powell, and Gary F. Moncrief. 2006. "The effects of term limits on state legislatures: A new survey of the 50 states." *Legislative Studies Quarterly* 31(1):105–134.

Carnes, Nicholas. 2013. *White-Collar Government: The Hidden Role of Class in Economic Policy Making*. University of Chicago Press.

Caro, Robert A. 1974. *The Power Broker: Robert Moses and the Fall of New York*. Alfred A. Knopf Incorporated.

Carpenter, Daniel P. 2002. *The Forging of Bureaucratic Autonomy: Reputations, Networks, and Policy Innovation in Executive Agencies, 1862–1928*. Princeton University Press.

Carpini, Michael X. Delli and Scott Keeter. 1996. *What Americans Know about Politics and Why It Matters*. Yale University Press.

Casas, Andreu, Matthew J. Denny and John Wilkerson. 2020. "More effective than we thought: Accounting for legislative hitchhikers reveals a more inclusive and productive lawmaking process." *American Journal of Political Science* 64(1):5–18.

Caughey, Devin and Christopher Warshaw. 2022. *Dynamic Democracy: Public Opinion, Elections, and Policymaking in the American States*. Chicago: University of Chicago Press.

Celock, John. 2013. "ALEC posts model legislation online." *Huffington Post*, www.huffpost.com/entry/alec-model-legislation_n_2885570.

Christenson, Dino P. and Douglas L. Kriner. 2019. "Does public opinion constrain presidential unilateralism?" *American Political Science Review* 113(4):1071–1077.

Christenson, Dino P. and Douglas L. Kriner. 2020. *The Myth of the Imperial Presidency: How Public Opinion Checks the Unilateral Executive*. University of Chicago Press.

Clough, Paul and Mark Stevenson. 2011. "Developing a corpus of plagiarised short answers." *Language Resources and Evaluation* 45(1):5–24.

Cook, Scott J. and David Fortunato. 2022. "The politics of police data: state legislative capacity and the transparency of state and substate agencies." *American Political Science Review* 117(1):280–295.

Coppock, Alexander. 2022. *Persuasion in Parallel: How Information Changes Minds about Politics*. University of Chicago Press.

Cox, Gary W. and Mathew D. McCubbins. 2005. *Setting the Agenda: Responsible Party Government in the US House of Representatives*. Cambridge University Press.

Crosson, Jesse M., Alexander C. Furnas, Timothy Lapira, and Casey Burgat. 2021. "Partisan competition and the decline in legislative capacity among congressional offices." *Legislative Studies Quarterly* 46(3):745–789.

Crosson, Jesse, Geoffrey Lorenz, Craig Volden, and Alan Wiseman. 2020. How Experienced Legislative Staff Contribute to Effective Lawmaking. In *Congress Overwhelmed: The Decline in Congressional Capacity and Prospects for Reform*, ed. Lee Drutman, Timothy M. LaPira, and Kevin Kosar. University of Chicago Press, pp. 363–396.

Curry, James M. 2015. *Legislating in the Dark: Information and Power in the House of Representatives*. University of Chicago Press.

Curry, James M. and Frances E. Lee. 2020. "What is regular order worth? Partisan lawmaking and congressional processes." *The Journal of Politics* 82(2):627–641.

de Figueiredo, John M. and Brian Kelleher Richter. 2014. "Advancing the empirical research on lobbying." *Annual Review of Political Science* 17(1):163–185.

Diamond, Alexis and Jasjeet S. Sekhon. 2013. "Genetic matching for estimating causal effects: A general multivariate matching method for achieving balance in observational studies." *Review of Economics and Statistics* 95(3):932–945.

Dorrell, Robert M. Jr. and Joshua M. Jansa. 2022. "Copy, paste, legislate, succeed? The effect of policy plagiarism on policy success." *Policy & Politics* 50(4):605–623.

Drutman, Lee. 2015. *The Business of America is Lobbying: How Corporations Became Politicized and Politics Became More Corporate*. Oxford University Press.

D.ür, Andreas. 2019. "How interest groups influence public opinion: Arguments matter more than the sources." *European Journal of Political Research* 58: 514–535.

Egbert, Bob and Michelle Anne Fistek. 2009. New Hampshire. In *Political Encyclopedia of U.S. States and Regions*, ed. Donald P. Haider-Markel. Oxford University Press, New York, pp. 34–50.

Engelhardt, Andrew M. 2020. "Racial attitudes through a partisan lens." *British Journal of Political Science* 51(3):451–472.

Erikson, Robert S., Gerald C. Wright, and John P. McIver. 1993. *Statehouse Democracy: Public Opinion and Policy in the American States*. Cambridge University Press.

Farhang, Sean. 2021. "Legislative capacity and administrative power under divided polarization." *Daedalus* 150(3):49–67.

Feinstein, Brian D. 2024. "Legitimizing agencies." *University of Chicago Law Review* 91(4):919–1019.

Fenno, Richard F. 1973. *Congressmen in Committees*. Little, Brown and Company.

Ferrari, Silvia and Francisco Cribari-Neto. 2004. "Beta regression for modelling rates and proportions." *Journal of Applied Statistics* 31(7):799–815.

Finocchiaro, Charles J. and Jeffery A. Jenkins. 2008. "In search of killer amendments in the modern US House." *Legislative Studies Quarterly* 33(2):263–294.

Fiorina, Morris P. 1989. *Congress: Keystone of the Washington Establishment*. Yale University Press.

Flesch, Rudolf and Alan J. Gould. 1949. *The Art of Readable Writing*. Vol. 8. Harper New York.

Flynn, D. J. and Laurel Harbridge. 2016. "How partisan conflict in Congress affects public opinion: Strategies, outcomes, and issue differences." *American Politics Research* 44(5):875–902.

Fouirnaies, Alexander. 2018. "When are agenda setters valuable?" *American Journal of Political Science* 62(1):176–191.

Fouirnaies, Alexander and Andrew B. Hall. 2018. "How do interest groups seek access to committees?" *American Journal of Political Science* 62(1): 132–147.

Fouirnaies, Alexander and Andrew B. Hall. 2022. "How do electoral incentives affect legislator behavior? Evidence from U.S. state legislatures." *American Political Science Review* 116(2):662–676.

Frantzich, Stephen. 1979. "Who makes our laws? The legislative effectiveness of members of the US Congress." *Legislative Studies Quarterly* 4(3): 409–428.

Gailmard, Sean and John W. Patty. 2013. *Learning while Governing: Expertise and Accountability in the Executive Branch*. University of Chicago Press.

Gaskins, Keesha. 2012. "The importance of state legislatures, redistricting, and civil rights." *Brennan Center for Justice*, https://tinyurl.com/2mzft47u.

Gilens, Martin. 2005. "Inequality and democratic responsiveness." *Public Opinion Quarterly* 69(5):778–796.

Gilens, Martin and Benjamin I. Page. 2005. "Testing theories of American politics: Elites, interest groups, and average citizens." *Perspectives on Politics* 12(3):564–581.

Gray, Virginia and David Lowery. 1996. *The Population Ecology of Interest Representation: Lobbying Communities in the American States*. University of Michigan Press.

Grumbach, Jacob. 2022. *Laboratories against Democracy: How National Parties Transformed State Politics*. Princeton University Press.

Hall, Richard L. and Alan V. Deardorff. 2006. "Lobbying as legislative subsidy." *American Political Science Review* 100(1):69–84.

Hansen, Eric R. and Joshua M. Jansa. 2021. "Complexity, resources and text borrowing in state legislatures." *Journal of Public Policy* 41(4): 752–775.

Harbridge, Laurel, Neil Malhotra, and Brian F. Harrison. 2014. "Public preferences for bipartisanship in the policymaking process." *Legislative Studies Quarterly* 39(3):327–355.

Harbridge-Yong, Laurel and Celia Paris. 2021. "You can't always get what you want: How majority-party agenda setting and ignored alternatives shape public attitudes." *Legislative Studies Quarterly* 46(2):323–356.

Harden, Jeffrey J. 2016. *Multidimensional Democracy: A Supply and Demand Theory of Representation in American Legislatures*. Cambridge University Press.

Hart, Grace E. 2016. "State legislative drafting manuals and statutory interpretation." *Yale Law Journal* 126(2):438–487.

Henderson, John and Sara Chatfield. 2011. "Who matches? Propensity scores and bias in the causal effects of education on participation." *The Journal of Politics* 73(3):646–658.

Hertel-Fernandez, Alex. 2019. *State Capture: How Conservative Activists, Big Businesses, and Wealthy Donors Reshaped the American States – and the Nation*. Oxford University Press.

Hertel-Fernandez, Alexander. 2014. "Who passes business's 'model bills'? Policy capacity and corporate influence in US state politics." *Perspectives on Politics* 12(3):582–602.

Heterington, Marc J. 2005. *Why Trust Matters: Declining Political Trust and the Demise of American Liberalism*. Princeton University Press.

Hibbing, John R. and Elizabeth Theiss-Morse. 2001. "Process preferences and American politics: What the people want government to be." *American Political Science Review* 95(1):145–153.

Hibbing, John R. and Elizabeth Theiss-Morse. 2002. *Stealth Democracy: Americans' Beliefs about How Government Should Work*. Cambridge: Cambridge University Press.

Hibbing, John R. and Elizabeth Theiss-Morse. 2004. *Stealth Democracy. Americans' Beliefs about How Government Should Work*. Cambridge University Press.

Hibbing, John R., Elizabeth Theiss-Morse, Matthew V. Hibbing, and David Fortunato. 2021. "Who do the people want to govern?" *Party Politics* 29(1).

Hinkle, Rachael K. 2015. "Into the words: Using statutory text to explore the impact of federal courts on state policy diffusion." *American Journal of Political Science* 59(4):1002–1021.

Hirsch, Alexander V. and Kenneth W. Shotts. 2018. "Policy-development monopolies: adverse consequences and institutional responses." *The Journal of Politics* 80(4):1339–1354.

Hirsch, Donald. 1989. *Drafting Federal Law*. US Government Printing Office.

Hoffman, Mitchell and Elizabeth Lyons. 2020. "A time to make laws and a time to fundraise? On the relation between salaries and time use for state politicians." *Canadian Journal of Economics* 53(3):1318–1358.

Huber, John D. and Charles R. Shipan. 2002. *Deliberate Discretion?: The Institutional Foundations of Bureaucratic Autonomy*. Cambridge University Press.

Huber, John D., Charles R. Shipan, and Madelaine Pfahler. 2001. "Legislatures and statutory control of bureaucracy." *American Journal of Political Science* 45(2):330–345.

Huber, John D. and Nolan McCarty. 2004. "Bureaucratic capacity, delegation, and political reform." *American Political Science Review* 98(3):481–494.

Hudson, D. Zachary. 2009. "A Case for Varying Interpretive Deference at the State Level." *Yale Law Journal* 119(2):373–382.

i Miquel, Gerard Padró and James M. Snyder Jr. 2006. "Legislative effectiveness and legislative careers." *Legislative Studies Quarterly* 31(3):347–381.

Jacobs, John. 1995. *A Rage for Justice: The Passion and Politics of Phillip Burton*. University of California Press.

Jansa, Joshua M., Eric R. Hansen, and Virginia H. Gray. 2018. "Copy and paste lawmaking: Legislative professionalism and policy reinvention in the States." *American Politics Research* 47(4):739–767.

Jenkins, Jeffery A. and Michael C. Munger. 2003. "Investigating the incidence of killer amendments in congress." *Journal of Politics* 65(2):498–517.

Jones, David R. 2013. "Do major policy enactments affect public evaluations of Congress? The case of health care reform." *Legislative Studies Quarterly* 38(2):185–204.

Junk, Wiebke Marie. 2019. "When diversity works: The effects of coalition composition on the success of lobbying coalitions." *American Journal of Political Science* 63(3):660–674.

Kalla, Joshua L. and David E. Broockman. 2016. "Campaign contributions facilitate access to congressional officials: A randomized field experiment." *American Journal of Political Science* 60(3):545–558.

Keefe, William J. 1968. The functions and powers of the state legislatures. In *State Legislatures in American Politics*, ed. Alexander Heard. Englewood Cliffs, N. J.: Prentice-Hall, for American Assembly, Columbia University.

Keele, Luke. 2010. "An overview of rbounds: An R. package for Rosenbaum bounds sensitivity analysis with matched data." *White Paper*. Columbus, OH. www.personal.psu.edu/ljk20/rbounds%20vignette.pdf.

Kimball, David C., Frank R. Baumgartner, Jeffrey M. Berry, Marie Hojnacki, Beth L. Leech, and Bryce Summary. 2012. "Who cares about the lobbying agenda?" *Interest Groups & Advocacy* 1:5–25.

Kincaid, J. Peter, Robert P. Fishburne Jr, Richard L. Rogers, and Brad S. Chissom. 1975. "Derivation of new readability formulas (Automated Readability Index, Fog Count, and Flesch Reading Ease Formula) for navy enlisted personnel." Technical Report, Naval Technical Training Command, Millington TN Research Branch.

Kirkland, Justin H. and Jeffrey J. Harden. 2022. *The Illusion of Accountability: Transparency and Representation in American Legislatures*. Cambridge University Press.

Klarner, Carl, William D. Berry, Thomas M. Carsey, Malcolm Jewell, Richard Niemi, Lynda Powell, and James Snyder. 2013. "State Legislative Election Returns (1967–2010)." *Ann Arbor, MI: Inter-university Consortium for Political and Social Research*.

Kousser, Thad. 2005. *Term Limits and the Dismantling of State Legislative Professionalism*. Cambridge University Press.

Krause, George A. and Neal D. Woods. 2014. Policy delegation, comparative institutional capacity, and administrative politics in the American states. In *The Oxford Handbook of State and Local Government*, ed. Donald P. Haider-Markel. Oxford University Press, New York, pp. 363–396.

Krupenkin, Masha. 2021. "Constituency size and evaluations of government." *Political Behavior* 43:451–472.

Lax, Jeffrey R. and Justin H. Phillips. 2012. "The democratic deficit in the states." *American Journal of Political Science* 56(1):148–166.

Lewallen, Jonathan. 2016. "Legislative Error and the 'Politics of Haste'." *PS: Political Science and Politics* 49(2):239–243.

Lewis, Jeffrey. N.d. "California Assembly and Senate Roll Call Votes, 1993 to the present." http://amypond.sscnet.ucla.edu/california/.

Lindblom, Charles Edward. 1980. *The Policy-Making Process*. Prentice-Hall.

Linder, Fridolin, Bruce A. Desmarais, Matthew Burgess, and Eugenia Giraudy. 2020. "Text as policy: Measuring policy similarity through bill text reuse." *Policy Studies Journal* 48(2):546–574.

Lipton, Eric and Ben Protess. 2013. "Banks' Lobbyists Help in Drafting Financial Bills." *New York Times* https://tinyurl.com/h7fuuu9z.

Little, Thomas H. and David B. Ogle. 2006. *The Legislative Branch of State Government: People, Process, and Politics*. ABC-CLIO, Inc.

Lowande, Kenneth. 2019. "Politicization and responsiveness in executive agencies." *The Journal of Politics* 81(1):33–48.

Lowande, Kenneth and Jon C. Rogowski. 2021. "Executive power in crisis." *American Political Science Review* 115(4):1406–1423.

Lowande, Kenneth, Melinda Ritchie, and Erinn Lauterbach. 2019. "Descriptive and substantive representation in Congress: Evidence from 80,000 Congressional Inquiries." *American Journal of Political Science* 63(3):644–659.

Lupia, Arthur. 1994. "Shortcuts versus encyclopedias: Information and voting behavior in California insurance reform elections." *American Political Science Review* 88(1):63–76.

Lyon, Caroline, James Malcolm, and Bob Dickerson. 2001. Detecting short passages of similar text in large document collections. In *Proceedings of the 2001 Conference on Empirical Methods in Natural Language Processing*, pp. 118–125.

Madison, James. 1788*a*. "Federalist No. 45: 'The Alleged Danger from the Powers of the Union to the State Governments Considered for the Independent Journal'." The Independent Journal, as reprinted in The Avalon Project, Yale Law School. Originally published under the pseudonym "Publius"; retrieved from Avalon Project. https://avalon.law.yale.edu/18th_century/fed45.asp.

Madison, James. 1788*b*. "Federalist No. 62: 'The Senate'." The New York Packet, as reprinted in The Avalon Project, Yale Law School. Originally published under the pseudonym "Publius"; retrieved from Avalon Project. https://avalon.law.yale.edu/18th_century/fed62.asp

Maghsoodloo, Saeed and Ching-Ying Huang. 2010. "Comparing the overlapping of two independent confidence intervals with a single confidence interval for two normal population parameters." *Journal of Statistical Planning and Inference* 140(11):3295–3305.

Mansbridge, Jane. 1992. A deliberative theory of interest representation. In *The Politics of Interests: Interest Groups Transformed*, ed. Mark Petracca. Westview.

Mansbridge, Jane. 2007. "Deliberative Democracy" or "Democratic Deliberation"? In *Deliberation, Participation and Democracy*, ed. Shawn W. Rosenberg. Palgrave Macmillan, pp. 251–271.

Martin, Lanny W. and Georg Vanberg. 2014. "Parties and policymaking in multiparty governments: The legislative median, ministerial autonomy, and the coalition compromise." *American Journal of Political Science* 58(4):979–996.

Masket, Seth E. 2009. *No Middle Ground: How Informal Party Organizations Control Nominations and Polarize Legislatures*. University of Michigan Press.

Masunaga, Samantha. 2015. "We're No. 8: California near top of world's largest economies." *Los Angeles Times*. www.latimes.com/business/la-fi-california-world-economy-20150702-story.html.

Mayhew, David R. 1975. *Congress: The Electoral Connection*. Yale University Press.

McKay, Amy Melissa. 2021. "Buying amendments? Lobbyists' campaign contributions and microlegislation in the creation of the Affordable Care Act." *Legislative Studies Quarterly* 45(2):327–360.

Meyers, John. 2015. "For California's powerful, following the law often means writing it yourself." *KQED: Public Media for Northern California*. https://tinyurl.com/36br2nym.

Michener, Jamila. 2018. *Fragmented Democracy: Medicaid, Federalism, and Unequal Politics*. Cambridge University Press.

Mooney, Christopher Z. 2009. "Term limits as a boon to legislative scholarship: A review." *State Politics and Policy Quarterly* 9(2):204–228.

Niskanen, William Arthur. 1971. *Bureaucracy and Representative Government*. Aldine, Atherton.

Nourse, Victoria and Jane S. Schacter. 2002. "The politics of legislative drafting: A Congressional case study." *New York University Law Review* 77(3): 575–623.

Nownes, Anthony J. and Patricia Freeman. 1998. "Interest group activity in the states." *The Journal of Politics* 60(1):86–112.

Noyes, Dan. 2015. "I.-Team examines bill that'd end California's ban on kangaroo products." *ABC7 News*. https://tinyurl.com/2f682sbm.

Olson, Michael P. and Jon C. Rogowski. 2020. "Legislative term limits and polarization." *Journal of Politics* 82(2):572–586.

OpenStates. 2016. "Open States Bulk Downloads." http://openstates.org/downloads/.

Parrillo, Nicholas R. 2013. "Leviathan and interpretive revolution: The administrative state, the judiciary, and the rise of legislative history, 1890–1950." *Yale Law Journal* 123:266.

Payson, Julia A. 2021. *When Cities Lobby: How Local Governments Compete for Power in State Politics*. Oxford University Press.

Pew Research Center. 2019. "How Americans See Problems of Trust." www.pewresearch.org/politics/2019/07/22/how-americans-see-problems-of-trust.

Potter, Rachel Augustine. 2017. "Slow-rolling, fast-tracking, and the pace of bureaucratic decisions in rulemaking." *The Journal of Politics* 79(3):841–855.

Rasmussen, Anne and Stefanie Reher. 2023. "(Inequality in) Interest group involvement and the legitimacy of policy making." *British Journal of Political Science* 53(1):45–64.

Reeves, Andrew and Jon C. Rogowski. 2018. "The public cost of unilateral action." *American Journal of Political Science* 62(2):424–440.

Reeves, Andrew and Jon C. Rogowski. 2020. *No Blank Check: Why the Public Dislikes Presidential Power and What It Means for Governing*. Cambridge University Press.

Reinsch, Paul Samuel. 1907. *American Legislatures and Legislative Methods*. Cornell University Library.

Reynolds, Molly E. 2020. The decline in Congressional capacity. In *Congress Overwhelmed: The Decline in Congressional Capacity and Prospects for Reform*, ed. Drutman, Lee, Timothy M. LaPira, and Kevin R. Kosar. Oxford University Press, New York, pp. 34–50.

Ritchie, Melinda N. 2018. "Back-channel representation: A study of the strategic communication of senators with the US Department of Labor." *The Journal of Politics* 80(1):240–253.

Ritchie, Melinda N. 2023. *Backdoor Lawmaking: Evading Obstacles in the US Congress*. Oxford University Press.
Roberts, Margaret E., Brandon M. Stewart, and Dustin Tingley. 2019. *stm: An R. Package for Structural Topic Models*. R. package version 1.3.6. https://cran.r-project.org/web/packages/stm/index.html
Roberts, Margaret E., Brandon M. Stewart, Dustin Tingley, Christopher Lucas, Jetson Leder-Luis, Shana Kushner Gadarian, Bethany Albertson, and David G. Rand. 2014. "Structural topic models for open-ended survey responses." *American Journal of Political Science* 58(4):1064–1082.
Rogers, Everett M. 2010. *Diffusion of Innovations*. Simon and Schuster.
Rogers, Steven. 2017. "Electoral accountability for state legislative roll calls and ideological representation." *American Political Science Review* 111(3): 555–571.
Rogers, Steven. 2023. *Accountability in State Legislatures*. University of Chicago Press.
Rosenbaum, Paul R. 2002. *Observational Studies*. Springer.
Rosenhall, Laurel. 2013. "California legislation often 'Sponsored' – or even written – by interest groups." *Sacramento Bee*, www.sacbee.com/news/politics-government/article2577337.html.
Rosenson, Beth A. 2005. *The Shadowlands of Conduct: Ethics and State Politics*. Georgetown University Press.
Rosenthal, Alan. 1981. "Legislative behavior and legislative oversight." *Legislative Studies Quarterly* 6(1):115–131.
Rosenthal, Alan. 1986. "The state of the Florida legislature." *Florida State University Law Review* 14(3):399–431.
Rosenthal, Alan. 2009. *Engines of Democracy: Politics & Policymaking in State Legislatures*. CQ Press.
Rosenthal, Alan and Rod Forth. 1978. "The assembly line: Law production in the American states." *Legislative Studies Quarterly* pp. 265–291.
Salisbury, Robert H. and Kenneth A. Shepsle. 1981. "U.S. Congressman as enterprise." *Legislative Studies Quarterly* 6(4):559–576.
Schattschneider, E. E. 1960. *The Semi-Sovereign People: A Realist's View of Democracy in America*. Holt, Rinehart, and Winston.
Schiller, Wendy J. 1995. "Senators as political entrepreneurs: Using bill sponsorship to shape legislative agendas." *American Journal of Political Science* 39(1):186–203.
Schlozman, Kay L. 2010. Who sings in the heavenly chorus? The shape of the organized interest system. In *The Oxford Handbook of American Political Parties and Interest Groups*, ed. Berry, Jeffrey M., L. Sandy Maisel, and George C. Edwards. Oxford University Press, New York, pp. 425–450.
Schlozman, Kay Lehman, Sidney Verba, and Henry E. Brady. 2012. *The Unheavenly Chorus: Unequal Political Voice and the Broken Promise of American Democracy*. Princeton University Press.
Schnakenberg, Keith E. 2017. "Informational lobbying and legislative voting." *American Journal of Political Science* 61(1):129–145.
Seifter, Miriam. 2019. "Understanding state agency independence." *University of Michigan Law Review*, 117(8):1537–1592.

Sekhon, Jasjeet S. 2011. "Multivariate and propensity score matching software with automated balance optimization: The Matching package for R." *Journal of Statistical Software* 42(7): 1–52.

Shobe, Jarrod. 2017. "Agencies as legislators: An empirical study of the role of agencies in the legislative process." *The George Washington Law Review* 85(2):451–535.

Shor, Boris and Nolan McCarty. 2011. "The ideological mapping of American legislatures." *American Political Science Review* 105(3):530–551.

Sinclair, Barbara. 1991. *Unorthodox Lawmaking: New Legislative Processes in the U.S. Congress*. Yale University Press.

Sinclair, Barbara. 1994. "House special rules and the institutional design controversy." *Legislative Studies Quarterly* 19(4):477–494.

Smith, Kevin B. 2012. *State and Local Government, 2012–2013 Edition*. CQ Press.

Spirling, Arthur. 2016. "Democratization and linguistic complexity: The effect of franchise extension on parliamentary discourse, 1832–1915." *The Journal of Politics* 78(1):120–136.

Squire, Peverill. 1992. "Legislative professionalization and membership diversity in state legislatures." *Legislative Studies Quarterly* 17(1):69–79.

Squire, Peverill. 2007. "Measuring state legislative professionalism: The Squire index revisited." *State Politics & Policy Quarterly* 7(2):211–227.

Squire, Peverill. 2017. "A Squire Index update." *State Politics & Policy Quarterly* 17(4):361–371.

Stokes, Leah Cardamore. 2020. *Short Circuiting Policy: Interest Groups and the Battle over Clean Energy and Climate Policy in the American States*. Oxford University Press.

Strolovitch, Dara Z. 2008. *Affirmative Advocacy: Race, Class, and Gender in Interest Group Politics*. University of Chicago Press.

Teodoro, Manuel P. 2011. *Bureaucratic Ambition: Careers, Motives, and the Innovative Administrator*. Johns Hopkins University Press.

Treul, Sarah A. and Rachel Porter. 2025. "Setting the Narrative: Modern Congressional Campaigns and Inexperience Success." https://rachelporter.org/assets/pdf/book_prospectus.pdf.

Treul, Sarah, Danielle M. Thomsen, Craig Volden, and Alan E. Wiseman. 2022. "The primary path for turning legislative effectiveness into electoral success." *The Journal of Politics* 84(3).

Tyler, Charles W. and Heather K. Gerken. 2022. "The myth of the laboratories of democracy." *Columbia University Law Review* 122:2187–2240.

Uttermark, Matthew J., Lauren A. Dula, Francesca Bové, and Kamryn Scott. 2023. "Contact and control: Engagement and influence among women of color state agency heads." *Public Administration Review* 84(2):308–322.

VanderMolen, Kathryn. 2017. "Stealth democracy revisited: reconsidering preferences for less visible government." *Political Research Quarterly* 70(3): 687–698.

Verba, Sidney, Kay Lehman Schlozman, and Henry E. Brady. 1995. *Voice and Equality: Civic Voluntarism in American Politics*. Harvard University Press.

Volden, Craig and Alan E. Wiseman. 2014. *Legislative Effectiveness in the United States Congress: The Lawmakers*. Cambridge University Press.

Walker, Jack L. 1969. "The diffusion of innovations among the American states." *American Political Science Review* 63(3):880–899.

Wawro, Gregory. 2001*a*. *Legislative Entrepreneurship in the U.S. House of Representatives*. University of Michigan Press.

Wawro, Gregory. 2001*b*. "A panel probit analysis of campaign contributions and roll-call votes." *American Journal of Political Science* 45(3):563–579.

Weingast, Barry R. 1989. "The political institutions of representative government: legislatures." *Journal of Institutional and Theoretical Economics (JITE)/Zeitschrift für die gesamte Staatswissenschaft* 145(4):693–703.

Wilkerson, John D. 1999. "'Killer' amendments in Congress." *American Political Science Review* 93(3):535–552.

Wilkerson, John, David Smith, and Nicholas Stramp. 2015. "Tracing the flow of policy ideas in legislatures: A text reuse approach." *American Journal of Political Science* 59(4):943–956.

Woods, Neal D. 2015. "Separation of powers and the politics of administrative rule review." *State Politics and Policy Quarterly* 15(3):345–365.

Woon, Jonathan. 2008. "Bill sponsorship in Congress: The moderating effect of agenda positions on legislative proposals." *The Journal of Politics* 70(1):201–216.

Workman, Samuel. 2015. *The Dynamics of Bureaucracy in the US Government: How Congress and Federal Agencies Process Information and Solve Problems*. Cambridge University Press.

Yackee, Jason Webb and Susan Webb Yackee. 2006. "A bias towards business? Assessing interest group influence on the U.S. bureaucracy." *Journal of Politics* 68(1):128–139.

Yackee, Jason Webb and Susan Webb Yackee. 2020. "The American State Administrators Project: A new 50-State, 50-Year data resource for scholars." *Public Administration Review* 81(3):240–253.

You, Hye Young. 2017. "Ex post lobbying." *The Journal of Politics* 79(4):1162–1176.

You, Hye Young. 2023. "Dynamic lobbying: Evidence from foreign lobbying in the U.S. Congress." *Economics & Politics* 35(2):445–469.

Index

For EU product safety concerns, contact us at Calle de José Abascal, 56–1°,
28003 Madrid, Spain or eugpsr@cambridge.org.

www.ingramcontent.com/pod-product-compliance
Ingram Content Group UK Ltd.
Pitfield, Milton Keynes, MK11 3LW, UK
UKHW042210080726
473066UK00008B/345

* 9 7 8 1 0 0 9 7 1 0 1 0 7 *